Twentieth-century Welsh Autobiography

Writing Wales in English

CREW series of Critical and Scholarly Studies
General Editor: Professor M. Wynn Thomas (CREW, University of Wales, Swansea)

This *CREW* series is dedicated to Emyr Humphreys, a major figure in the literary culture of modern Wales, a founding patron of the *Centre for Research into the English Literature and Language of Wales*, and, along with Gillian Clarke and Seamus Heaney, one of *CREW's* Honorary Associates. Grateful thanks are extended to Richard Dynevor for making this series possible.

Other titles in the series
Kirsti Bohata, *Postcolonialism Revisited* (0-7083-1892-4)
Stephen Knight, *A Hundred Years of Fiction* (0-7083-1846-0)

Twentieth-century Autobiography

Writing Wales in English

BARBARA PRYS-WILLIAMS

UNIVERSITY OF WALES PRESS
CARDIFF
2004

British Library Cataloguing-in-Publication Data
A catalogue record for this book is available from the British Library.

ISBN 0–7083–1891–6

THE *A*SSOCIATION FOR
*W*ELSH *W*RITING IN *E*NGLISH
*C*YMDEITHAS *L*ÊN *S*AESNEG *C*YMRU

Recommended text

Published with the financial asistance of the Welsh Books Council

Printed in Wales by Gwasg Dinefwr, Llandybïe

For my family: Allan; Catrin and Dan; Kirsten and Timothy; and in loving memory of my parents, John and Heulwen Davies, dwellers in a mining valley.

CONTENTS

General Editor's Preface

The aim of this series is to produce a body of scholarly and critical work that reflects the richness and variety of the English-language literature of modern Wales. Drawing upon the expertise both of established specialists and of younger scholars, it will seek to take advantage of the concepts, models and discourses current in the best contemporary studies to promote a better understanding of the literature's significance, viewed not only as an expression of Welsh culture but also as an instance of modern literatures in English world-wide. In addition, it will seek to make available the scholarly materials (such as bibliographies) necessary for this kind of advanced, informed study.

M. Wynn Thomas,
Director, CREW (*Centre for Research into the English Literature and Language of Wales*)
University of Wales Swansea

Acknowledgements

Some of the material in this book has appeared in earlier forms in other publications. I am grateful to Dr Tony Brown, editor of *Welsh Writing in English*, both for what his editorial skills have taught me over the years and for permission to reproduce material which appeared in my papers on R. S. Thomas and Rhys Davies in that journal. My thanks are due to Professor Meic Stephens, editor of *Rhys Davies: Decoding the Hare*, for generously allowing me to reproduce material from my paper in that work. I have explored some of the ideas contained in this book in articles, review articles and reviews in the *New Welsh Review*. I thank its editor, Dr Francesca Rhydderch, for permission to draw on these.

I am grateful to Cassandra Davis for permission to quote from the works of Margiad Evans; to Vivian Davies for permission to quote from the works of B. L. Coombes; to Orion Publishing for permission to quote from letters by B. L. Coombes and Victor Gollancz contained in the editorial file for *These Poor Hands* (published by Gollancz); to Lesley Berry Coburn for permission to quote from the works of Ron Berry; to Jeffrey Robinson for permission to quote from works by Gwyn Thomas; to Mary Parnell for permission to quote from the working papers of Michael Parnell, Gwyn Thomas's biographer; to Gwydion Thomas and Kunjana Thomas for permission to quote from the works of R. S. Thomas, © Kunjana Thomas 2001. Quotations from *Bad Blood* are reprinted by permission of HarperCollins Publishers Ltd © Lorna Sage 2000.

I have been most grateful for expert and committed help in mining particular archives. At the National Library of Wales, Dr Ceridwen Lloyd-Morgan's scholarly help and extensive knowledge of uncatalogued material has been of notable assistance to me. Elisabeth Bennett, of the South Wales Coalfield Collection at the University of Wales Swansea, has been unstinting with her time and knowledge in matters concerning B. L. Coombes and documentation of the south Wales mining experience in the 1930s. Mike Petty, at the time publishing director of the Gollancz imprint of Orion Publishing, put himself out considerably to retrieve for me the editorial file of the communications between

Victor Gollancz and B. L. Coombes and allowed me to photocopy large parts of it.

This book is the culmination of a ten-year immersion in the academic process. Three people have been crucial in their influence and support:

Professor M. Wynn Thomas, FBA, peerless teacher, first awakened my interest in and enthusiasm for aspects of Welsh Writing in English, most particularly the depths of R. S. Thomas's poetry. He was an enabling supervisor of the master's dissertation and doctoral thesis from which this book has emerged.

I could not have handled the in-depth psychoanalytic engagement without a secure background in psychoanalytic therapy myself. For what this has done to illuminate my own human experience I have a great deal to thank Jonathan Pope. As a separate process, he has been most generous in discussing with me my various hypotheses as they have evolved, although the responsibility for the final version is, of course, mine.

I owe most to my husband, Allan Prys-Williams, for his endless patience, for all manner of support and encouragement, for providing and wrestling with a variety of software, for giving houseroom to the range of autobiographical personae with whom I have been preoccupied for several years and for ambling after me down some of the divergent byways into which they have led me. Without him, this book could not have been written.

Barbara Prys-Williams
January 2004

Author's note
Italics within quotations are the writer's own emphasis, unless otherwise indicated.

ABBREVIATIONS

Attach1   John Bowlby, *Attachment and Loss 1: Attachment* (vol. 1 of 3 vols, Harmondsworth: Penguin, 1971)

Attach2   John Bowlby, *Attachment and Loss 2: Separation: Anger and Anxiety* (vol. 2 of 3 vols, Harmondsworth: Penguin, 1975)

Attach3   John Bowlby, *Attachment and Loss 3: Loss: Sadness and Depression* (vol. 3 of 3 vols, Harmondsworth: Penguin, 1981)

Fictions   Paul John Eakin, *Fictions in Autobiography: Studies in the Art of Self-Invention* (Princeton, NJ: Princeton University Press, 1985)

'Full'   B. J. Mandel, 'Full of Life Now', in James Olney (ed.), *Autobiography: Essays Theoretical and Critical* (Princeton: Princeton University Press, 1980)

Gifts   Isabel Briggs Myers and Peter B. Myers, *Gifts Differing: Understanding Personality Type* (Palo Alto, CA: Consulting Psychologists Press, Inc., 1993)

Metaphors James Olney, *Metaphors of Self: The Meaning of Autobiography* (Princeton, NJ: Princeton University Press, 1972)

'Pact'   Philippe Lejeune, 'The Autobiographical Pact', in *On Autobiography* (Minneapolis: University of Minnesota Press, 1989)

Touching   Paul John Eakin, *Touching the World: Reference in Autobiography* (Princeton, NJ: Princeton University Press, 1992)

Location of holding libraries of archives consulted:

National Library of Wales, Aberystwyth (NLW).
South Wales Coalfield Collection, University of Wales Swansea.
Harry Ransom Humanities Research Centre at the University of Texas at Austin.

It seems that the entire Gollancz archive has now been incorporated into the Littlehampton Book Services Archive at Littlehampton, Sussex.

1

Introduction

In this study of some twentieth-century Welsh autobiographies in English, I have chosen my subjects according to my personal judgement of the intrinsic interest of their autobiographical offerings rather than from a desire to represent particular Welsh experiences or propensities in that period. Yet the trawl has proved to be varied, including men and women, novelists and poets, representatives of the middle class and working class, individuals from rural as well as industrial communities, and border personalities as well as figures from the coalfield and north Wales. The lives of the writers selected span the whole century.

Each of the writers considered here communicates a vivid sense of what it was like to live in their particular society if you were them. The views of Wales are lively and memorable but distinctly idiosyncratic. Consistency of outlook is hardly to be expected between authors: depictions of the industrial Rhondda, for example, range from lost Eldorado to Valley of the Bones. Moreover, writers such as Rhys Davies and B. L. Coombes who are often labelled 'objective' are shown to have slanted their material for personal reasons, while overtly subjective autobiographers, such as Lorna Sage, Ron Berry and Gwyn Thomas, provide intense and emotionally convincing pictures of what it felt like, as individuals, to experience particular Welsh cultures at particular moments in history. These are powerful personal constructions of a time and a place. They should not, however, be mistaken for accurate historical record. Ensuing generations need to be on their guard against converting such striking narratives into too believing a sense of the Welsh past.

The writing of good autobiography requires an encounter with oneself that can involve the need to confront potent elements from one's past, a sort of wrestling with personal dragons. At times, for example, aware autobiographers have a sense of powerful unconscious forces that have to be grappled with in attempting a meaningful interpretation of their lives – forces or memories that may have been repressed or distorted because of their potential to cause pain. The value as autobiography of the works considered here is seen as directly proportional to the wholeheartedness with which their writers attempt to answer the questions 'Who am I?', and 'How did I become what I am?'

Gwyn Thomas found writing his commissioned autobiography extraordinarily difficult and painful: it seems to have taken him too close to unconscious material that had been repressed because it was too distressing to contemplate. Lorna Sage struggles to reclaim her own story from the pejorative constructions put on it by others, as the title of her autobiography, *Bad Blood*, implies. Her dragons were the restrictive codes dealing with the nature and position of women in the 1950s and 1960s. Rhys Davies, though aware of his dragons and their nature, refuses to wrestle publicly with them. Between draft and published work he eradicates accounts of areas of behaviour over which he feels vulnerable, particularly his homosexuality (for which he implicitly offers Freudian interpretations). Ron Berry writes with the passionate involvement of one who knows that he is 'going to clay', aware that he is as much of an enigma to himself as to the world. R. S. Thomas, writing in the shadow of his wife's last illness, is forced to look death in the eye and comes to see that he has overcome his own lifelong dread of it. Margiad Evans feels herself to be diminished and profoundly changed after the onset of epilepsy but, even in the grip of anguish, she confronts her fears as she struggles to describe her changed perceptions. Miner-writer B. L. Coombes puts up substantial barriers between his own life and the various narratives he writes about himself. While his professed motivation was to reveal to an ignorant and indifferent world the human cost of coal – to fight the dragons of owner-greed and hard-heartedness – archival delving would seem to suggest that his deeper motivation was successfully to become 'a writer', to which end his life story became a highly malleable commodity.

It has been interesting to uncover potent ideological forces at work at key times in the century. The early drafts, at least, of Rhys Davies's autobiography reveal the degree of excitement and release he experienced in the 1920s in taking on board Freud's liberating views on human sexuality. My long engagement with archival material involving B. L. Coombes has revealed that his 'autobiography', *These Poor Hands*, is shaped by an awareness of what would be successfully marketable in the ethos created by the Left Book Club in the 1930s, when the solidarity, heroism and decency of working men were seen as a powerful force in the fight against Fascism. Pacifist R. S. Thomas, writing in the aftermath of the Chernobyl disaster, sees the creation of the nuclear cloud over Hiroshima as equal in its mythic enormity to the Fall of Man. Lorna Sage, beneficiary of the feminist revolution, shapes her material in a way which may arouse outrage in the reader at the stifling of female potential in the earlier part of the century.

My main focus has been an analysis of the sense of self as enacted and discerned by my chosen writers. This has often been a problematic exercise. Diane Bjorklund has argued ably that a paradigm shift in autobiographical writing got under way in the late nineteenth century, when the new science of psychology radically changed beliefs about human motivation. As time passed, autobiographers began to discern, with Freud, that 'each one of us . . . is not even master in his own house' and that each 'must remain content with the veriest scraps of information about what is going on unconsciously in his own mind'.[1] For several of my authors, my analyses detect both 'calculated self-portraiture' and 'unintentional self-betrayal',[2] as well as sometimes an awareness in writers of unsounded depths that may resist being raised to consciousness. For each of these writers, I have used the tools of psychoanalysis to attempt to unlock troubled areas of the writer's sense of identity, which, while often noted by them, have sometimes seemed inaccessible to them at the time of writing.

Psychoanalytic references have needed to be wide-ranging in this study. Freud's initial theoretical formulations were in some cases expanded, in some cases modified by later workers. The extent to which early pioneers in the field were required to erect their theories using scientific concepts currently available in late nineteenth-century Vienna and Switzerland is sometimes forgotten. It is hardly surprising that more than a century of developed insights into ethology and Darwinian evolution has changed the paradigms used in describing how a living and intelligent organism can handle information from, adapt to and internalize its experience of the world. John Bowlby's extended exposition of attachment theory has been particularly valuable, most notably in my analysis of Gwyn Thomas. The introvert/extravert distinction in personality type formulated by Jung, and later expanded as part of the Myers Briggs Type Indicator, has been useful for several of my subjects, most strikingly for R. S. Thomas.[3]

A major concern of this study has been an attempt to investigate how it felt to inhabit the skin of each of my subjects, to try to establish for each what Gerard Manley Hopkins described as 'my consciousness and feeling of myself, that taste of myself, of *I* and *me* above and in all things, which is more distinctive than the smell of walnut leaf and camphor'.[4] Margiad Evans's perspectives on self, written at several different points in her life, have been particularly moving. Her fictionalized account of the agonies of unrequited Oedipal love in adolescence and early maturity, which mirrored her actual situation at the time, gave way to the security and self-acceptance of married happiness, bringing with it the rootedness which allowed her to develop the ability to be an acute observer of nature. The onset of epilepsy frighteningly undermined her sense of identity, but, even in that pain, she sought to describe her sense of self so that others might understand both the terror and radical loss of self-esteem many epileptics suffer. The 'taste of self' was particularly clearly communicated by Ron Berry, the cadences of his language and his idiolect helping one feel that in an important sense the medium was the very man. Several of my writers created telling metaphors of self. Ron Berry's sense of himself as an embodiment of pent-up aggression is wonderfully evoked in his image of 'a solitary piranha amongst inedible weaver [fish]'. Gwyn Thomas coins images of alienation, declaring, for example, that the sophisticates of the *Brains Trust* aroused in him 'a strong desire to send home for my leper's bell and hood'. Rhys Davies, in an early draft, in an emphasis later deleted, identifies himself with the Wandering Jew who is accursed and doomed to wander the earth.

The sense of self as communicated reveals not only the pulse of personality but also characteristic ways of looking at things. Margiad Evans feels the zenith of her selfhood is achieved, paradoxically, when she loses her sense of self through interfusion with nature and becomes the most exact observing, recording instrument. Ron Berry's sense of identity is nurtured by vivid and acute sense-impressions. Through his potent image-making, R. S. Thomas seems closely in touch with unconscious processes, indeed with the life of the whole psyche. Gwyn Thomas flourishes by indirection, digression and meander, delighting in the oblique viewpoint. Lorna Sage's characteristic stance is innately analytical.

Any autobiography must represent a phenomenal exercise in selection. My study has revealed several instances of external factors dictating the shaping of a life story. Such crucial moulding elements have derived from an editor's sense of what the market needs and wants, what will sell or what will advance a cause. Sometimes standpoints have been suggested strongly to particular authors. The American editor of Gwyn Thomas's autobiography, for example, insisted on the inclusion of particular areas of his public experience as a playwright and television personality: the first draft Thomas submitted had ended at the point when he left teaching.

The most impressive autobiographies have been those where the writing, one feels, has been as much for the author's own enlightenment as to entertain or instruct a reader. For at least part of her autobiographical project, Lorna Sage writes in the (undisclosed) knowledge that she is dying prematurely and engages, as she seeks to know herself, in a tracing of cause and effect which leads her back through generations. Many recreate epiphanic moments from which, they now see, the course of their lives changed. Lorna Sage re-experiences the power of the moment when, having recently given birth at the age of sixteen, she stepped over the excluding boundaries drawn by her headmistress and entered the school to attempt A level exams, from which her entire future flowering as an academic, intellectual and writer followed. R. S. Thomas portrays his arrival at what was to be his final church at Aberdaron as a spiritual homecoming tinged with mystical illumination: henceforth his poetry becomes increasingly focused on his search for an absent God. Ron Berry, after one horrendous wartime trip in the merchant navy where he is exposed to every sort of depravity, never again accepts authority or subscribes to ideas of honour or patriotism. B. L. Coombes, alone of the writers in my study, composes the exemplary life so dear to previous generations of autobiographers. When, because of a publisher's perceived risk of a libel action, he interpolates a fictional rendering of a mine accident, his depiction of self – in incidents that never happened – is as a particularly nurturing and generous friend to a former fellow worker.

For each of my autobiographers, experiences of Wales – social, cultural, linguistic or historical – impinged significantly on the sense of self each developed. Berry and Gwyn Thomas were born at a time when aspirational families in Wales were starting to speak only English, seen as the language of advancement, to their children. The twelfth child in his family, the first six and the parents speaking Welsh from preference, Gwyn Thomas comes to experience Welsh as the language of exclusion. Fielded as a representative Welshman in many media contexts, he held views on the nature of Welshness which had grown from complex and unrecognized conflicts in himself, and caused frequent offence. Ron Berry saw Welsh as the language of control, his parents using it to share incomprehensible secrets. For R. S. Thomas, Welsh became the language of the heart, although, as an adult learner, he was never able to write poetry in it. Rhys Davies symbolically identified his homeland with the Welsh flannel it produced, seemingly designed to suffocate instinctual urges, and he saw his 'cul-de-sac' valley as something to be escaped from. Lorna Sage, growing up in the small, detached part of Flintshire which ran only to villages, saw it become 'more and more islanded in time' as the twentieth century advanced. Although the values of her Border area were those of the complacent yeomanry, she becomes enviously aware, through her annual visits to her grandmother's extended family in the Rhondda, that there are parts of Wales where her educational talents and ambitions would have been cherished.

Class positioning was an important means of demarcating of identity for most of the writers considered. Lorna Sage depicts the Hanmer area of the 1940s as feudal in outlook. That her grandfather, a Church in Wales vicar, was accorded the status of a gentleman, gave her prestige; she found, on her father's return from the war, the move to nuclear-family living in a council house most painful. Rhys Davies describes his petit bourgeois status as a son of a shopkeeper amongst the children of miners with considerable satisfaction, and has a keen eye for class placing throughout his autobiography. Gwyn Thomas attributes his considerable unease and sense of alienation at Oxford to a sense of self that is inextricably linked to his working-class origins. In *These Poor Hands*, B. L. Coombes displays unswerving class loyalty and anger at the inability of the owners to see their workers as anything but hands, generators of profit, valuable only as long as they have muscle-power.

Historical forces are shown to be factors potent in the shaping of achieved identity. Ron Berry's adult, knee-jerk resistance to authority started in his family of origin but grew to intransigent dimensions in the wartime climate, when Bevin's wartime Essential Works Order gave officialdom the power to insist on his working in the silicosis-inducing hard heading of the mine, a virtual death sentence. His very survival beyond young manhood had depended on a sense of self which had resisted such decrees of authority. Lorna Sage, who was to become a respected academic and writer, escaped into higher education by the merest whisker. Although her own Border area was slow to respond, the social changes that were to culminate in the swinging Sixties combined with Sage's undoubted abilities to persuade the authorities at the University of Durham that it was worth changing 'conventual college rules on [her] account' and admitting a married woman for the first time.[5] For all her intelligence and determination, had Lorna Sage been just a few years older, she could have been trapped for life by her early pregnancy and marriage. B. L. Coombes's chance to become a miner-writer came about in a historical climate that elevated the solidarity of the working man as part of the Thirties movement which sought to counter Fascism.

Attachment to the physical landscape of a dear part of Wales, an area perceived as native patch or landscape of the heart, is a compelling force in most of my subjects. For Margiad Evans, the Wye valley and the vista of the mountains of Wales are apprehended as the landscape of security and joy. They were imprinted in this way on her consciousness from the first year she spent there, at the age of eleven, when she became, for the first time in her life, the beloved favourite of someone – her aunt – at a time of family unhappiness and insecurity. R. S. Thomas is most deeply attached to place and, through his keen awareness of how time has shaped particular beloved spots, has a powerful sense of connection with times past. The in-migrant, Coombes, mole-like spending long working hours underground, often on double shifts of sixteen hours, cherishes the delight and refreshment derived from a regular walk to a nearby waterfall. Ron Berry wandered in memory the mountain tops that hem in the Rhondda, evoking with pure delight the memory of 'wheatears [. . .] and two planing skylarks'. Gwyn Thomas's love of place seems to have been more generalized but he frequently confesses to his deep insecurity when required to travel more than a few miles from his natal patch. For Lorna Sage, the deep attachment is to a particular building, the vicarage at Hanmer, which was her earliest home, ejection from which caused her considerable anxiety and an enduring sense of loss.

Several of my subjects have been unusually aware of what the particular idiosyncrasies of their bodies have contributed to their sense of self. Neuman has fascinatingly drawn attention to 'this near effacement of bodies in autobiography' as a form of cultural 'repression'.[6] Many of my subjects, however, write in a most illuminating way about what their bodies made them bear and of how one's own physical features powerfully influence the sense of who or what one is. Gwyn Thomas describes a period of intense, near-suicidal misery and draws it to a close by noting that he had been suffering from an overactive thyroid gland which then received surgical correction, with some alleviation of black moods. From B. L. Coombes we have an unusual sense of many aspects of physical identity: the immutable night and day rhythms of the human body, which make night shifts so difficult, the awareness of one's skeletal and muscular make-up brought by the contortions required in working a narrow seam. From Lorna Sage we have an evocative sense of how large the physical and hormonal changes of adolescence loomed in her life and of how deeply they affected her mood. The feeling of being trapped by the traitorous fertility of one's own body is most tellingly conveyed: one self, the physical, had imprisoned another, more important self, the aspirant intellectual, possibly denying her the chance of fulfilment through an academic life. Margiad Evans draws us into a terrifying awareness of the loss of a sense of self, resulting both from an impairment of memory after epileptic fits and from the changes in the nature of her perceptions.

Finally, the success of an autobiography may depend on how well it can help the reader understand possible valuable ways of living a life. In a very rich field for potential study, those autobiographers chosen for inclusion here have inspired me through the personal meaning they have found in the self and the history that shaped it. Lorna Sage, professor of English and an Establishment figure in her world, used much of her final life-energy to depict the suffering of a particular sort of growing up and to affirm the possibility of rich survival as a bright beacon for others. Particular sorts of exploited life depicted, through the sheer abnormality and intensity of the endurance, developed ways of relating that are movingly deep. For Coombes and, particularly, Berry, the dangers of the mining experience, where dependence on one's working partner has to be total, brought about levels of human trust that, at times, made particular sorts of male bonding the ultimate human experience for them. As a brain tumour tightens its grip, Margiad Evans uses her diminishing power to arouse in the reader, particularly the intended audience of doctors, pity for and empathy with both the tormented inner world of many epileptics and their social exclusion. The reader is left feeling that meaning and use can be wrung from any human situation.

Many of my subjects experienced a 'laming of the soul' to a lesser or greater degree in early childhood.[7] The lifelong neediness which resulted for many of them seems to have been an important impetus to writing about their own lives in various and often highly constructed forms. By engaging with their lives, at some cost, many of my subjects gained insight into and, importantly, a sense of power over or control of the past. Most interestingly, the least publicly searching autobiographers in this study, Rhys Davies and Gwyn Thomas, in their continual mesmeric fascination with their childhood environment in their fiction, reveal, perhaps more than any of my other subjects, that they simply could not leave the past alone. It may be significant that some of the most committed self-examination in the works studied here was written towards the end of the writer's life. An important result of engaged confessional autobiography is its seeming tendency to lay ghosts.

2

Hare or Houdini?: Rhys Davies (1901–1978)

While many of the best autobiographers succeed both in exploring their experience for their own enlightenment and in moving on from this to paint a bold and revealing self-portrait for the world's inspection, for others there may be a crucial failure of nerve in moving from private understanding to public recording. Indeed, Rhys Davies put off until old age his attempt explicitly to image himself to himself and to the world in *Print of a Hare's Foot*, subtitled 'An Autobiographical Beginning', published in 1969 when he was sixty-eight.[1] The very title suggests Davies saw himself as an elusive hare, aiming to bolt beyond the limits of an observer's vision before he has been properly seen and categorized. The published version of *Print of a Hare's Foot* reads as a remarkably urbane work with little sense of the interiority of Davies's experience. Fortunately, the earlier drafts are available for study and these help the reader construct a much fuller picture of the man. As one notes what Davies found it necessary to delete for reasons that do not seem to be aesthetic, and as one discovers how regularly he repositions material so that its original, revealing emphasis is lost, one builds up a much clearer sense of the vulnerability of the man lurking behind formidable defences. The first section of this chapter focuses, in the main, on the published version of *Print of a Hare's Foot*, providing some preliminary interpretation against which the draft versions will emerge more tellingly. The second section analyses what new information one gains about Davies's personality from the drafts. The concluding section attempts to construct a model of personality that takes into account and interprets what has been noted in a way which will, it is hoped, increase understanding of *Print of a Hare's Foot* and, indeed, of Rhys Davies's fiction.

In *Print of a Hare's Foot*, Davies most successfully places his individual life within the nexus of the powerful historical forces which impinged upon him and his community. He vividly traces the social history of a part of the Rhondda from pre-industrial (as seen through the eyes of Dr William Price, Llantrisant, both 'libertarian hero' and 'atavistic relic') to post-industrial times.[2] Ostensibly, the time-span covered in detail is from the turn of the nineteenth century to the middle of the Depression in the 1930s, yet, as the actual vantage-point of writing is the late 1960s, the experiences of that decade would appear to contribute to the defeated mood of the final chapter of the published work. The 1960s had seen the closure of seventy-four pits in south Wales, including the Cambrian, in Clydach Vale, after an explosion there in 1965 which had killed thirty-one miners. Thus Davies records his memories of his own mining community at a time when the focal point and *raison d'être* of his village had already ceased to be. We experience, too, through particular characters represented in detail, the human reality of social movement in south Wales in the first forty years of the twentieth century: the Welsh-speaking maid, Esther, driven by grim poverty in west Wales into service in the Rhondda; Jim Reilly, son of an Irish immigrant, adjusting with difficulty to some Welsh norms; Aldo and Vanna, part of the Italian influx which established purveyors of delectable ice cream throughout the Valleys; Caerphilly Jones, part of the diaspora of the 1930s, escaping hunger in the Valleys by taking the King's shilling in the Horse Guards. Yet, for the most part, the mood is of record, not of commemoration.

As Davies documents historical movements which shaped his community, he describes, too, how he learnt to position himself within that society. In the early chapters, we see Davies smugly aware of his niche, above that of the ordinary working man, in the petit bourgeois position of a shopkeeper's family. Although he simulates surprise at the 'dread thing in life, class consciousness' (104) which he claims to have discovered on moving to London, his family send out the appropriate signals of their higher-than-average rank in the world through the semiotics of dress and possessions. Davies was clothed appropriately for chapel in an Eton collar – 'as a member of the lower middle class I never wore the celluloid kind, which required no laundering' (17) – and sat in the socially superior position of his family's 'rented pew' (17). The employment of a maid was another social marker. His sense of who he is and his social position are intricately enmeshed.

In *Print of a Hare's Foot*, Davies gives a lively sense of the attractions of being socially accepted, while making clear his admiration for free spirits, such as William Price and D. H. Lawrence, who seemed able to dispense with social acceptability altogether. He seems particularly aware of how the granting of primacy to one's sexual needs in entering a relationship might affect one's social placing, and in his delineations of Vanna, Esther and Madame S. he explores the ways in which different cultures and traditions come to different accommodations in this matter. Italian Vanna has a 'gleam in [her] dancing eye' as she reveals her 'forbidden mystery' (39) to Davies after their child-hood mock-marriage in the coke oven. A few months later, 'she put her hair up much earlier in life than was the practice with Welsh girls' (40) and, shortly after that, was whisked back to Turin to finish her growing up under the fiercer Italian sexual codes for nubile girls and the strict supervision of her grandmother. Davies clearly sees the binding force of sexual convention in limiting life possibilities here. In his portrayal of the family maid, Esther, he depicts a woman who fears where the power of her sexuality might lead her when, after an impoverished upbringing, her greatest need is for security. When a strike is threatened, she sees clearly what marriage to a miner might involve and returns to west Wales. Some four years later, she comes back to the Rhondda triumphantly on a visit, 'dressily well-off' (63), married to a much older man who has provided her with 'a bay-windowed house' well away from 'the unbridled sea' (63). The adolescent Davies retains a lively memory of the electric charge he experienced as a child when he explored her intimate person on the one night when he shared a bed with her. Now she is totally hemmed in and contained. 'Under a wide hat containing a sharp-eyed bird with outspread wings, she sat with an erectness conveying . . . the discip-line of a lengthy corset' (63). The fixed bird with outstretched wings surely suggests the freezing of any aspiration for a fuller emotional life. Moving into a wider world, Davies, in his portrayal of Madame S., his landlady in the south of France, shows how other, warmer-blooded cultures can reconcile the needs of good sexual adjustment with the desired niche of social placing that the marriage contract brings. Madame S. entertains a lover in the room adja-cent to his for exactly one hour every Friday afternoon. Davies is amazed and instructed by the 'choral ritual' (121) of their unbridled lovemaking and 'the Gallic thoroughness which, like the native talent for forcing all usages out of a vegetable, extracts full value from the provisions of nature in men and women' (121). Only once does he catch sight of the lover, dressed in *bleu de travail*, unmistakably denoting his peasant or working-class status. Madame S.'s husband, a clerk in a municipal office, assures her lower-middle-class status, while her lover provides an outlet for her highly sensual nature. Davies is amused when, after Madame S. has put herself out to be helpful, he invites her for a morning aperitif at a café: he notes 'a perceptible drawing-up of her frontage' and an 'expression of deprecating rebuke' (142), her refusal implying that 'a respectable married Frenchwoman did not sit in a public place drinking with a young man acquaintance' (142). This is a culture where public and private codes are allowably quite different. Davies captures beautifully the French bourgeois preoccupation with having everything exactly *comme il faut* in the public domain.

As Davies observes and conceptualizes from a late-adult perspective what sexual need and social placing have done to limit others, there is a distinct, if guarded, tracing of his own sexual development. Overtly, Davies attributes his huge sense of guilt to his chapel formation, and in his adolescence achieved relief when he 'found a less guilt-ridden religious creed' in transferring from Nonconformist Welsh-speaking Gosen to the Anglican church of St Thomas (81). Nonconformism does not have the reputation of allowing people to live happily with their sexuality, and Davies had perhaps reason to be less happy than many. David Callard reproaches him for being, on the evidence of his friend Urquhart, '100% homosexual' yet, in *Print of a Hare's Foot*, 'writing much to hint otherwise'.[3] Certainly, he never declares his homosexuality overtly in *Print of a Hare's Foot*. Yet what he does write of his early sexual experiences seems to show a shaping where homosexuality might be a likely outcome. As we shall see later, Davies makes explicit that he found Freud's theories, as expounded in the London of the 1920s, personally very liberating. Indeed, at many points in *Print of a Hare's Foot* Davies seems to explain himself to himself – and to readers alert to this coded communication – in Freudian terms. Freud writes of his conviction that the choice of sexual orientation is made in adolescence.[4] The models of heterosexual identity that Davies offers us as he moves towards adolescence often depict the female in a relationship as threatening and often emasculating. Chronologically, his first overt heterosexual experience is with the maid Esther with whom he has, on his assertion, just once to share a bed, receiving an 'eerie shock' as he explores her 'electrically tingling bush' (47) while she is asleep. At this early stage, very much the young master, his guilt at his action – which was a sort of theft – is containable, although when Esther decides to leave the Rhondda, Davies records 'Somewhere far away in me I felt an oddly welcome acceptance of her going' (62). However, years later, coruscating guilt is felt when Esther returns to visit, very much the fine lady. 'Had she *known*?' (63) he asks himself in torment. When he returns from a short walk, Esther has left, leaving as a gift a plucked and eviscerated duck (64). Davies shapes this observation to form a climactic end to the chapter.

Davies's next heterosexual adventure is the mock marriage to Vanna in the coke oven, arranged by the manipulative Idwal. After the ceremony, Idwal retires, ostensibly to keep guard, but when Vanna whips up her skirt to reveal all, a convincing voice from outside booms that Sergeant Richards is there, ready to make an arrest. Heterosexual interest is again consciously linked with the idea of punishable wrongdoing. Perhaps the most interesting and powerful indication of his sexual shaping, however, is given in the incident of Mrs Blow's pear-tree. Idwal involves Davies in a scrumping adventure. As Davies swings up the big pear-tree, he sees 'golden flasks hung plump among the arms of leaves' (42), perceiving the pears first sensually as breasts. Then 'my hand closed round a cool little belly and the fleshy shape, free-of-charge for its plucking, excited me' (42). In this moment of heightened sexual awareness, Mrs Blow appears bellowing 'Thief! Police!' and so great is Davies's terror that he urinates there and then in the tree. This level of panic seems indicative of a particular psychic vulnerability. He has been caught in what he would see as a lascivious act by a female authority figure.

From the examples cited, heterosexual sex is closely linked in Davies's mind as he writes with acts of theft or trespass. An aspect of a child's nurture that is often offered as a precipitator of the homosexual state is that, within the family situation, the mother is dominant and the father weak. The child fails to resolve the Oedipal stage, as most males do, by moving on from intense love of the mother to fear of the castrating power of the father-as-rival, to use the Freudian model, and then to identifying with the father as role model. Heterosexuality then becomes unthinkable because, at an unconscious level, it involves a kind of theft, a sort of violation of the mother. Mrs Blow's appearance as Davies is on the point of sensually capturing a 'fleshy shape', envisioned as a female body, arouses enormous guilt and fear. Inwardly, then, he is consolidating a view of the female as domineering, controlling and, as we shall see later, predatory, while outwardly he seems to be making a 'normal' progress through adolescence, following models of a particular sort of adult identity based on externals: he takes to cigarettes, buys his own shirts and acquires a silver-topped malacca cane and spats. An important rite of passage remains to be negotiated; Davies depicts himself finally losing his virginity to a woman on the sand dunes at Porthcawl.

It seems to be in ignominious retreat from a sighting of this woman in Cardiff that Davies discovers in an intuitive way what his sexual orientation might be. At this point, the tale virtually becomes a conversion narrative. He has that day bought a copy of Wilde's *Salome* with the Beardsley drawings.[5] 'Random little bombs go off inside one with secret detonations . . . Delight restored my nerves' as he looks at 'these sinuous drawings of perverse yet truthful human beings' (95). Evidently Davies felt an imaginative awakening and a strong sense of affinity with these brilliant – yet perverse and nasty – drawings illustrating a text in which Wilde has depicted Salome using her enormous sexual power over her stepfather, Herod. Through her wiles, she achieves the death of John the Baptist, who has spurned her. On his death, she lavishes a horrifying, necrophiliac love on his severed head. The drawings are overtly erotic, showing the considerable sexual power of Salome and of Herodias, her mother, and through them Beardsley creates a series of images of potent women producing arousal in men – Herod, servants, slaves – without any hope of consummation. Davies makes his own idiosyncratic leap in interpreting the drawings: 'even I could tell that its illustrator . . . made peculiar fun of [Wilde's text]. . . The alarming majesty of our Jehovah and other powerful biblical characters went awry and melted like wax' (95). That Herodias and Salome were contemptible figures of corruption seems to have passed him by. Because Davies seems to have been prone to experiencing women as authority figures, he delights in seeing Beardsley 'sending up' the evil matriarch Herodias and her wile-full daughter. When that authority crumbles, for Davies, the whole religious structure with its guilt-arousing tendencies collapses too. One can only speculate, from the vigour and delight of Davies's response to Beardsley, that the drawings and Wilde's text reinforced in him a growing sense of alienation from the trap that women represented – and, at the end of Part One of *Print of a Hare's Foot*, Davies sees traps all around him.

If, in leaving the Rhondda in 1920, Davies is in search of fulfilment, he gives no stronger sense in Part Two than he did in Part One that it will be achieved through heterosexual love. He writes with incredulity of Franz, who achieves congress with a known-by-sight journalist at the Café Royal in 'an old-style [telephone] booth of stolid wood with two small glass panels in the door' (107) and is then trapped into marriage by this woman who 'ferreted his identity' (107) and unleashes 'a bombardment of phone-calls and telegrams' (108) until he capitulates. Davies visits a brothel in Germany to inspect but not to participate. Although, on the evidence of the pubic-hair lice he mentions and 'the lyrical night' (125) which produced them, Davies is evidently sexually active, he tells us nothing of the identity or sex of the partner in this presumably rather sleazy liaison. He has a wide range of homosexual acquaintances, ranging from 'unknowns', like the German Ernst in Nice, to Norman Douglas and Hart Crane.

Although Davies at no time explicitly acknowledges his homosexuality, his developing orientation can be traced in the ways indicated and in a further humorous clue, where the reader is required to match two pieces of information, rather like cards in a game of Pelmanism. Early in Part Two, Davies acclaims Freud as 'a newly canonised redeemer' (101) in the London of the 1920s and he would doubtless have been aware of the significance Freud imputes to particular symbolic forms. Davies confesses an obsessive attachment to a cash box 'I used to carry about everywhere when I was much younger'. It was 'a black-and-gold tin box' with 'beautifully-fitting trays'. He explains, 'Early anxiety, rooted in guilt, had manifested itself in fear of loss of my beloved box' (87). Freudians would see in this attachment to the box with its beautifully fitting trays a strong identification with female genitalia. That Davies is aware of what he is suggesting seems likely as, some forty pages later, he seems euphemistically to image the vagina as a money box. The child Rosamund in Nice is said to steal from tips left for lavatory attendants and to conceal the coins in 'that very private money box' (123). That the box Davies so treasures is a cash box provides a further, teasing conundrum. Freud argues that miserliness is a later manifestation of an anally retentive personality. Davies was known to be frugal, even parsimonious. He leaves the interpreting reader floundering between these two possibilities: to which orifice is he alluding? One feels that Davies enjoys the power of manipulating and discomfiting the reader.

So guarded a depiction of his sexual orientation gives interesting insights into Davies's very private personality. He would seem to offer a further, cultural, explanation for his reticence. A recurrent theme in *Print of a Hare's Foot* is the way in which Davies's Welsh Valleys conditioning tended to stifle any strong instinctual life and how moving to a sense of fulfilled identity involved leaving behind the narrow, claustrophobic models on offer in his cul-de-sac valley. In the introductory chapter, we see how, as a boy, Davies felt 'manacl[ed]' (17) in the itchy Welsh flannel shirt he was forced to wear to chapel. In a neat and (surely) exuberantly fictive balancing episode in the final chapter, an elderly collier's wife speaks of the days when men, her husband included, 'used to wear those Welsh flannel underpants with tapes to tie below the knee . . . Striped, they were, bright stripes' (174). Flannel, for Davies, represents all in Welsh life that depresses the instinctual and, from this concluding episode, we surmise he is alluding to the forces he sees in Welsh life that stifle joyous sexual fulfilment. His autobiographical journey has involved a progressive moving outwards from this base.

If the content of *Print of a Hare's Foot* is guarded and coded, the polished elegance of its style seems a further controlling device, leaving minimal risk of unintended self-disclosure. Each of the sixteen chapters shows Davies exercising the acquired skills of a lifetime as a short-story writer, imposing coherence, closure, form on the amorphousness of life as it was lived and inevitably introducing a fictive dimension. The remarkable concreteness of detail of the telling and the firmness of the narrative line as it shapes towards the closure of each chapter give a distinct sense that this is 'life as short story'.

My study of *Print of a Hare's Foot* was almost complete, when, in a visit to
the National Library of Wales in Aberystwyth, I found my perspective radically altered and my understanding deepened after unearthing earlier drafts
of the work. There are five drafts to which I refer in what follows, all holograph in pencil: the first, loose-leaf, a fragment of fifty-one pages, henceforth
referred to as 'D1 frag.'; the second, complete, apart from occasional missing
pages, henceforth referred to as 'D2'; a thirty-five page fragment of a third
draft, written in the second volume of draft 2, henceforth referred to as
'D3 frag.'; and complete fourth and fifth drafts (apart from some missing
pages), referred to henceforth as 'D4' and 'D5' respectively. Each of the
three complete drafts contains a final chapter, 'Country', which was dropped
just before publication.[6] In the discussion which follows, *Print of a Hare's
Foot* is used to represent the published form of the book.

Before evaluating the drafts, it seems essential to try to formulate what jus-
tifiable expectations can be brought to one's reading of autobiography, a
genre which has attracted a great deal of critical interest and comment over
the last thirty years. Philippe Lejeune posits a contract or pact, whether
explicit or implicit, 'proposed by the author to the reader, a contract which
determines the mode of reading the text'.[7] The author invites the reader to
read with particular expectations. In the rules Elizabeth Bruss formulates in
her attempt at a generic definition she includes:

> Under existing conventions, a claim is made for the truth value of what the auto-
> biography reports – no matter how difficult that truth value might be to ascertain,
> whether the report treats of private experiences or publicly observable occasions . . .
> The autobiographer purports to believe in what he asserts.[8]

Barrett J. Mandel arrives at a particularly helpful judgement:

> An honest autobiography puts its illusion of the past forward in good faith, not
> suspecting that it is but one angle of perception. The good faith is the ratification
> that the particular creation speaks as well as could any creation for the author's
> present sense of where he or she has been and the meaning of it all.[9]

To what extent does Rhys Davies enter into such an autobiographical pact?
The title-page declares *Print of a Hare's Foot: An Autobiographical Beginning*
and delivers an account of the earlier part of the author's life. Further, the
name inscribed on the title-page as author is the name inscribed in the text
as protagonist: included in the text is a letter from D. H. Lawrence to the
narrator which begins 'Dear Rhys Davies' (*Print of a Hare's Foot*, 127). The

dust-jacket of the first edition describes the work as 'informal autobiography'. In the opening page, Davies describes the incidents which trigger 'an unsealing of the past' and the uncovering of 'buried memory'. The way Davies attempts to market the work is surely an indication of how he intends it to be read. Just before publication of *Print of a Hare's Foot*, he attempted to sell the 'Esther' chapter to the *Southern Review*. The response thanks him 'for giving me the opportunity of reading this excerpt from your autobiography'.[10] At no point in his text does Davies repudiate an autobiographical pact.

A study of the drafts brings the reader to the unavoidable conclusion that Davies is a very unreliable narrator in matters which concern his private experience. Davies had, on occasion, little concern for matters of fact or for recording consistent emotional responses to people or situations as the text evolves. In 'D1 frag.', both he and Idwal climb the pear-tree. They are caught by the owner (at this point referred to as Mrs Cook), Davies believes that he has been recognized and 'badly wanted to water' but manages to contain himself and drops down into the garden, to be told off by the irate woman, who later complains to his mother. Davies states that, after this, 'the unrea-sonably malevolent dislike of Mrs Cook endured for long'. He records 'mak-ing fun of her', 'jeering at her dropsical behind' and playing practical jokes on her ('D1 frag.', 11). There is no mention of Mrs Cook's death or funeral. By 'D2', his initial action becomes more culpable – he urinates into the tree – and his emotional response more commendable – after the incident he now accords Mrs Cook 'an embarrassed respect' and declares 'she was no longer a target for derisive humour'. He ends the 'D2' account of her with a descrip-tion of her 'moderate funeral' (21) when 'night shift colliers' (that is, those free to come without inconvenience or loss of pay) turned out to pay tribute 'to the widow of a collier killed down under' ('D2', 20). Davies concludes the section with some general comments about miners' funerals, which can be very impressive when club guilds turn out with their banners. By 'D4', Mrs Cook's funeral itself becomes large-scale, resplendent 'with a panoply of great banners' (31). In this draft, Davies asserts he feels guilt over the pear-tree theft and urination and is glad to see this impressive recognition of Mrs Cook in a large-scale funeral (31). By *Print of a Hare's Foot* (44–5), the lady in question, by now referred to as Mrs Blow, has the grand funeral which her husband had merited. On this occasion, he is recorded as having died of silicosis in a home over the mountain. Many of the funeral details were ori-ginally positioned for quite another funeral, now deleted. Davies himself is penitently centre-stage as the funeral moves off: 'My small presence among the pack of onlookers, most of them grown-ups, was all I could offer' (*Print of a Hare's Foot*, 45). Thus between 'D1 frag.' and *Print of a Hare's Foot* there has been a complete turnabout on personal feeling about the owner of the pear-tree, very different versions of what happened in it, and a magnificent scaling-up of a possibly imaginary funeral.

The slipperiness on matters of fact is pervasive. Davies will change a word to its opposite or add a 'not' between drafts. He makes four changes in the number of pairs of shoes a dressy 'Gentleman Collier' is alleged to possess. Some of his changes suggest an astonishing shallowness of emotional response. His friend Jim is the human being to whom Davies portrays himself as having been closest in his growing up. In an early draft ('D2', 91), Jim is recorded as having died of silicosis in his thirties. In the published work, Davies exploits his friend's death (*Print of a Hare's Foot*, 75). Here Jim is described as dying in his teens in a mine accident, allowing Davies to portray himself as a sensitive boy finally taking in the immensity of his loss and, in a tender chapter ending, dashing at the last minute to the funeral of his friend.

At times Davies shifts from third-party reportage to personally endorse the authenticity of a story. In 'D2' (138), eastern European Franz and a woman journalist achieve sexual congress in the otherwise empty lounge of the 1917 club. By *Print of a Hare's Foot* (107), Davies is personally vouching for the happening, as Franz is described as leaving the table where Davies is sitting to go upstairs, where the act now takes place in a two-paned telephone box. Further, guilt is a persistent theme in *Print of a Hare's Foot*, but it may well be one that Davies found it convenient to develop in a literary sense. In 'D2', this sentence is interpolated: 'I was not conscious of guilt for a long while, although its strong underswell lay in our religion' (8A). Yet by *Print of a Hare's Foot* (17, 37), we have a very early evocation of how early and deeply his chapel experiences imbued Davies with guilt.

As one engages with *Print of a Hare's Foot*, one is aware that every syllable is considered, weighed and mostly evaluated in terms of its intended effect on an exactly positioned reader. That he means us to read his escapade in the pear-tree and his discomfiture in front of Mrs Blow in Freudian terms is made absolutely clear when one discovers that Davies abandons a neutral description of the pears in 'D4' and inserts a deliberately eroticized evocation of breasts and 'cool little bellies' in 'D5' (53). The episode is invention, on the factual level, as we have shown, but is, perhaps, an attempt to encode a psychic truth of how terrifying – to the point of involuntary urination – Davies found any possibility of heterosexual engagement in a world dominated by authoritarian women. Similarly, although Rosamund's vaginal 'money box' appears in 'D4' (171), the balancing cash-box, very codedly suggestive of Davies's anality and identification with female sexual equipment, is quite deliberately inserted as late as 'D5' (134–5). One can almost feel the presence of the ironic writer manipulating and then evaluating the reader.

It is in the area of sexuality that the drafts seem most revealing. Although Davies seems exuberantly relaxed in discussing sexuality in general terms, he lets no explicit reference to his own homosexuality into the public domain. In 'D2', Davies describes very early and in great detail the 'Gentleman Collier' who is clearly something of a homosexual role-model for him. This collier is:

> no longer really young but still unmarried . . . He was alleged to possess nineteen pairs of shoes which he polished to resplendency every Sunday and treading our streets trimly in a pair of these, wore a slim-waisted mauve velvet smoking jacket, fanciful neckwear and kid gloves long after our evil winter winds became balmy with spring. ('D2', 8E) . . . Whatever people said about the dressy Gentleman Collier – one of them ran 'He's got his father's fixtures and his mother's tastes' – he paid his bills and kept himself in clean and tidy order. ('D2', 8ff)

By *Print of a Hare's Foot*, he is assigned only a minimal walk-on part, in a scene illustrative of the sort of brawls that take place in the Davies family shop. Davies has removed any traces of his boyhood fascination with someone who resembled what he might have felt himself to be. Further, Davies systematically excised all traces of even homoerotic interest between drafts and published work.

His interest in sexual matters in a general way, however, is allowed through to *Print of a Hare's Foot*. He acclaims Freud as 'the newly canonised redeemer' of that 1920s post-war society which 'coruscated with intimations of complete personal liberty' (*Print of a Hare's Foot*, 101). Freud's belief in the force of the sexual drive, which he saw as the strongest human motivational force, and his analysis of the neurotic illnesses which can follow a too-ferocious repression of it must have seemed to offer carte blanche for promiscuous sex to those early, delighted receivers of his findings. In 'D4' (218), a sentence which occurs in a description of Bloomsbury in the 1920s, and which Davies deletes, reads 'Another virtue was its discriminating awareness of puritanism, derived from the still-fresh breezes of psychoanalysis.' Freud's Vienna was the very model of seeming propriety and respectability, yet he found it to be seething with sexual energy beneath the surface. Suddenly Davies sees his chapel-instilled puritanism as no sort of God-given absolute but merely a repressive construct set up against wholly natural sexual drives. He sees Wales as being as repressed as turn-of-the-century Vienna: 'In Wales, sex as a subject of conversation was strictly taboo. It was a thing lying under a great weight of flannel blankets and it belonged to the deepest dark' ('D2', 168).

Retrospectively Davies is able to construct a realistic illustration of a Freudian normative figure in a grandfather whose sexual drive appears in both public repression and impetuous action. A particular section in 'D2' highlights Davies's sense of adolescent troubled sexuality within this very repressive society. He has described having his nose broken by stone-throwing boys and being gently ministered to by a young woman (who later goes mad from unrequited love) ('D2', 79–80). He becomes tormented by nightmares. In a generally frail state he is sent to convalesce at his grandparents' house at Ynysybwl. There, the 'clean religious quiet' was dominated by 'the portentous tick tock' of the grandfather clock (clearly seen by Davies as an objective correlative for his stern grandfather), 'its rhythm at night less a threat than a solemn warning not to neglect discipline' ('D2', 83). The specific area in which discipline might be required is clear from the description of the 'genital pendulum and dim weights' of that clock. The mood is as near to distress as we ever get from Davies, and an awareness that Freud closely identified the nose with the penis helps us interpret the wretchedness he is feeling over his nascent sexual identity as he nurses his damaged nose in this oppressive household. The passage continues:

> My grandfather frightened me. I thought of him and her weighed down under their enormously heavy patchwork quilt night after night while the religious ticktocking of the clock went on and on for eternity but such a grey, deacon loving bed was beyond any crystallisation of my imagination. Yet some years after my visit when my grandmother died untimely, he would not wait the customary twelve months of decent mourning and within a few weeks anarchically married a buxom widow on the sly/quiet.[11] My mother wept into a Turkish towel when news of the furtive act reached her – a full-sized weeping of all the shocked daughters in the world. ('D2', 86–7)

From his late adult perspective, Davies knows that those who live by the tenets of puritanism are not exempt from the anarchic forces of their own sexuality. In 'D2' the connections can be clearly traced between Davies's memory of his adolescent dismayed but growing awareness of the power of sex, his consciousness of the ferocious discipline that his grandfather exerts over his household, to the extent, the adolescent believed, of the banishing of any carnal contact, and the universal amazement when carnality rampant is finally revealed in this pillar of the chapel. Although the relating of the actual events is carried through to *Print of a Hare's Foot*, deletions ensure that these clear points are not made. What is symbolically resonant in a draft largely becomes mere plot or local colour in *Print of a Hare's Foot*.

But Davies's strongest interest in Freudian theory seems to be to do with neurosis. In 'D5' (308) he observes 'But pleasure for me was varied people, especially if they were problematical – and who isn't – or dire with failings or, best of all, ruined', and indeed he seems to relish the collection of neurotics he depicts, using this term explicitly for several of the characters he presents. It will be remembered that Freud saw sex as an anarchic power of tremendous strength which civilization, as it evolved, attempted to keep in check by imposing repressive defences. Individuals, in trying to accept the strong, inhibitory demands of society, may reject at the conscious level desires that society considers wrong and immoral. These repressed desires still have power, however, and, if frustration levels are increased, can break through and result in antisocial acts. Alternatively, when instinctual energy is denied outlet, a person's defence mechanisms can become more and more extreme, resulting in neurotic behaviour. The most striking example presented by Davies is Erasmus, in the final chapter of the drafts, who is rescued by his sister Rhoda after 'the serious adultery' ('D4', 281) of his wife and becomes a chronic, chairbound invalid, presumably as a defence against the unbridled nature of sex. However, from his chair Erasmus researches Welsh folk customs, including the unbelievable *Hir Wen Gwd*, allegedly an old Pembrokeshire custom, which involved removing a corpse from its coffin just before the funeral and hauling it right to the top of its own chimney on ropes as a sort of farewell to life.[12] Davies seems to delight in the imaginative displacement of the phallic and ejaculatory in neurotic Erasmus. We also meet deeply neurotic eastern European Franz, who achieves sexual congress without any social preliminary with a journalist in the 1917 club lounge ('D2', 138), which, in the next full draft, has metamorphosed into a two-paned telephone box ('D4', 155). Further, Davies sees Esther's arm's-length treatment of her devoted Rhondda boyfriend as deeply neurotic.

Indeed, in spite of considerable preoccupation with sex in *Print of a Hare's Foot* and its drafts, the works are remarkable for the lack of feeling displayed by the main protagonist. Occasionally Davies is an appalled spectator of what feeling can do to others: for example, at a funeral seeing 'a woman's exposed face streaming with unashamed tears' ('D2', 98); or Esther, after she has intervened on her brother's behalf in a riot, '[it] petrified, my first glimpse of a woman demolished by emotional excess' ('D2', 60). He remembers that his boy-self was scornful of Gwilym, who allowed himself to be in thrall to their maid, Esther. Depending on the content of a message delivered to the young man by Davies, 'his swarthy, strong-boned face would either close into blankness or brim into a smile. My wondering contempt grew' ('D2', 68). Davies's version of events in *Print of a Hare's Foot* often seems to reveal dissociation from pain. As he describes the undoubted torment he suffered as a boy in his itchy flannel shirt in chapel, being bombarded with terrifying *hwyl*, it is as though he is not there in the experience. 'Adult saints of the past endured a comparable martyrdom' (*Print of a Hare's Foot* 16), he jokes of his childhood Sunday mornings.

However, the same period is recorded in stronger language in 'D2' where a recurrent motif of the horror of anything imprisoning is apparent. In chapter 1, Davies traces the beginning of his whole autobiographical project to a visit to Carmarthen, where, in the market, he notes with alarm a roll of the flannel which had so tormented him as a child. He also notes (in a none too subtle symbol, immediately deleted) 'a crumbling old gaol placed warningly in [Carmarthen's] centre' ('D2', 2). He goes back in memory to 'the dreadful Sundays' agonies of a manacled boy', remembering 'the robust shirt, slipped on by my mother's capable hands', before 'something almost as ruthless [deleted] manacling followed' (5). He writes of his Eton collar as though it were a neck fetter and declares, in a deleted sentence, that 'exposition of the Gospel required such manacled tribute' (6). He evokes the whole experience of being a child in coldly appalled language:

> But there is a period of growth when man is a miserably ignorant nobody almost totally unable to free himself of ignoble/ancient fetters, when he is moribund, lost in a dread no-man's land, incarcerated in a jail of submission to authority of which he has no rational understanding. This happens in early boyhood roughly between the ages of five and twelve [ten]. ('D2', 7–8)

The horrified images of constraint are remarkably revealing and, although he later refers to the Wordsworthian 'shades of the prison house', there is no sense of a time when the world was 'apparelled in celestial light' for Davies. In a later passage he writes with admiration of Dr William Price, who tried to emancipate people from what Price saw as the blighting power of Welsh chapels and 'the groaning sounds of guilt coming from within those shackling, imprisoning walls' ('D2', 43). Finally, at the point of making life decisions about what work he should do, Davies sees the colliery as 'a final jail' ('D2', 144). Although in 'D2' (145) the sentence 'I was my own interior master now' appears with coded emphasis, embedded in a paragraph where Davies describes his purchase and treasuring of a rhyme sheet of Blake's poem 'Never Seek to Tell Thy Love', by 'D4' the words are given unmistakable prominence, becoming the opening sentence of Part Two and a ringing

declaration of his sense of emancipation on leaving the Rhondda. An incident appearing only in 'D1frag.' (15), which tells of his being held down
and anaesthetized on the kitchen table for an operation, finds Davies, at
times, almost inarticulate with a remembered terror that he cannot bear to
formulate:

> I was laid flat on the kitchen table . . . I can still see the hovering of the mask of
> wadding, smell the chloroform . . . It was the sudden assault that branded me
> indelibly, this proof of the illusion of freedom and the will. This death . . . this
> prison. I struggled against obliteration; was mercilessly held down by the legs
> and arms.

The idea of being tied down, having to submit to someone else's authority,
brings out the strongest language we experience in *Print of a Hare's Foot* and
its drafts. Many of the early references to jail and manacling disappear by
Print of a Hare's Foot.

Interestingly, too, Davies vividly communicates a sense of horror of
entrapment in relationships in the way he juxtaposes two situations in 'D2'.
He describes himself fleeing from his lady of Porthcawl who had relieved
him of his virginity, and sees his 'fear or self-preservation or whatever'
('D2', 138) as being like that of the eastern European refugee, who, having
achieved sexual congress with an almost unknown woman, finds himself
bombarded by her attentions until he capitulates into marriage. It is probable
that Davies finds the parallel too revealing, and by 'D4' the anecdote has
been shifted to Part Two, removing all the emphasis it originally delivered
about his own fear of being trapped by a relationship. Further, some family
ties are perceived as frighteningly constricting. When visiting Carmarthen-
shire relations, Davies is dismayed by Erasmus and Rhoda's sibling relationship: 'His sister's submissive harkening to him is oppressive to me. They are
imprisoned in a tight cramp of family bondage' ('D4', 289). Most interestingly, in describing the excitement of the freedom of London, he writes
'Homosexuality, a term I did not know until I went to London, was not a thing
to be shut away [in Wormwood Scrubs – deleted]' ('D4', 154). In view of
Davies's obvious horror of any sense of being imprisoned, trapped, not his
own person, this gives a telling insight into what active homosexuality might
have felt like for him during the period when it was illegal. Although some of
his changes will have been made for aesthetic reasons, Davies seems aware
from his deletions and removal of emphases that such a dread of entrapment
could be pathological, and is not prepared to allow something so revealing to
stand.

As a defensive protection, Davies habitually adopts the stance of 'Now you see me, now you don't'. As we have already seen, there is a drive to fragment, so that the clear message of the drafts might be lost, ensuring that he is not trapped by what he seems to have said. In the published work, he seems to have had a need to present himself as poised, debonair, unknown to inner anguish. In an early draft ('D2', 147), Davies ends Part One – the point at which he definitively leaves the Rhondda for London – with an account of himself watching an old pedlar they called the Wandering Jew toiling up a mountain with a heavy burden on his back. Davies recognizes that his own moving on will involve his exploring the nature of the undefined burden he knows himself to be carrying. By the published version, this climactic and appropriate ending to Part One has been replaced by a bland and unconvincing account of a jaunty Rhys Davies relishing the thought of London. Davies's nerve seems to have failed him at the thought of identifying himself with the mythical Wandering Jew, who is accursed and condemned to wander the world until the Second Coming, though such a figure might accurately have reflected his genuine feelings at this point of departure. Similarly, he abandons the use of his trunk as a motif symbolizing his compulsion to pack up and move on at regular intervals, possibly because he has come to recognize such needs as pathological.

A further striking motif, fully preserved in *Print of a Hare's Foot*, is the 'Ledger of Old Accounts' in the shop owned by Davies's parents, a six-inch-thick tome in which were recorded the debts of the miners during strike periods, a tracing that was preserved even beyond death. Although his tone is always equable as he describes her, it seems that Davies's mother was an unrelenting debt collector: 'Untainted by the romantic gullibility of my father, she swooped drastically now and again' (*Print of a Hare's Foot*, 23). In other contexts, he twice uses the word 'ruthless' of her ('D3frag.', 20 and 'D2', 5).

In *Print of a Hare's Foot* Davies shows that he cannot allow himself to be in anyone's debt: 'I became ashamed of being poor. I would not borrow money even from my parents, and when D. H. Lawrence heard of my plight from a friend and sent a cheque for ten pounds, I stupidly refused it' (155). Perhaps the most interesting passage in any of the drafts is one which seems powerfully to encapsulate the characteristics in Davies we have been observing in the last few pages. The episode seems to provide a paradigm for the way in which Davies configures his feelings and, as it is deeply revealing, it comes as no surprise that the passage disappears after the second draft:

Half the people remained for ever in bad debt because of the long Cambrian strike. But the father of another boy in my class [schoolfriend – half deleted] cut his throat with a razor in a shed down their back garden. In aspect, they were the best turned-out family in the place and did not mix with the others: two aloof twin girls with a calm diplomatic poise and their hair put up early, their tall graceful brother with his considered air of not really being present in our noisy/scruffy class, their slender mother always taking trips to Cardiff and wearing something new – her feather boas, esp. a pink one, were especially flaunted and she wore them like an actress (people said it was her mania for costly clothes for herself and three children that brought the disaster) and the quiet father, a clerk in the colliery office who slit his throat from ear to ear in an ivy-smothered shed. I watched the meagre 'private' funeral passing below our upstairs window. There was no singing. A few men walked before the hearse, behind it, my fourteen-year-old fellow pupil, stepping with a strange, elegant dignity, perfectly dressed. He was the man of his family now. To my astonishment and admiration, he carried a smart, rolled umbrella, planting it on the road with easy resolution. ('D2', 88–9)

The passage is striking on many points. A man has responded to huge debts incurred by his dependants by killing himself in a horrific manner in an ivy-covered shed, the creeping plant symbolizing the parasitic nature of human relationships, as we see from the way Davies uses it elsewhere.[13] As suicide was illegal at this time, the funeral was small and shamefaced. Yet what remains with Davies is not the sense of squalor and pain but the stylish way the son distances himself from it all with 'his smart, rolled umbrella, planting it on the road with easy resolution'. It seems to be the sort of urbane detachment Davies himself seeks to achieve in life and certainly adopts effortlessly in his stories. The horror of being trapped, manacled, imprisoned, the need to be constantly on the move to avoid dependent relationships, the awareness that being in debt is a way of being bound hand and foot in someone's power, all coalesce into a life solution that Davies seems to see as a luminous positive: detachment. Again and again Davies describes himself as remote inside his private lighthouse. What could be more securely aloof, less subject to 'parasitic' demands of relationships, and yet more able to give warning of danger?

How we respond to a particular autobiography may depend on what we have felt about self-disclosure in other, similar works we have read, particularly those of the same period. J. R. Ackerley, literary editor of *The Listener* and a deeply respected figure in the London world of letters, published his autobiography *My Father and Myself* in 1968[14] and, although there is congruence with Davies in age, the time-scale covered, the London literary milieu and promiscuous homosexuality,[15] the contrast with *Print of a Hare's Foot* could not be more striking. Ackerley's response to his deep-rooted sense of being an enigma to himself is to excavate as strenuously as he knows how and then to display the results frankly, feeling that in this way either he or others may achieve understanding of his complexities, and so increase the general sum of knowledge of the human condition. He writes openly of his sexual relation-ships, revealing that the Horse Guards, who were very poorly paid, were a regular source of homosexual prostitutes. Comparing Ackerley's frank analy-sis with Davies's bland chapter on the guardsman, Caerphilly Jones, almost certainly the nearest he comes to describing a homosexual partner – when he marries, Caerphilly presents Davies with a single-bed mattress – one is very struck by the difference between Davies and Ackerley.

However, when one compares *Print of a Hare's Foot* with the earlier drafts and notes the deletions and revisions, a much stronger sense of the pulse of personality – and, it has to be said, of the areas of pathology of that person-ality – emerges. There are questions which surface insistently. Why did Davies have so little regard for literal truth? Why did he find it necessary to cover his tracks by fragmenting, omitting and editing what had been clear in the drafts? Why does he need to be quite so manipulative and controlling? Why is there such dissociation from feeling and such shallow depiction of feeling? Why, in his autobiography, as so often in his stories, does he turn descriptions of passion into farce, as in his tale of Madame S. and her *coq au vin* lover (*Print of a Hare's Foot*, 126) or his account of the ardent transvestite couple which culminates in a funeral in drag ('D4', 240)? Why does he seem to relish voyeuristic imaginings, as when he transfers the passionate encounter between eastern European Franz and his known-by-sight journalist from the lounge of the 1917 club ('D2', 138), to a telephone booth with two glass panes ('D4', 155)? Whence the horror of entrapment? Why is he so obsessed with funerals and why, as in so many of his stories, does he end his own draft autobiography with an utterly macabre tale – in this case, of the *Hir Wen Gwd* custom where corpses are dragged up chimneys ('D5', 315–18)? Why does he find it so necessary to subvert death? Why is there virtually never a charge of real feeling passing from writer to reader? My contention for the remain-der of this chapter will be that it assists and clarifies the reading of his work to consider whether Davies was, in the technical sense of the term, a narcis-sist. As technical descriptions of the condition are sometimes expressed coldly and even, seemingly, judgementally, it is important to emphasize at this stage that narcissism is a very painful state, often fixing the sufferer on a point between the Scylla of perceived entrapment in relationships and the Charybdis of loneliness.[16]

There seems to be general agreement that the state is caused by a particular traumatic event or cumulative trauma, brought about by the emotional character of a parent, which causes the sufferer to turn inwards to self love at the very time when s/he would normally be beginning to develop object relations in the world beyond herself/himself.[17] Kernberg finds that:

Chronically cold parental figures, with covert but intense aggression are very frequent features of the background of these patients. A composite picture of a number of cases . . . shows consistently a parental figure who functions well on the surface in a superficially well-organized home, but with a degree of callousness, indifference and non verbalized spiteful aggression. [We remember how Davies's 'ruthless' mother 'swooped drastically' on defaulters from the 'Ledger of Old Accounts' and what an imaginative charge this carried for Davies.] Their histories reveal that each patient possessed some inherent quality which could have objectively aroused the envy or admiration of others . . . Sometimes it was the cold, hostile mother's narcissistic use of the child which made him 'special' and set him off on the road in a search of a compensatory admiration and greatness . . . For example, two patients were used by their mothers as a kind of 'object of art' being dressed up and exposed to public admiration in an almost grotesque way. [We remember Davies's middle-class Eton collar and his 'little Lord Fauntleroy' suit, mentioned at the beginning of *Print of a Hare's Foot* and at the beginning and end of all the complete drafts, an outfit which must have made him remarkable, even grotesque, amongst miners' children. Davies's narcissistic grandiosity shows itself clearly in his presenting himself throughout the autobiography as an only child, whereas in fact he was the fifth of six. Resplendent in a middle-class Eton collar, he saw himself as 'seated alone in my mother's rented pew in a Congregational chapel' (*Print of a Hare's Foot*, 17).] . . . The greatest fear of these patients is to be dependent on anyone else . . . and the development of a situation in which they do feel dependent immediately brings back the basic threatening situation of early childhood. [We note with what hostility Davies remembered the period between the ages of five and ten, when 'in a jail of submission to authority'.][18]

Christopher Lasch summarizes succinctly the characteristics of pathological narcissism from a comprehensive overview of the clinical literature.[19] He records that sufferers lack a capacity to mourn, particularly their parents, 'because of their rage against lost objects [people]' (37). Their terror of emotional dependence and what can be an exploitative approach to other people result in superficial and deeply unsatisfying relationships (40). They tend to be sexually promiscuous rather than repressed, looking for 'instantaneous intimacy' and seeking 'emotional titillation rather than involvement' (40). They depend on a 'vicarious warmth provided by others' while fearfully avoiding dependence (33). As traumatic damage has started in the pre-Oedipal stage of psychic development, narcissists often have a huge sense of oral deprivation which results in unsatisfied oral cravings (33, 37). They have a profound sense of inner emptiness and 'a boundless repressed rage' (33). They are terrified of ageing and death (38).

How good a fit does the narcissist model seem to be for what we can discern of Davies? This study has already drawn frequent attention to his need to be totally independent, avoiding the entrapment he saw in close relationships by being constantly on the move. An inability to mourn, combined with a strong sense of repressed anger, would explain why Davies deals so sketchily with his parents in *Print of a Hare's Foot*. The exploitative literary use he made of his friend Jim's death could be explained in a similar way: without the deepening of the emotional process that grief brings, Davies would not have felt constrained from disposing of his friend in a way that made, by his lights, for the best story, spotlighting Davies himself narcissistically centre-stage at that funeral. We remember that the climax of 'A Human Condition' involves a bereft husband, after a morning of obsessive drinking, gazing into the grave into which his wife's body has just been lowered before tumbling in on top of the coffin and, in so doing, parting company with his false teeth.[20] Davies could hardly be argued to be showing much empathy with grief.

In considering whether Davies's sexual relations reveal a similar sort of shallowness, or even the outright promiscuity Lasch includes as a narcissistic characteristic, we have the evidence of David Callard that these took the form 'of casual, often mercenary, contacts with Guardsmen'.[21] It is possible that 'vicarious warmth provided by others' would be delivered by the sort of voyeuristic imaginings already alluded to, and more fully worked out in such characters as Mrs Vine in 'The Chosen One' (*Collected Stories II*, 258) as she spies on Rufus, bathing naked, through field glasses. 'Unsatisfied oral cravings' might explain Davies's interest in a lascivious engagement with food, particularly in his predatory female characters,[22] and the sort of oral dependence that can be assuaged by cigarettes. Davies was a lifelong smoker and died of lung cancer. 'Boundless repressed rage' erupts regularly and unappeasably in his stories, where the delivery of savage revenge brings climactic satisfaction for a character. Particularly significant in this regard is 'The Last Struggle' (*CSII*, 32–41), the horrific tale of a miner who is entombed and, although left for dead, fights his way out with amazing pertinacity, only to find his wife has gone on holiday with the insurance money to find herself a new man. He brutally brings her to submission through the power of his will. 'The Wages of Love' (*Collected Stories I*, 202–8) shows the merciless revenge her family is prepared to exact on Olga for being a lady of easy virtue, while all the while feathering their nests with the proceeds of her life of sin.

There is no doubt at all that Rhys Davies understood most deeply what a 'profound sense of inner emptiness' felt like, and I rate 'Boy with a Trumpet' (*CSII*, 93–104), in which he engages with that feeling, amongst his very best stories. In the young boy protagonist Davies paints a most compassionate picture of narcissistic pain. A young boy brought up in an orphanage is discharged from the army after a suicide attempt. He is unable to love and he knows his lack: 'he had no instinctive love to give out in return for attempts of affection: it had never been born in him' (95). In his inner desolation, 'like a young hungry wolf sniffing the edge of the dark, he howled desolately inside himself' (97). He declares to a prostitute with whom he shares a house, 'I have no faith, no belief and I can't accept the world – I can't feel it' (102). He likes being with prostitutes because 'their calm acceptance of the world as disintegration eased him'. In a moving interchange the prostitute observes:

'You're too lonely, that's what it is.'

'Will you let me –'

'What?' she asked, more alert. The light was finishing, her face was dim.

'Put my mouth to your breast?'

'No', she said at once. 'It wouldn't be any use, anyhow.' (104)

The boy is not making sexual advances but is asking for succour of his infant needs, never properly nurtured. Turning away in despair from her refusal, he takes the narcissistic option, as did the boy narrator in 'The Dark World' (*CSI*, 253), and projects his own inner desolation on the world. 'He saw himself the inhabitant of a wilderness where withered hands could lift in guidance no more. There were no more voices and all the paps of the earth were dry' (104).

But perhaps the most interesting of the characteristics in relation to Davies is that narcissists are terrified at the thought of ageing and death. As a writer shapes his autobiography, imposing coherence and closure, thoughts of that final, unavoidable closure to his life story can hardly be dodged. Davies manages to sidestep this by limiting the time-span of his autobiography to the first thirty-five years of his life, although the man who held the pen was himself

sixty-eight. Funerals, however, abound in *Print of a Hare's Foot*, and there
are further ones in the drafts; Death, played by a knockabout comedian, is one
of the main characters in his stories. An analysis of death and funerals in the
stories quickly reveals how little of a real sense of the finality of death Davies
allows himself. A sister sits up in her coffin and so is not dead; a body is
buried with great pomp by a guilty widow and then it is discovered her real
husband is alive and well; a man's drinking mates propose to carry his coffin
the four uphill miles to the cemetery, but, after many refreshment stops en
route, arrive without it; a woman's fiancé dies away from home and the coffin
goes missing so that she never has a body to grieve over; a woman dies and
her companion leaves her body sitting in the chair for months while claiming
her pension; a man is entombed for a week but fights his way out, by which
time his wife has spent the insurance money.[23] Again and again there is no
body to bury or the wrong body. In this Houdini universe, death and grief can
be thoroughly disconnected from each other. Surely, too, there is a denial of
death as we see people escape that ultimate entrapment.

Psychoanalytic insights do, indeed, offer illumination on puzzling features
in Davies the writer. The narcissism hypothesis, further, helps to explain
another interesting idiosyncrasy observed in Davies – his ability to receive
intense and erotic pleasure from what he sees. His description of his early
response to ballet is particularly interesting. He describes 'the barbarically
primary colours' which 'gave much more than visual impact; colour shot
down the throat, attacked the spine, poked up an erotic tumult' (*Print of a
Hare's Foot*, 109). He further describes ballet as 'a sweet depravity of the
eyes' and 'a permissible cultural aphrodisiac' ('D2', 157). He makes quite
clear the complete primacy the sense of sight has for him when he describes
his pleasure in sitting in the Café Royal thus:

> Although I had long left corporeal adolescence, I listened less at those loqua-
> cious tables than received/absorbed visually. I received much less through my
> ears (deafened) by bullying sermons (and exalted oratorios) than through my
> ever-famished (starved) eyes. (Voyeur?) ('D2', 165)

We have already noted voyeuristic imaginings and how Davies transformed
an open act of sexual congress into one that could provide a voyeuristic fris-
son by transporting it from a lounge to a two-paned telephone box. It is possible to surmise that sight stood in for other senses in his make-up. In his
analysis of narcissism, Heinz Kohut explains that a child deprived in his early
physical needs, both oral and tactile, by a cold or rejecting mother can seek to
compensate through the visual sense:

By looking at the mother and being looked at by her, the child attempts not only to obtain the narcissistic gratifications that are in tune with the visual sensory modality but also strives to substitute for failures that had occurred in the realm of physical (oral and tactile) contact or closeness.[24]

Kohut describes a young man who had been grossly deprived of tactile stimulation in infancy but who had been able, 'early in his life, to shift his need for tactile stimulation to the visual area . . . The visual stimulation seems to have been sufficient to support the nucleus of a self which in general maintained its cohesiveness'.[25] When Davies describes his eyes as 'ever-famished' he seems to suggest that he recognizes visual stimulus is as necessary to him as food.

A study of Rhys Davies's autobiographical process has, it is hoped, illuminated the extent to which unconscious process and personal vulnerability work upon the picture a writer paints of himself and his society. Ultimately, the researcher is left with a palimpsest effect: an image of what Rhys Davies was projecting in the early drafts, and a further image generated by discovering in what ways the first image had been made safe by its author. Crafted by a writer of undoubted ability, Rhys Davies's central image of a repressed Valleys culture is a powerful creation but, as we have shown, it is perceived from the stance of a detached narcissist, not through truly objective eyes. Davies makes his repression pervasive and external, symbolized by the shackles of the chapel and the constraints of Welsh flannel, and experiences its shattering in a way he cannot or will not make explicit when he experiences the Beardsley drawings of *Salome* and the Wilde text. It is probable that these externals were in fact objective correlatives for inner states, brought about by the potent combination of Davies's narcissism and, at the time of his first seeing the Beardsley drawings, his unacknowledged homosexuality. A reader working with a sympathetic model of Davies's psychology in mind is likely to find their reading of his autobiographical text much enhanced.

3

Writing it Out: Margiad Evans (1909–1958)

Margiad Evans, born Peggy Whistler in Uxbridge of English parents, appears here because of her passionate identification with the Welsh Border area. Acclaimed novelist in the 1930s, short-story writer, minute observer and recorder of the natural scene, she has further claim to attention here through the fascinating range and, finally, the self-giving depth of her autobiographical writing. Her autobiographical novel, *The Wooden Doctor* (1933), seems to be an attempt to bed down painfully significant experience, and is an interesting variant on the *Bildungsroman* in its concern to trace the struggle to come to terms with female sexuality.[1] In some of her last autobiographical works she endeavours to dredge meaning from serious disability and, finally, from the process of dying, as she strives to use her writerly skills to communicate to the world, in *A Ray of Darkness* (1952),[2] and to the medical profession, in the unpublished autobiographical essay, 'The Nightingale Silenced' (1954),[3] some sense of the distress, disorientation and fear a major epileptic often endures, as well as the altered perception and erosion of meaningful selfhood this state can produce. Set against this, the unpublished 'The Immortal Hospital' (1957),[4] written in the shadow of death, is a glowing affirmation of the power of early love to shape, mould and provide consolation in the harshest circumstances, as Margiad Evans returns in memory to a precious year of childhood spent with her aunt Fran (Annie in real life) on the Welsh Borders.[5]

Margiad Evans's autobiographical writing from different phases of her life movingly allows the reader to trace the psychic development that a female human being needs to accomplish over a lifespan in order to achieve secure rootedness in her sexuality and in the world. The surviving, unpublished journals of her early adult years (1933–9) reveal an emotional life of considerable pain and difficulty: a largely tempestuous relationship with her mother; an alcoholic father; the final taming of an overpowering unrequited love for her doctor (the eponymous protagonist of her heavily autobiographical novel *The Wooden Doctor*); and, subsequently, continuing calf-love for another unattainable older man, her publisher, Basil Blackwell.[6] For many years, in parallel with her longing for the love of Blackwell, she had a largely unhappy lesbian relationship with Ruth Farr. From all this, there is a sense of coming into safe haven as she emerged into mature adult love through marriage to Michael Williams in 1940.

Margiad Evans was, in pen-name and, I believe, in one of her writerly personae, an elective Welshwoman, intensely attached to a particular part of the Welsh Border area. For reasons which will be explored progressively, Peggy Whistler, deeply unhappy in her early adult life, had a particular need to create personae with which to face the world. As the adoption of a new name could be taken to be the declaration of a desired identity, it seems important to explore her likely degree of attraction to a specifically Welsh one, although it would be a rash undertaking to attempt to establish incontrovertibly what lies at the basis of a creative writer's love of place.

Indubitably, powerful emotional needs were met in Margiad Evans's childhood by and in the Border area. My analysis of *The Wooden Doctor* will highlight the degree of misery and emotional deprivation Peggy Whistler experienced as a result of her father's alcoholism. At the end of her life, she recalls, in 'The Immortal Hospital', that her strong identification with the Border area started at the age of nine at a time of major family upheaval, when her father had just retired early because of what has been described as 'ill-health perhaps not unconnected with alcohol' (Lloyd-Morgan, 8). Surprisingly, as she is 'the least favoured among his three girls', she is chosen as her father's companion for a visit to his sister's farm at Benhall near the river Wye. She recalls, on the point of being drawn away from the river at the moment of departure, 'in a passion of tears' sobbing 'Oh don't, don't take me away from this place. Oh, Dad, can't I stay *here*?' ('The Immortal Hospital', 17). Two years later, at a time when the Whistler family has no permanent home, and after Peggy has had a deeply unhappy period at boarding school, she has a year, from March 1920, with her sister Nancy at Benhall, a time which she experiences as blissfully happy, her sister much less so. As she describes the period in 'The Immortal Hospital', a feature of central importance in an experience that she describes with rapture is that she was deeply loved by her Aunt Fran and was her special child for the duration of the stay ('The Immortal Hospital', 9). What such security represented for 'the nervous creature' she remembers herself to have been, 'distraught not with nightmares but with passions and distortions of passions, weary even at eleven years old with too much feeling' can only be guessed at ('The Immortal Hospital', 21).

At the end of that year, in 1921, the Whistler family set up home at Lavender Cottage, within walking distance of Benhall. When, after the father's death fifteen years later, the family have to leave Lavender Cottage, Margiad Evans describes the depth of her attachment in her journal:

> Leave this house and leave this place where I was born? Yes, though I'm 27 and I came when I was twelve, I was born here . . . I ask myself by what accident I was born away from these people? What rupture with Fate made me an alien walking on these hills? ('Journal 2', 62v)

'Alien' in one sense, indeed she was. Clare Morgan has suggestively argued that Margiad Evans is primarily an English Romantic writer, wedded to the idea of the sublime in nature rather than to a particular landscape.[7] Although Margiad Evans's journal records the intense lifting of the heart she regularly experienced on catching sight of the Welsh mountains spread out against the sky, often from the Hereford road as she returned home after an absence,[8] her love of Wales would indeed, as Morgan suggests, seem to stem from an imaginative affinity and a romantic attachment to the idea of the country rather than from any extensive experience of its reality. One can imagine, however, that during her year at Benhall, the mountains of Wales became imprinted on her consciousness as part of the landscape of security and joy.

She feels herself, then, to have been a nervous and vulnerable child. The young adult who grew from these beginnings seems to have had a need to try out for herself different ways of being and, as we shall see, even to attempt to manipulate members of her immediate family into particular roles. As Peggy Whistler eased her way into the persona of Margiad Evans, the Brontë sisters seem to have been both early role-models and writerly influences in several respects. Most obviously, the Brontës' strong identification with their Yorkshire setting matched Evans's sense of being inspired by and rooted in the Welsh Border area. Evans shared Emily Brontë's fascination with Byronic heroes. Dearnley describes Evans as 'fascinated, ultimately obsessed by Emily Brontë' and finds 'the main character of [Evans's novel *Turf or Stone*] essentially Heathcliff' (18). It is possible to see how Margiad Evans's own early experience would make the creation of such a character attractive, even therapeutic. In *The Wooden Doctor*, she writes of the child Arabella and her sister's 'terror and disgust' as they stand 'shivering behind bolted doors with our hands over our ears that we might not hear [our father] scream of the horrors that he saw' (xvi). One can imagine that the creation of Easter Probert [in *Turf or Stone*], an eroticized version of a terrifying, strong yet needy male, might in some way earth a charge of horror from childhood.[9]

However, certainly the most intriguing tracing of Margiad Evans's pre-occupation with the Brontës comes in a letter of 28 July 1963 from Arthur Calder Marshall, communicating with Arnold Thorpe, Margiad Evans's prospective biographer, about a visit he had paid to the Whistler home at Bridstow. He writes:

> [On visiting Bridstow] I found that I was precipitated into a drama of the Brontës. Haworth had been translated to Herefordshire. Margiad was quite certainly Emily. Sian was rather reluctantly Charlotte. She had almost no literary talent but was forced to exploit what she had. Anne was, unfortunately, not playing ball. [There is also a brother whom Calder Marshall humorously depicts as being alarmed at the possibility of having to play Branwell.] The generating station of this Brontë was Peggy Whistler who for some reason could not bear to be Peggy Whistler but had to be Margiad Evans.
>
> Please don't think that I am despising this, even though there was a strong element of play acting in it. For some reason she had to play act – which she did not do very well.[10]

Calder Marshall's impression, recollected thirty years later, is hardly a factual record, but the general picture given is of a piece with other evidence concerning that time. Certainly, Margiad Evans encouraged her sister Nancy to adopt the name Sian Evans and to write, although her journal reveals that she suffered torments of jealousy and an enduring sense of threat that Sian would overtake her as a more successful writer.[11] The psychological 'pay-off' she may have received from the notion of a 'Welsh' writing family, analogous to the Yorkshire Brontës, may have provided some compensation for these very painful feelings. At about this time, in the first draft of *The Wooden Doctor*, in parts later excised, she twice alludes to her protagonist self as Welsh.[12]

Perhaps the most striking emotional need that seems to have been answered for Evans by reinventing her family as a Welsh equivalent of the Brontës came from another area of vulnerability: family life at Haworth was rendered deeply unhappy in the final three years of Branwell's life through his alcoholism and his addiction to opium, just as Margiad Evans conveys in *The Wooden Doctor* that her father's alcoholism totally overshadowed her young life. One can imagine that there was powerful encouragement for her in the way the Brontë sisters transcended such adverse circumstances to forge an enduring reputation. Thus, the persona Margiad Evans may have seemed to promise much.

Margiad Evans destroyed her early journals in 1934. The earliest extant journals, 1933–9, covering the period when she was aged twenty-three to thirty, reveal further 'trying on' of personae, as though seeking to answer the question, 'Who or what am I?' She sometimes writes in French, as though aspiring to a more vibrantly artistic register or a cosmopolitan poise but the effect is rather spoilt, even for herself, when she is aware of her insecure command of grammar, particularly gender.[13] There is often a pleasurable flirtation with a bohemian identity.[14] While it is beyond question that Margiad Evans was very unhappy for long periods at this time, there is undoubtedly, too, an exhibitionist streak in what she writes. On occasion, she catches herself out in the self-indulgence, and a climax of romantically expressed anger about elements of suspected betrayal in the relationship with Ruth Farr collapses into farce: 'May . . . the spiders spin in her windows, the weeds choke her flowers, the owls fly blindly by day. Python passion . . . Aw shit!' ('Journal 1', 59). Such humorous self-deflation is, however, rare.

The Wooden Doctor could be regarded as Margiad Evans's major, published, autobiographical act, in spite of her conventional disclaimer that 'all characters in the book are purely imaginary'. Arabella Warden, the heroine, is the same age at various stages of the book as Margiad Evans was in accomplishing similar stages, and shares her author's artistic and literary talents. The life of each is overshadowed by an alcoholic father and a mother with considerable musical gifts, who is only intermittently supportive. The late adolescence and early adult life of each is traumatized by agonizing attacks of cystitis. Each, while living in the Welsh Border area, spends a period as a pupil teacher at a school in France. Each lives for a time with a cousin in Oxfordshire, and stays on a farm in north Wales to finish writing a first book. Both Arabella and Margiad Evans cherish an unrequited, obsessive love for their middle-aged Irish doctor. Further, Margiad Evans entitles her 1935–9 journal *Arabella's Voice*, and she is known as Arabella to her publisher, Basil Blackwell. In the first draft, she frequently forgets her assumed identity, Arabella, and has people address her as Miss Whistler and Peggy, while the Irish doctor is referred to by his real-life name of Dr Dunlop. Inevitably, however, there is some simplifying and reshaping of her actual life-circumstances. Several years later, Margiad Evans records in her journal: 'Very late last night I read *The Wooden Doctor*. What pain I was in when I wrote that. It was like standing in my own grave to read it' ('Journal 2', 145v). She evidently feels that she is looking back on a period of her own life.

However, as, in *The Wooden Doctor*, Margiad Evans is dealing with very recent painful events in her life and is evoking particular significant figures in an unflattering way, the marketing of the book as a novel seems to have been inevitable. The Prelude declares: 'My father did more than drink occasionally; he was a habitual and incurable drunkard. No word was ever more accurately or deservedly applied; no family was ever rendered more miserable by its justice' (*The Wooden Doctor*, xvi). The mother is repeatedly revealed as unsupportive in crucially important areas. Furthermore, the doctor for whom Margiad cherishes a long-term unrequited love would have been easily identifiable. She rather blows her cover by dedicating the book to the 'Wooden Doctor', so described because of her perception of his impassive reaction to her declaration of love, but also, perhaps, to indicate his iconic significance: the first draft had entitled the book 'The Divine Image'. It is possible to identify a range of conceivable motives, both conscious and unconscious, for writing in the way she did. At one time she records in her journal: 'I write all this *because I want to forget it*. I always write what I want to get rid of' ('Journal 2', 117). Just as Virginia Woolf finally purged herself of her obsessive memories of her beloved mother, who died when she was thirteen, by making her glowingly external and real in *To the Lighthouse*, so, perhaps, Margiad Evans hoped that the writing of the book would distance the events it dealt with and diminish their pain. Her journal records that she sent Dr Dunlop proof copies of *The Wooden Doctor* and was surprised to receive no response ('Journal 1', 2, 3v). It seems possible that she hoped that, by revealing to him the extent of her suffering, she would stir him to some recognition and response. The strongest motivation, however, would seem to have been an attempt to come to terms with the experience and to derive comfort from fuller understanding.

Adoption of a fictional mode gives Margiad Evans particular freedom in patterning her experience poetically, symbolically. She is a strongly intuitive writer, trusting what floats up from her deepest unconscious processes. In my engagement with *The Wooden Doctor*, a Freudian framework of interpretation and later developments from this have been indispensable tools, particularly in tracing the power of Oedipal feeling at work in Margiad Evans. However, one cannot determine with any certainty whether what becomes clear to the initiated reader was also transparent to the writer, as was clearly the case in the use by Rhys Davies of Freudian concepts; in the light of subsequent journal entries, probably not. Yet, as one continues through the journals, tracing Margiad Evans's subsequent compulsive need of a further father-figure-as-love-object in Basil Blackwell, in a second reading of *The Wooden Doctor* one becomes aware that the writer has perhaps known more than she can consciously access.

The Prelude sets the scene, with some elucidation of situations and events which precede the main action. The Warden family live in a private hell, isolated in their neighbourhood by the father's alcoholism. Their doctor, middle-aged and unmarried, is one of their rare visitors and is a soothing and beneficent presence. Arabella, the narrator, is the middle child, apprehensively on the threshold of puberty. We become quickly aware that she has no opinion of her own physical allure in relation to her two sisters: 'Our relations said Catherine was beautiful and Esther promised well in spite of her deplorable tendency to make the worst of herself but I should always be plain (x).' The Prelude vividly encapsulates the course of the father's alcoholism and its effect on the family. Margiad Evans, later to become a most exact observer of nature in its minutest manifestations, describes how the mother's efforts to protect the children from the effects of the father's alcoholism are subverted, partly by the father's tendency to roam 'and partly because our perceptions were really abnormally acute' (xvi). It is startling to consider that the highly developed powers of observation may have been fostered as a survival strategy in youth in the family of a violent alcoholic.

> As we grew older, there was less violence, and by that time, very little could touch us . . . Where we had feared and hated we now pitied and despised: our father's attitude reacted to the change. His health gave way, he became quieter in his degradation, in his ruin more complete. (xvii)

In the course of the Prelude and the first few pages of the novel proper, Arabella moves from the age of twelve to sixteen and her point of departure for the wider world. Nothing that she has seen in her own family has caused her to feel confident in her own sexuality or sanguine of the potential for fulfilment in the relationship between the sexes. In the middle of the night before Arabella is due to leave for a period as a pupil teacher in France, her father returns in a particularly horrifying state of drunkenness:

> Desperately, wearily, sternly, with all her heart my mother cried:
>
> 'See the horrors of a drunken man'.
>
> I looked for all my life. (4)

The final sentence is resonantly telling. At this point, the doctor implicitly moves into position as a substitute parent:

The next day I was too ill to travel, and the doctor came. All that I craved, all the things existence had so far denied me, I found in him, and in him only . . .

After he had gone, I slept till midnight when a furious gale awoke me . . . Sheltered from the frenzied uproar without, the lamp upon the table by my bed burned steadily without a flicker. (4–6)

In a functioning family, a primary parenting role is the nurture and protection of the young. In Arabella's family of origin, the father is often frightening and unpredictable; the mother can do little to preserve a safe and loving environment. Neither is to be trusted in terms of establishing secure boundaries. In Arabella's perception, the doctor moves in as surrogate protector, in whose shelter the flame of life can burn more securely.

Her time in France is bitterly unhappy. An innocent friendship with a young Englishman offends the bourgeois proprieties of the headteacher, and Arabella's mother accepts the Frenchwoman's version of events without discussion. Mrs Warden is capricious and impulsive in subsequent decisions. It is the doctor who realizes the importance of release from the school for Arabella and, with wholesome gales of laughter, gives her the means of effecting it.

In Part Two, Arabella discovers her talent as an artist and, through it, the perceived power of female sexuality. Interestingly, in a reaction similar to the one we have already observed in Rhys Davies, she is 'pierced by delight' and 'her imagination leapt' (75) when she comes upon some of Aubrey Beardsley's more notorious drawings. It is the sense of contained power that seems to fascinate her: 'this curbed riot, this dammed river, how it bore me away' (75).

Her talent recognized, she is sent to art school: 'We drew skulls and vases and a girl who wore all her clothes. A nude model was unprocurable' (76). Where she has discovered in herself a yearning to explore the power of human sexuality, at one remove, through the safety of drawing, and to investigate imaginatively her sense of what the female body may be a site for, she is given what she perceives as tame objects to draw, only to develop the skill of draughtsmanship. At this point, Arabella is clearly needing to pass through a Lacanian mirror-stage: to gaze at a mature female form, draw it and to own it as part of her perceived identity. She is not given the means to achieve this. Winning her parents' approval, she completes her first artistic commission and is on the threshold of adult life and a career. She takes the canary's cage out into the garden. 'I saw the sky through the bars of his cage' (76). Later, she takes off all her clothes; 'the garden was so deep in leaves'. That night she is overcome by agonizing pain. The acceptance of adult status seems to produce conflict (77). In one who has perceived within the family the hell that the gaining of mature adult sexuality can unleash, this is hardly surprising. The doctor comes and diagnoses cystitis.

For someone as emotionally deprived as Arabella, her illness provides a considerable pay-off, guaranteeing the continuing care and consideration of a consistent fatherly human being and justification for regression. Her first tentative and innocent experience with someone of the opposite sex, the young Englishman in France, has ended in misunderstanding and disgrace. Beardsley has taught her something further of the power of female sexuality. On the verge of adult life, as her first commission is completed, she becomes agonizingly afflicted in an area that would make any genital engagement problematic. Given that Arabella is a fictional character, it is possible that it is no coincidence that the author here makes it impossible for her to engage in any serious sexual expression.

Returning home, Arabella again becomes ill:

> I had another attack and our father had a roaring drinking bout. Esther and I could not restrain our shouts of derision. To quench the stream of abuse we pretended to have hysterics and yelled and laughed till our father sat down in his armchair . . . He ejaculated softly:
>
> 'You little bitches, you *bloody* little bitches.'
>
> I banged on the piano with my fists. Esther's enormous eyes were wide and black, all her features were sharpened, strained. Our mother wept. (92–3)

It is a nightmare scenario. Psychoanalysts argue that the achievement of mature adult sexuality, genital sexuality, is dependent on having first experienced powerful love for the parent or other carer of the opposite sex in early childhood at the Oedipal stage. Indeed, this intense relationship has been seen to have profound and central significance in future personality development. This love is normally safely and flirtatiously touched into life again in adolescence as, during normal development, the young person moves inexorably onwards to becoming a free-standing sexual being. The evidence of Margiad Evans's journals, as we shall see, seems to indicate that she became fixated at the Oedipal stage, needing to draw in surrogate fathers to fulfil an overwhelming emotional need, before she could move onwards. This climactic exchange with Arabella's drunken father is an important representative scene in the unfolding autobiographical work, making clear why Arabella is inescapably drawn into an overwhelming love for the supportive, reliable and utterly consistent doctor.

While in hospital for tests for cystitis, as she observes the face of a dying woman, she becomes aware of the depth of her alienation from her own mother and that the 'Wooden Doctor' is her only emotional support (105). Later, as the tests are extremely painful, she becomes aware of her female body as a site of anguish. On returning home, when she has to report that no discernible cause for her illness has been found, her mother coldly attributes her problem to nerves. Minutes later, she lavishes endearments and protests her love: 'I did not believe her. Esther yawned and refilled the teapot. Our eyes met with deep understanding' (119). Arabella comes to view herself more and more as unattractive and undesirable. At last she acknowledges in her own heart that she deeply loves the doctor and, henceforth, significantly, refers to him as 'Papa Doctor' (124). Such a naming seems to acknowledge an awareness of his unavailability to her as a sexual partner. It seems plain that she is aware at some level that she has directed her passionate feelings in a safe direction. Still unconsciously at the Oedipal stage, genital consummation is not a goal.

Part Two builds to a climax as she crosses the Rubicon of declaring her love, presumably by letter. Visiting him soon after this, she is gently told: 'My dear, it's impossible; autumn cannot mate with spring–' (140). Returning to her cousin's house desolate, she is tormented by the fullness of the loving relationship she sees between her cousin and her husband. The depth of misery is very real, but, after the passage of time, she believes that she has moved on. Later, when staying at a farm in Caernarfonshire to complete her first book, she has a love affair with a young Englishman, Oliver, and they plan to marry. She completes her book at the farm and that very night is attacked again by cystitis but this does not darken her mood of triumphant achievement. Yet, in the final page of the book, she returns home and meets the 'Wooden Doctor' (often referred to as 'the Irishman') by chance in the street. The final ten lines of the book are reproduced in full:

'Arabella, are ye back again?'

'Oh Papa –' I stammered.

It looks absurd written down, the conviction that I could not marry any other man. Yet it came upon me very suddenly.

It only remained to tell Oliver.

*****

All this took place some time ago.

My book was published.

Oliver sends me red tulips on my birthday.

And the Irishman married a young girl a few months after my return.

*****

And that's the end.

The reactions to the book were largely approving. The *TLS* reviewer on 23 March 1933 found Arabella and her author 'something akin'. He concludes his comments:

> Fate intervenes when happiness seems nearest and all her world falls to pieces before her consuming, hopeless love. There is no end to the story. The study of the fatal nature which can rely on nothing but its own strength should have many readers.

With the advantage of hindsight, well beyond the end of Margiad Evans's life and taking the tenor and content of her later writing into account, it is possible to be more sanguine, to see that in *The Wooden Doctor* she is passing through a necessary developmental stage. Given the fraught nature of her early environment, Margiad Evans's devotion to the qualities of tenderness, reliability and encouragement that she found in her 'Papa Doctor' had to be allowed to run its course. The doctor has been the container of her intense feelings during her growing up, the means by which she could project and externalize the pain experienced within her family of origin. Yet she has understood that there has been both projection and idealizing in her love of him. At the end of the draft version she ponders:

> I cannot describe what he meant to me . . . Previous misery melted under his thoughtful, penetrating gaze. With him I was a child and my youth adored him. Nevertheless he was for many years a friend of fancy rather than of fact, a fancy that circling unsteadily in its fledgling flight alighted on him from the first. (*The Wooden Doctor*, draft, 240)

Through this image she seems to acknowledge that her neediness was so great that it was almost a matter of chance whom her love fixed upon.

In many respects, *The Wooden Doctor* is a study in humiliation. In a journal entry for 13 March 1933, Margiad imagines the mockery her depiction of her relationship with Dr Dunlop will provoke amongst her acquaintances:

> Last night Percy took my proofs screaming he would bring them back this morning – of course he did not and when fancy pictures himself and Tony Alexander and their rabble crew laughing over those pages, I feel it, I feel it in my pride. Thus my long love and my Irishman. ('Journal 1', 5v)

Towards the end of *The Wooden Doctor*, she anticipates just this sort of experience:

> An ardent devotion offered, politely declined and handed back very little the worse for wear . . . judge me, a woman who will set that down against her own name, who will betray her own passion, and refrain from mocking at it hanging crucified, only because she knows many people who can spit farther and scourge more powerfully . . .

> Good person, I am writing a history of humiliation and loss. It is for me: it is mine. (*The Wooden Doctor*, 160)

The evidence points to the likelihood that Arabella contained a large measure of Margiad Evans's view of herself in 1932.

At the time Dr Flaherty is Arabella's obsessively perceived Other, and he seems to hold for her some part of a personality she ultimately will need to integrate for herself. He is used as an external superego. After the mother's harsh judgement of the episode with the young Englishman in France, Arabella observes:

> The Irishman [Dr Flaherty] would not have judged so harshly, nor so cruelly condemned . . .

> He has called himself my Father Confessor: he was more. Against vice, brutality, stupidity, evil, I weighed this one man whose puissant image was the strongest influence in my life, and he more than balanced all. (*The Wooden Doctor*, 56–7)

The fictional Dr Flaherty must rank high on any scale of hugely idealized characters in literature. When, in the real world, Dr Dunlop married, he drew a line under some aspects of his relationship with his young patient, and it is evident from his widow's testimony that Margiad Evans found it very hard to accept the new situation, writing and phoning frequently, in spite of requests that she desist (Lloyd-Morgan, 37). As her relationship with Dunlop was powerfully Oedipal, it did not prove to be possible for her to move on from it merely through an act of will. However, while her journal from 1934 onwards reveals continuing intermittent thoughts of Dr Dunlop, it also divulges that she seems to have found it possible to transfer her intense feelings to another container, another safe, unavailable, powerful man, Basil Blackwell, her publisher. In the weeks before Godfrey Whistler's death of liver failure, even when she is deeply involved in a relationship with Ruth Farr, Evans twice recognizes the stark need she has of Basil Blackwell: 'I am undergoing a blind, instinctive craving for the Professor – it's as though he has something I must have to reach my whole self' ('Journal 2', 14v). Later: 'What has made of the Professor a gate I *must* pass through?' ('Journal 2', 15v). The tone is puzzled, but at some level she seems to understand that she is in the grip of a strong psychic need.

If one reads in chronological sequence the first draft of *The Wooden Doctor*, the published version, the extant early diaries in sequence and the much later 'The Immortal Hospital', which deals with her childhood, one cannot fail to be struck by Margiad Evans's tendency to idealize or denigrate, and by how violently her feelings veer between these two poles. In *The Wooden Doctor* the father is at first feared and loathed, then pitied and despised; by the journals of 1934 onwards he is regarded more tolerantly and sympathetically, and it is the mother who is viewed with rage and disgust. In 'The Immortal Hospital' Margiad Evans's childhood relationship with her sister Sian/Nancy is rhapsodically idealized; in the journals she often cannot contain her irritation, dislike and jealousy.[15] The swings of feeling for Ruth Farr, with whom she has a lesbian relationship over several years, regularly move from hate to passionate declaration of love: 'She was a traitor in her mother's womb and her bones grew in guile' ('Journal 1', 85v); and a bold, large statement standing proud on the page: 'Ruth, I love you dearly always' ('Journal 2', 86).

Margiad Evans obviously finds it hard to deal with ambivalence, to hold simultaneously the possibility of love and hate for the same person. Melanie Klein teaches us that this, too, is to do with a developmental stage. Kleinians argue that at first the infant has a concept of good – the generously provided, available breast – and bad – the torturing, withholding breast, when the baby's needs are not immediately answered. The violence of the small baby's feelings lead to a splitting, so that the good is kept apart from the bad, lest the violently experienced bad has the power to destroy the good. An important developmental stage is reached – the depressive stage, as Klein terms it – when the child is able to realize that the good and bad attributes belong to the same person and learns to cope with ambivalence. This stage is reached when a baby receives 'good enough' mothering, where the mother is strong enough to bear the infant's hostile projections and reflect back something that is perceived by the baby as loving.[16]

It is all too common for someone who has been poorly nurtured to blame herself for perceived inadequacies and to idealize ineffective caregivers. The description of herself that Margiad Evans gives early in this chapter suggests that at eleven she was an insecure, nervous child. She remembers that 'so dear was [my mother] to me that until I was sixteen, I could never leave her without tears' ('The Immortal Hospital', 17). It is possible that she misinterprets her remembered distress: it seems more likely that she was showing signs of what John Bowlby describes as anxious attachment, which is an acute worry over the accessibility and responsiveness of a protective attachment figure, developed as a result of bitter experience. Drawing on the studies of others, Bowlby summarizes predisposing characteristics for anxious attachment, of which three seem of particular relevance to Margiad Evans's childhood circumstances.[17] A very unsettled home life with changes of caregiver and frequent shifts of residence was one factor, being constantly compared unfavourably with one's siblings another, and quarrels between parents and mutual disparagement a third.[18] We remember that Margiad Evans's father took early retirement on grounds of alcoholism-induced ill-health when she was nine, that she had a very unhappy period at boarding school when she was ten, and moved to Benhall for a year at eleven before settling at Lavender Cottage with her parents at twelve, to observe Godfrey Whistler's deterioration. The Prelude to *The Wooden Doctor* suggests that Arabella's relations saw her as the least promising of the three sisters in terms of appearance and commented on their observation. As an adult when, with her sister Betty, Margiad visits Aunt Nell in Uxbridge, the town where she was born, she observes Nell's love for Betty with some distress: 'Aunt Nell gave Betty mustard and cress, eggs and a green pot of hyacinths. She loves her. That's plain to see. My throat feels so tight tonight. I think perhaps I shall be sick' ('Journal 1', 34). The mother, however, was the primary caregiver, and the picture that emerges of Margiad Evans's mother from 'The Immortal Hospital' does not encourage any objective view of a close and loving bond. Written when Margiad Evans knew herself to be dying, it memorializes with great gratitude the loving care and tenderness she received from Aunt Fran in her year at Benhall which, we get a strong impression, was a new experience for her. 'Once more I seem to feel Aunt Fran bending towards me with such a look, that had she not died of pneumonia soon after my marriage some of life's suffering had been softened towards me or even spared' ('The Immortal Hospital', 45). Margiad's parents mocked Aunt Fran's taste in clothes for children. Margiad Evans comments: 'It may have been in bad taste but it was in good love . . . For the affection that went into the selection was what the child Margiad instinctively liked, and *not* the clothes themselves' ('The Immortal Hospital', 48). Margiad's mother visited when they had been with Aunt Fran almost a year: 'Sian seemed hardly to notice her . . . but to me she might have brought what is now called "an emotional conflict" if it had not been that my peace was too deep and my surroundings too happy' ('The Immortal Hospital', 49). When, at the end of a year, the younger sisters returned to their parents at Lavender Cottage:

> the scrapping of those brilliant clothes in a bonfire of rather unkind laughter caused me pain. When they threw away certain things they were almost throwing me away. A *me* they could not recapture for myself: a peace like a summer's day, so long, so long, long ago: an innocence, reliance and quietness never to be regained in subsequent days. ('The Immortal Hospital', 48–9)

These descriptions of a powerful and ungentle character unaware of, or perhaps even uncaring of, what is deeply important to her child are consistent with the view given of Arabella's mother in *The Wooden Doctor*. The bitter quarrels between Margiad Evans and her mother in adult life, recorded in the journals, perhaps had their seeds in this childhood. It seems likely that an inability to deal with ambivalence, a need to see people as black or white, to idealize or denigrate, was a consequence of Margiad Evans's nurture as an infant.

For the most part, the earliest extant journals from 1933–9 make distressing reading. There is a horrifying sense of the hell that family life can become when lack of means requires incompatible people to live together. 'This *is* an unhappy home', Margiad writes of the Whistler household in July 1933 ('Journal 1', 10). Margiad Evans, while yearning for Blackwell, becomes deeply enmeshed in a relationship with Ruth Farr from April 1934. There are appalling rows, about this and other matters, and on several occasions Mrs Whistler abandons the family for several weeks, to the seeming relief of Margiad, Nancy and their father. The darkness, suffering, pessimism and the sterility of relationships in her novel, *Creed* (1936), give a fair indication of her state of mind in this period. A not untypical mood is expressed:

What am I pouring out here but self, self, rotten self feeding on self, burying self, throwing self up and eating self again. The days crawl on me like snails. What is there to live for but more misery and further sleep? . . . I never go out. I never work. I am ugly, dirty, now indifferent, now frenzied. My eyes pick out all that is horrible, sad, feverishly disordered. ('Journal 2', 43)

She sees the need for the journal as a means of capturing and, to some degree, pinioning otherwise free-floating despair:

I must keep up this book or the last vague control will be gone . . . But approaching this book and writing in it is like dressing a wound or a repulsive sore, such a sore as I pictured last night in my side, a grey hole creeping with maggots which bit and bit at the edges. Surely it's better to write *that* than carry it in my mind. ('Journal 1', 72v)

She certainly wrote in the hope of penetrating the puzzle of herself: 'It's hopeless, impossible to come to grips with myself – like trying to cast up accounts that will never meet. I can't get at myself, and *nobody* can get at me' ('Journal 1', 56). In January 1939 she acknowledges the cathartic effect of writing in her journal: 'Why don't I write more? For the relief now is like weeping to an aching heart' ('Journal 2', 148v). Margiad Evans's journals in the period 1934–8 seem to reveal a driving need to externalize particular moods. They seem largely to change in content from about January 1939. They become less a receptacle for pent-up feelings and more a means of recording something otherwise evanescent, of interpreting, of celebrating. Although it is a psychological truism that, in times of external threat, depressive states can improve dramatically, this would seem to provide only a small part of the explanation of the change in her journals. A more profound metamorphosis came about from experiencing the certainty that she was loved, as her relationship with Michael Williams developed.

Without any doubt the recovery of her childhood deep attunedness to nature – originally in itself possibly a sort of emotional displacement – comes about in part through the merging of personality in love with someone who shared her love of nature. From about January 1939, there is a great increase in the frequency and amount of natural description in her journals. At this period, Mrs Whistler was living in Ross and, when staying with her mother, Margiad Evans and Michael Williams were able to have long walks in the surrounding countryside. These times played an important part in their deepening relationship. In a recognizably autobiographical short story, 'The Ruin', which Margiad Evans wrote in 1946, she describes the difficult period of readjustment of a young couple who have been separated for several years by the husband's war service. Out together, they revel in the profusion of primroses, the trout in the sparkling streams. The woman inwardly rejoices:

> Together again, together again . . . Their worlds had fused . . .

> 'Of us two', she meditated, 'it's he who has the strongest power to interpret. Though as *I'm* the writer, no-one knows it except myself. Oh, my imagination needs him dreadfully.'[19]

She writes something similar in *Autobiography*:

> I often feel when M— suddenly speaks like that that he thinks from inside Nature, that he has some thought with it flowing with it. To go with him into the fields is to see further than my own sight, and to understand without effort, from within . . . He has thoughts, simple, in no way elaborate or strange, which he can make me see, as I see the birds and the cloud and the moonlight.[20]

Indubitably, Margiad Evans's perception of the natural world was extended and deepened by this relationship. Her published *Autobiography*, very largely detailed accounts of her response to nature, is a reworking or edited version of her journal during the war years.

She becomes aware that in her response to nature she is 'reliving the first perception of my life, how I am interwoven with my childhood' (*Autobiography*, 80) and it is again the memories of the blissful year with Aunt Fran that she recalls, as she evokes the close relationship with her sister Sian/Nancy that grew during that year:

> But I was thinking how I was alive up to about thirteen – and how vivid and pure and *true* were the things I saw and did . . . Existence since has been a smoke and a jargon until a short while ago when I found the same early beauty as early still. Living with M— has let me find myself entirely, let me go back, never I hope to be lost again . . . (*Autobiography*, 81)

It was in times of deep emotional security that Margiad Evans became rooted enough to have the potential to be a visionary observer of nature.

Happiness in a relationship at last seemed to release Margiad Evans into a mode of being that she considered her true self. In October 1940, at the age of thirty-one, she married Michael Williams, who was many years *younger* than she was. In writing to him in January 1943, she expresses her awareness of what that marriage has meant to her: 'Oh my dear dear young man, what a restoration our marriage has been to me' (quoted by Lloyd-Morgan, 86).

After her marriage, Margiad Evans lived for the next seven years in a small cottage at Llangarron, near Ross, three miles from the Welsh border, where some of her best writing was completed. During the time when Michael Williams was on active service, on board ships in the Mediterranean, she wrote letters to him almost daily, hundreds of which survive, and these, in many respects, took the place of her detailed journals.

Secure in being loved, Margiad Evans lived in circumstances that were at last conducive to her coming into the safe haven of a mature, authentic identity. At the beginning of *Autobiography* she rejoices in solitude: 'Oh the happiness of being alone – it's like having only one door to yourself and that bolted and firm walls round' (1). The personality is intact, protected, at peace. A journal entry in February 1943 has her showing a most unusual tenderness and acceptance of herself:

One night in February.

I am an introvert. Not a physical one, but an introvert for all that. Tonight I am so happy. I want nothing but myself. I close my book *Darkness and Dawn* and sigh looking at the lamp which is smoking and has a blackened chimney. Dear Arabella. Dear, dear self. The nurturing in my being, the star shine and wood burning, they are all in harmony with myself.[21]

Much stress in the years before her marriage was caused by her inability to have the defended space so essential to one of an introvert orientation.[22]

Margiad Evans's autobiographical writings of the war period are structured on the principle of daily record. Her journal entries and letters to her husband would be written at night after hard work, often in the fields beet-hoeing or apple- and pear-picking, moments of imaginative space wrenched from an often exhausting routine. Intriguingly, during the period of the nature writing, she became aware of the sense of self as a burden she would wish to relinquish. Her greatest happiness comes with awareness of loss of individuality: 'Such a lovely unconscious day. I never once remembered that there was such a person as myself and that I was there chopping and sawing logs and gathering faggots . . . The only assertion of existence was blood warmth' (*Autobiography*, 3). Further: 'I don't wrap myself in solitude, I go naked in it. I discard my particularity, I discard myself' (*Autobiography*, 103). She makes it movingly apparent that through her relationship with nature in the day's tasks and chores, she manages to divest herself of emotional pain:

'Often and often walking up and down between the coppice and the stile, by looking into the wide field I have cleared my soul of pain' (*Autobiography*, 151). As she writes, she is revealing the intense joy to be had in the process of attention and the delight in noting the significance of a myriad details. On virtually any page of *Autobiography*, the reader is being taught how to observe, the meaning of what she sees and what lies beyond it: 'As I sit here by the wall I find the continuity, the connection between all living things' (*Autobiography*, 92). The ultimate aim of the rapt observation is interfusion. 'The intense desire to be united with Nature grows in me with the impossibility of achieving it or comprehending the longing. Rarely for a moment it happens: but constantly and every day I want it without ceasing' (*Autobiography*, 139). The goal of this particular self is the mystic's absorption into the infinite.

Margiad Evans had one-sided relationships with two idealized and powerful men, which remained constant over long periods. The level of idealization of the 'Wooden Doctor' made the relationship in reality intensely unsatisfying, given that idealization is a defensive formation against aggressive feelings, in this case for her parents. Her way of relating to these distant, unavailable men was through splitting off her good self and projecting it, leaving for herself a morass of despairing feelings. Maturing beyond the need of an Oedipal relationship, Evans establishes a happy marriage relationship with someone not at all in the category of father, who shares her delight in nature. At last, in nature, she has a link with something greater than herself that can truly sustain her and be a container for her intense feelings. However, tragically, after the onset of epilepsy, when medication destroyed her ability to relate to nature in the same way, it becomes evident that she has understood the projective mechanism at work in that relationship, too:

> And because Nature and weather and landscape had failed, I knew everything had, for people like myself cannot live long sanely without that powering from one kind of being into another. No, not love, sexual or maternal, replaces it. That my projection of conscious life into plants, animals, trees, the land, even, in all its contours, was *scientifically* illogical I knew, but it made no difference to my not being able to exist without it. ('The Nightingale Silenced', 40)

Indeed, the onset of epilepsy transformed the way Margiad Evans understood and constructed the world and her place in it. The *TLS* reviewer of *A Ray of Darkness* (5 December 1952) compares the upheaval in her scheme of things with what Darwin experienced off the coast of Chile, when he witnessed an earthquake, after which the earth never again seemed to him a secure place.

Two works, one by Robert Murphy and another by Oliver Sacks, have been useful in helping me conceptualize the way the advent of serious disability undermines and alters the existing sense of self. Robert Murphy, a professor of anthropology, was found, in middle life, to have a spinal tumour which gradually rendered him quadraplegic. Using anthropological perspectives, he looked, in *The Body Silent*, at what happens to an individual's status in society and to his or her perception of self when afflicted by serious disability.[23] In *The Man Who Mistook his Wife for a Hat*, Oliver Sacks, with a different focus, shows the tremendous struggle people with neurological disorders put up to preserve identity in adverse circumstances.[24]

Margiad Evans explores with particular intensity her perception of how epilepsy changed her life in two works: *A Ray of Darkness* (1952) and the unpublished 'The Nightingale Silenced' (1954). *A Ray of Darkness* is shaped into three parts. In Part One Margiad Evans outlines, with hindsight, all the premonitory symptoms of emerging epilepsy, and explores the difficulties of ever knowing, from within one's own subjectivity, what is normal. In Part Two, 'The Other Side of the Wave', during an evening of tranquil domestic activity, she moves irrevocably across a great divide: in undergoing her first fit, she becomes an epileptic and her status in the world and her perception of herself are changed for ever. She further discovers that, at the age of forty-two, she is pregnant for the first time. After a period of tormenting doubt, it is decided that her epilepsy is not inheritable and the pregnancy is allowed to continue. The third part describes the different, less frequent and more frightening nature of the fits under medication. Evans struggles obsessively to attribute personal meaning to the onset of epilepsy, refusing the doctor's ready-made explanation.

Using Murphy's analytical approach, it seems productive to set Evans's feelings about and observations of her changed state in the wider framework of how society and the individual within society are seen to cope with disability. Murphy shows how a formal occasion, which conferred on him a particular academic honour, served as a rite of passage for him. As a high-ranking academic, he makes the transition from one social identity to another, as he re-emerges in his world as a paraplegic in a wheelchair (65). Margiad Evans attempts to negotiate a similar passage. From the moment, an hour after her first fit, when she becomes aware that her lapse of unconsciousness has involved incontinence, she 'knows' that she has had an epileptic fit, 'an inner certainty to which it was necessary to confess once a day' (*A Ray of Darkness*, 86). Her letters to her extended family 'grow angrier and angrier' (*A Ray of Darkness*, 99), as her blood relations resist very energetically any such diagnosis: 'One cannot blame this attitude. It is natural that one's blood relations should not welcome a disease such as epilepsy into their circle. They are bound to protest against the idea of it' (*A Ray of Darkness*, 98). She is left in a liminal state because of their non-acceptance, although she has a vivid sense of the category to which she properly belongs. She had regularly visited an epileptic colony near her sister's home 'and saw the poor children and the sad, bitter battered faces of the older inhabitants and the "different" ones of the younger' (*A Ray of Darkness*, 37) and believes that she 'should have been all the time' one of them. She confers a near-priestly function on the consultant who confirms that she has epilepsy: 'And I walked out of the Institute as a person harbouring epilepsy, it was true, but free of false hopes and quite clearly defined as myself by another's firmness, directness, courage and knowledge' (*A Ray of Darkness*, 106). She reifies her disease: she is an epileptic, not a human being who sometimes has fits.

Quoting Ernest Goffman, Murphy describes his own radical loss of self-esteem, his sense of 'stigma' and 'spoiled identity', once disabled (77). He knows the aura of contamination can become attached to other members of the family, too. This seems to have been Evans's experience. Calder Marshall, who corresponded with her at the time of the publication of *A Ray of Darkness*, feels 'it was clear that Margiad had fallen out with all her family as a result of that brave book' (letter to Thorpe, 28 July 1963). Presumably members of the family disliked the prominence given to a stigmatizing disease, and feared contamination themselves.

Murphy further refers to Gliedman and Ross's view that the disabled person becomes 'the Other – a living symbol of failure, frailty and emasculation; a counterpoint to normality, a figure whose very humanity is questionable' (100). Indeed, Margiad Evans finds it hard to maintain a positive frame of mind when 'attacked by the world in its ignorance and hatred of the sick. "If you can't be well, get out of my sight" is the natural if unexpressed reaction of the healthy to the unhealthy' (*A Ray of Darkness*, 107). She feels particular horror at the sudden onset of fits and the loss of control, 'of falling down and rolling about like an animal. It is horribly repugnant. Even more horrifying was the idea of coming round alone and finding the stamp of your animalism all around you with no-one to welcome you to yourself again' (*A Ray of Darkness*, 99). Murphy is very daunted by the effect of his illness on his status as a member of society 'for it visited upon [him] a disease of social relations' (3). Evans, too, is aware of a shift in her social acceptability. She describes having a fit while in hospital soon after the birth of her child, and desperately needing reassurance and explanation, because of the utter confusion caused by the blanks in her memory:

I made the other women call the nurse, I made her ring up my husband. 'Poor man' I heard her say, and when she returned it was not unkindly but in rather a satisfied manner she told me she had not been able to get through to him. (*A Ray of Darkness*, 153)

Through the eyes of others, Evans perceives herself as a burden, an encumbrance. Murphy further shows how lack of autonomy and unreciprocated dependence on others bring debasement of status (155). Indeed, in 'The Nightingale Silenced', Evans expresses her sense of humiliation at not being able to create a restful home for her husband: 'This shame helped to make me bad-tempered but it seemed I could not confess how dependent I felt without a total breakdown' (31). Because she might be a danger to herself or her baby during a fit or in the state of confusion which followed, she could not be left alone. In the moment of truth when she first determines she has had an epileptic fit, her first horrified thought is: 'A fit, to a healthy woman, on whose ability to live alone so much depended!' (*A Ray of Darkness*, 81). One feels that in writing 'The Nightingale Silenced', in particular, she is attempting to move from dependence to reciprocity: to offer the world insights that will be of benefit to a category of people, epileptics, but also to human understanding in general.

While Murphy uses his professional training as an anthropologist to evaluate the subjectivity and the status of the disabled from his own situation as a quadraplegic, the consuming interest of neurologist Oliver Sacks, in *The Man Who Mistook His Wife for a Hat*, is in how the neurological disorders affect the sense of self and what compensatory efforts particular selves make to retain their sense of identity. He declares at the outset that:

Neurology's favourite word is 'deficit', denoting an impairment or incapacity of neurological function . . . But it must be said from the outset that a disease is never mere loss or excess – that there is always a reaction on the part of the affected organism or individual, to restore, replace, to compensate for and preserve its identity, however strange the means may be. (1)

Although Evans sadly declares: 'It must be far easier, I think, to be born an epileptic than to become one – to have to accustom yourself to losing yourself' (*A Ray of Darkness*, 36), she, too, strives to preserve a recognizable core of self. The terrifying aspects of epilepsy, as she first experienced it, were to do with the suddenness of its onset, the loss of control it produced, and the amnesia and disorientation that followed in its wake. Each of the first four well-spread fits had a different 'homely and comfortable remembrance'

(*A Ray of Darkness*, 169), such as a jug or spoon, associated with it, 'embedded in [its] horror'. 'As long as I had these images, and the attacks remained far enough apart for forgetfulness *and* memory to combine, each retained a kind of separate personality' (169). These images helped Evans to come to some sort of uneasy accommodation with her condition. They offered her a semblance of control over her situation by giving her the power to register each fit separately in memory, although this ability was later lost. Another means of maintaining a cohesive identity, against the worst the disease could do to fragment it, was through writing. It seems probable that writing *A Ray of Darkness* one year after the onset of epilepsy was symbolically important. The work encapsulated and preserved the nature of that momentous experience, some of it transcribed from journals. A very frightening aspect of her fits when under medication was that consciousness was prolonged into the fit, and Evans regularly had the sensation of seeming to disintegrate into two or more entities. As her view of self was centrally as an author, a communicator, to fashion a book from the actual experiences which caused fragmentation was to fashion a new mosaic of self from those fragments. Yet she is aware of a profound change. In times when the epilepsy is quiescent: 'the drugs I have to take to prevent the discharges of the epilepsy make me apathetic, have faded, dulled and dimmed the powers of the imagination and concentration. Restless but helpless, no action seems worth taking' ('The Nightingale Silenced', 189). The intense, vibrant delight in nature is gone: she has even lost the freedom to be alone in nature and the projective powers which enabled interfusion have dulled. Indeed, the nightingale is silenced.

Erosion of memory was, for Margiad Evans, perhaps the most undermining aspect of her illness. One of the most interesting case histories Oliver Sacks recounts in *The Man Who Mistook His Wife for a Hat* is that of Jimmie, who has lost the greater part of his memory and, with that, his past, his moorings in time. Sacks prefaces the chapter with an epigraph from Luis Buñuel's *Memoirs*:

> You have to begin to lose your memory, if only in bits and pieces, to realise that memory is what makes our lives. Life without memory is no life at all . . . Our memory is our coherence, our reason, our feeling, even our action. Without it, we are nothing. (*The Man Who Mistook His Wife for a Hat*, 22)

For Evans, the loss of a sense of continuity of identity was one of the consequences of the memory losses caused by the epilepsy. On occasion, during a minor attack, she was left without any understanding of the significance of objects. Once, when offered pills by a nurse, she did not know what to do with them. She 'found such vacancy horrifying' ('The Nightingale Silenced', 24). She can believe herself to be surfacing from sleep in circumstances of total normalcy, her head beside her husband's on the pillow, only to be told she has just had another fit. Of this experience she affirms:

> Ever since I have been incredulous of all things firm and material. The light has held patches of invisible blackness. Time has become as rotten as worm-eaten wood, the earth under me is full of trapdoors . . . Sight, hearing, touch, consciousness, torn from one like a nest from a bird. (*A Ray of Darkness*, 122)

Clearly, deficits of memory could be a source of anguish. By a particularly cruel quirk of fate, recall could also become a bitter torment. The medication which reduced the actual number of fits prolonged consciousness into an attack, regularly inflicting upon her a sense of horror she would never forget: 'Lest neurologists imagine they can cure . . . let them absorb this one point: *that you cannot cure memory*. And that no person whose mind is imprinted with such memories is ever wholly healthy again' ('The Nightingale Silenced', 75). Memory, then, would seem to be the most essential attribute of a firm sense of identity: its impairment can undermine a sense of symbolic coherence in a very distressing way. Explaining this, Evans describes how:

> In certain moods it seems I slip in and out of [time's] meshes as a sardine through a herring net. Having once discovered periods of *action* which I could not remember, the trust which normal people rest in their own continuity has left me. (*A Ray of Darkness*, 182)

In the cataclysmic upheaval in her universe, she has lost a sense of the flow of time.

The diminishment of her capacities brought with it a shift in how she constructed her world. In 'The Nightingale Silenced' she writes: 'It is a commonplace to say that the world is not a real place but real only as the brain is capable of conceiving it' (16). Her consultant has indicated his belief that her fits have been caused by a slight scarring of the brain tissue, probably the result of a childhood fall from a horse. In fact, in her final years, an exploratory operation reveals that a brain tumour has been the cause of the whole problem. Yet Evans is driven to try to make her own sense of the disease that afflicts her. If the attacks are indeed a consequence of something fortuitous, there is no hope of having any control over them. If, however, they are a result of some failing in her, she may, unconsciously, believe that there is a possibility of achieving remission or control through effort. She returns again and again to her possible culpability, blaming too weak a loyalty to her Muse (*A Ray of Darkness*, 173) and pondering 'Can epilepsy be a physical unconscious awareness of a spiritual lack?' (*A Ray of Darkness*, 180). Murphy offers a convincing rationale for the sort of hypothesis-building Margiad Evans undertakes:

> There is, then, a need for order in all humans that impels us to search for systemic coherence in both nature and society and, when we can find none, to invent it . . . It is an empirical fact that the mind seeks to impose systems of some kind of order upon all it surveys. It is a property of all peoples and all cultures . . . I would suggest . . . that it derives secondarily from our deepest biological urge, the instinct for self-preservation. We look for order because it makes predictability possible and we seek predictability to avoid danger in an essentially perilous world. Our fondest illusion is that we can reduce risk by making the unanticipated predictable, and by exerting human control over the contingencies of life. (*The Body Silent*, 29)

Epilepsy transformed Evans's world. Initially, one of the most distressing aspects for the reader of *A Ray of Darkness* and 'The Nightingale Silenced' is the insight one gains into the loss of self-esteem the disease has inflicted on the writer. Her writing would seem to be an important attempt to improve her self-concept as a result of a need 'to testify . . . to raise up myself and others like me' ('The Nightingale Silenced', 2). She writes *A Ray of Darkness* from her own need to communicate, being allowed little or no cathartic relief through discussing her illness with family or friends. By the time of 'The Nightingale Silenced', however, she is consciously writing for doctors.

She believes there is a need of such a work, for she knows of no modern account of epilepsy apart from what Dostoevsky diffused throughout his works and, as Sacks quotes Dostoevsky's delighted assurance: 'You all, healthy people, can't imagine the happiness which we epileptics feel during the second before a fit' (*The Man Who Mistook His Wife for a Hat*, 137), it is evident that his testimony cannot speak for one like Margiad Evans, for whom 'within each seizure is embedded an embryonic second of such terror that body and mind recoil from any association with it' (*A Ray of Darkness*, 14). As her fits worsen, a new anguish intervenes. 'The actual visual appearance [of a thing] was unchanged but the visual value was altered' ('The Nightingale Silenced', 19). A cherry tree in bloom can look the same but feel terrifyingly different, and within her home 'a terror amounting to panic seemed to emanate from every piece of furniture, every book' ('The Nightingale Silenced', 26–7). Through her own distress, Margiad Evans has learnt intense compassion for others in her state. Her very laudable aim in 'The Nightingale Silenced' is to have clinicians appreciate the nature of the torment that afflicted people may undergo in the universe of human suffering that is epilepsy.

Idris Parry shows admiration for both her courage and her writerly skill.[25] He feels *A Ray of Darkness* is a disturbing, moving book which more than delivers on Kafka's stipulation: 'A book must be an axe for the frozen sea in us' ('Margiad Evans', 225). As Margiad Evans struggles to communicate the often tormented nature of her subjectivity in her two works on epilepsy, she succeeds again and again in transmitting and transmuting the pain of it, so that it stands as a type for all suffering of a similar kind.

4

Miners into Writers: B. L. Coombes (1893–1974) and Ron Berry (1920–1997)

The mining valleys bulk large in the popular myth of Wales in the twentieth century. As a society, they feature in the narratives of several authors in this book, particularly those of Rhys Davies and Gwyn Thomas. Accounts of what it was like to be a miner, however, are rarer. This chapter will consider the autobiographical work of two colliers, B. L. Coombes and Ron Berry, whose most important offerings, *These Poor Hands*[1] and *History is What You Live*,[2] were published in 1939 and 1998 respectively. Coombes's book acquired iconic status. His declared intention of raising consciousness of the human cost of coal was more than realized, for *These Poor Hands* sold nearly 50,000 copies in the first six months as a Gollancz Left Book Club choice. Between them, these two works cover a time from the boom period of the coalfield, through the industrial turbulence of the 1920s and depression of the 1930s, down to the rapid decline and near-complete demise of the industry in the later part of the twentieth century.

As autobiographers they could not be more different. A prime motivation for Berry seems to have been to engage in a genuine search to try to explain his perplexing self to himself. His dealings with the reader seem honest and in keeping with the character he reveals. With impish glee he signals a large area of omission some ten pages before the end of the book, when he owns that he has a wife and three children, not earlier or further mentioned in any way (136). Coombes, however, is a carefully constructed exemplary worker, 1930s style. It has taken extensive archival research to reveal the sometimes considerable gulf between his various autobiographical assertions and his lived life.

But to begin at the beginning. It seems strangely necessary to give an insight into the subjective experience of that allegedly objective evaluating instrument, the critic. Wolfgang Iser argues:

> This 'transfer' of the text to reader is often regarded as being brought about solely by the text. Any successful transfer however – though initiated by the text – depends on the extent to which this text can activate the individual reader's faculties of perceiving and processing.[3]

The idiosyncratic experience of the reader, then, may facilitate or impede assimilation of a particular text. The mining community in which I myself grew up had been of real importance to me. My father was a doctor, dealing with the full, distressing range of mining diseases and accidents. Because of the long psychiatric illness of my mother, the loving support of that village community was of crucial importance to me as a child. In my middle age, the published version of *These Poor Hands* gave me some sense of the nature of the working life of the community of which I had been part and reawakened my own early memories of it. I came to *These Poor Hands* early in my researches on autobiography and returned to it again and again over a five-year period, successive discoveries involving extensive rewriting. I offer first a record of my initial and – as it now seems to me – innocent appraisal of Coombes as autobiographer, with some adjustments of perspective from a slightly later date. A depiction of the persona of the published *These Poor Hands* seems a useful starting point, because this is the received version that has entered Welsh social history. Throughout, I place Coombes's name in quotation marks to distance the persona of the autobiography from the real person.

In the opening of *These Poor Hands*, 'Coombes' presents himself as an impoverished farm lad. The first chapter is masterly in the way it evokes the misery and chill deprivation of the life of the rural proletariat, huddling in damp clothes near a fire of damp logs, as 'the winter wind rushed across the Herefordshire fields where the swedes rotted in heaps' (7) because transporting them to market was not cost-effective. The feudal structure of rural life kept each in his preordained niche, with the gentleman farmer exerting great power through the tied cottage system, 'where he could, and often did, make [workers] homeless and wageless for the least opposition to his wishes' (13) and with the squire at the apex of the pyramid, for whom the very church bells 'pealed in earnest' (13) only when his carriage and pair was seen to round the turn. Coombes paints a bleak picture of unremitting toil for small return for those who did not own land. From this disheartening environment, he describes his fascination with the warm glow in the night sky, identified for him as the Bessemer works at Dowlais, which comes to represent in his mind's eye the fairer prospect of industrial labour. There was hope, too, for a more egalitarian society: 'Ain't got to call no manner of man sir up there' (10).

In chapter 1, the rural introduction to the industrial allegro, 'Coombes' grooms us into a way of perceiving and identifying that is strongly class based. On his arrival at Treclewyd, 'Coombes', presented as a total newcomer to the industrial scene, is struck by the warmth: he notes the bright dazzle of brasswork in the homes and 'a fire that filled the grate as high as was safe and its white heat showed in the reflection of the fender' (20). The reader is most skilfully drawn into an awareness of what made a move to the new way of life attractive to an enterprising young man from a dank rural heartland.

First and foremost, 'Coombes' perceives himself as a worker. The title of his autobiography comes loaded with the intertextual resonance of Dickens's *Hard Times*, where the lives of the exploited industrial 'hands' of Coketown are depicted in their drudgery and misery. In these pre-nationalization days, 'Coombes' documents exhaustively the callous indifference of profit-bent owners to all matters of human justice for their hands, and how men at all levels of management must collude in profit-for-owners as the only good. For this reason, he perceives an unbridgeable gap between workers and management. He is sickened by management's habitual behaviour after strikes:

> It seems to me to be a most unfair thing to penalise the men's officials after a strike. They only carry out the mandate of the men they represent (187) ... [After a strike the manager] would not allow the chairman or the check weigher to come on the colliery property (189) ... [This] was the fourth check weigher – elected to see that the men get fair play in coal-weighing – I have known whom the colliery companies have dismissed. (189)

He outlines dispassionately all the ways he has seen workers cheated or done down by officials. He describes how he and a companion, in the naivety and energy of youth, are deceived into cooperating by breaking all production records when a normally intractable seam becomes, briefly, easy to work:

> We realised, when it was too late that we had been the cause of the rate being fixed so low that the men were always afterwards driven like slaves in an attempt to force them to earn as near their [minimum] money as possible. (86)

When officials came to measure work done, on which payment would depend,

> their intention was . . . to badger the workman in every way, to talk about his
> interests, to frighten or fluster him – anything to make him forget some item in
> the measuring. After they had once passed it would be very difficult to get paid
> for it. (49)

If the miner took the company to court to insist on payment of the minimum wage, retribution would often come by the contaminating of his truck with stones or slag, for which he could be sacked (50). When a worker as a committee representative complained to an official about ambulance arrangements and the neglected state of airways, he was framed by a letter to Whitehall, which everyone knew to be forged, and dismissed (219–20). Miners were regularly made to work whole shifts of overtime and were not paid for their work (126). There seemed to be good evidence that the owners were in league with the Labour Exchange, the provider of dole-money, to ensure that workers were made to toil at levels below the dole entitlement (215). When mine accidents occurred that could have been attributed to official laxity, the evidence was often tampered with to imply either negligence on the part of those killed or the generous provision of items, such as pit props, the lack of which had actually caused the accident (27, 253). Miners were daily required to take inordinate risks through inadequate provision of those same pit props, and made to take heavy electric cables into gassy or very wet situations where explosions or electrocution might result (111–17). The financial value of an animal could merit more care for it than for a man: a pit pony was worth £40, whereas bachelor Jack, mainstay of his family's finances in fact, merited only funeral expenses when he was killed (60–1). The catalogue of callous indifference on the part of officials builds to a moving climax in the penultimate chapter of *These Poor Hands*, when we hear Billy tell 'Coombes' of Hutch's death. We have grown to know Billy and Hutch as endearing individuals in the course of the book. 'Coombes' affirms: 'I had the affection for Billy that every workman feels for a mate who has shared years at a dangerous job with him' (246). Billy describes how he and Hutch, as repairers in a new job up north, are forced by a fireman to work very soon after a rockfall, when another collapse is threatening. The fireman refuses to allow them to shore up the roof before starting the work of clearing, and Hutch is killed (248–51). The telling of this by 'Coombes' engages fully with Billy's pain and the grief he feels for the bereft family, with whom he and his family had lived very closely in shared accommodation. We understand and feel Billy's powerlessness: had he told of the fireman's negligence at the inquest, Hutch's family would have been denied compensation (254–5). The chapter ends with Billy asking 'Coombes' to speak for him at his colliery, so that he may have the hope of returning to familiar faces. 'Coombes' agrees. ' "I knew you would when I came", he answered, and I was grateful for this tribute from my old mate' (257). Through such feeling means, 'Coombes' presents how deeply his sense of self is enmeshed in his role of working man, engaged in important, dangerous and productive work with others, whom he has learnt to trust and love and on whom his life has often depended. His class identification – a feeling rather than a doctrinaire belief – is established as being a fundamental part of how he sees himself.

Certainly, some of the sense 'Coombes' has of class solidarity and an unpolitical sense of class enmity came from his growing awareness of what the accident rate was underground, once he had trained as an ambulanceman and was regularly called away from his mining work to treat injured people. In his later years as a miner, safety measures were increasingly ignored, as Welsh coal lost its traditional markets and management desperately pushed the workers in the search for speed and higher productivity. 'Coombes' becomes one of the early 'machine men', a job he hated, in charge of an enormously powerful cutting machine, and was obliged to work a double shift to the point of utter exhaustion and falling asleep at his dangerous post (108–25). Although mechanical cutting eased the physical labour of mining, it very much increased the dangers, as the high noise-level made it impossible to hear the early-warning creaking and shifting that often preceded a roof collapse, dust levels were much higher, raising the risk of what came to be known as pneumoconiosis, and the power cable often leaked electricity.

'Coombes' affirms in a variety of ways his warm commitment to comradeship as an abiding human blessing. He observes with approval from the first day in Treclewyd that: 'There was none of the "keep away from this place, I pay rent for it" about these people, as is the case in the English farming areas' (22). He is moved by the generous-spirited way those who had been able to save, through having several wage-earners in the family, would visit during a strike and 'after they had gone money would be found in places where only they could have placed it. When we sent it after them, they would deny all knowledge of it. It would be used to help in cases where the need was urgent' (79). 'Coombes' observes the painful progress around the pub of the silicotic ex-miner Dai, near death and trying to make some money for his family through selling raffle tickets for his gramophone: he notes that 'the three who are miners buy without any hesitation . . . you will never see a miner refuse help to another who is sick or injured, for it may be his own turn next' (238). When Billy, a fellow machine-cutter, is persuaded to return to work before the strike is ended, 'Coombes' compassionately observes that Billy, who has six children, 'was living in an isolated cottage on the mountainside . . . [He] did not have the support of other men living near, as we did' (185). He is appalled by the Labour Exchange's attempt to get men to seek work at a distance from their community. Such a man was forced to:

> Go away from the people he knew and counted as friends, who would smoke their pipe of tobacco with him while they talked of the better times that they had enjoyed together. Go to some strange area where he would feel himself a stranger and an interloper . . . Go to be a stranger in the house, in the work and in the street. (150)

He indicates that the Coombes family have made it a rule 'that if we have anything in our house, no beggar shall ask for food in vain' (223). On one occasion he discloses that he was part of a group travelling to work on a charabanc; on a particular morning they go and wake up a late-sleeping boy. During that shift the same boy is sent by his slipshod butty to borrow a hatchet from 'Coombes'. 'The boy asked so nicely I could not refuse him', he declares. Ten minutes later the boy is killed by a roof-fall. 'Coombes' observes, 'I have always been glad I loaned him my hatchet, or I would have felt that I withheld the thing that might have saved his life' (168). He identifies habitually with his fellow workers: 'Coombes' walked the four miles to the colliery when he was working at a particular time, on Friday, pay-day, exulting in 'the grand day' and feeling 'the wonder of such a day right in my bones', yet aware that 'underneath that mountain that is over to my right more than a thousand of my mates are shut away from the sight of this day' (228–9).

After the abnormal, subterranean, dangerous life 'Coombes' led so much of the time, he describes the need of normal, human, intimate life asserting itself particularly strongly. The delight 'Coombes' expresses in the nesting process, when he and his wife finally achieved two ten-square-foot rooms of their own, is touching, given the manifold disadvantages of that home. Just after the war, 'we had a wonderful stroke of luck – so unexpected that we could scarcely believe it to be anything but a dream: we got a house to ourselves' (130). The house flooded regularly; coal deliveries had to be carried through the prized front room; they had rampant beetle infestation, and the tiny house was next door to a noisy public house. At last, however, they had achieved privacy, something 'Coombes' sees as a deep human need frequently not met in the circumstances of a miner's life, and 'could talk without being overheard . . . We counted it as almost a palace, and, besides, there was a small garden' (131). 'Coombes' values this seemingly normal satisfaction highly, being aware that 'people there were prepared to go to any extreme in bribing or paying extra rent to get a house that became vacant' (130). He writes tenderly of the birth of his son, 'thinking how small and helpless he looked' (171), and of his first tentative steps walking and exploring the natural world. Through the life of this average miner, so often trapped into working sixteen hours a day underground, some glimmers of the deep human satisfaction and nurturing 'Coombes' gained from his family life shine through.

Miner 'Coombes' may be, crawling through darkness and filth for much of his working life, but he believes he has as much capacity to respond to beauty as any man. He is intensely responsive to beauty in nature: 'the dew of morning sparkl[ing] from a thousand leaves' (38) after his first night shift. An eighty-foot waterfall, 'not a mile from the drab village yet unknown to most natives', seemed 'a wide veil of water, the spray from which kissed the primrose roots amongst the rocky sides to a new life and beauty' (55). A miner incarcerated in darkness for much of his life reveals poignantly how moved he is by visual beauty.

From 'Coombes' we gain a sense of many aspects of physical identity. From him, we come to understand something of the hard-wired, compelling, night and day rhythms of the human body which are impossible to deny:

> I had thought that night and day were alike underground but it was not so. It is always dark, but Nature cannot be deceived and when the time is night man craves for sleep. When the morning comes to the outside world, he revives again, as I did. (37)

Further, the body never adapts entirely to sleeping by day:

> Jack [declared] there was little hope that I would ever sleep properly by day. He was quite right, and even today I notice that the beginning of each night shift shows the men weary and disheartened by the lack of proper rest and that all are hoping that the week-end will come soon so they can have a real night's sleep. (41)

A particular awareness of one's physical make-up comes with the unusual contortions and exertions a miner's work may require:

> I soon found that a different kind of strength was needed than the one I had developed. My legs became cramped, my arms ached and the back of my hands had the skin rubbed off by pressing my knees against them to force the shovel under the coal. (35)

'Coombes', in his early forties when writing *These Poor Hands*, is sensitive to the distressing awareness in older miners that their strength is ebbing and their whole sense of human value is linked to their muscle-power:

> Then, again, when one starts to think, it must surely be realised that every passing week makes one older . . . I watch how the few men who are old come to work; how weary they look, how their faces seem almost as grey as their hair; how desperate they are that the officials shall not think they are slower at the work than the younger men. (222)

In this harsh world, human usefulness depends on physical fitness: 'There is no place in our industry for the ill or the injured, no matter how that incapacity may be caused. A working man is only of any value as long as he can do a hard day's work' (222).

In *These Poor Hands*, the sense of self 'Coombes' displays is largely defined by the nature of his work: his sense of being an exploited unit of labour, creating profit for the owners and suffering danger and indignity in that cause, and his experience of the overpowering reality of comradeship as a great good in that life.

Although I had felt moved and informed in my early readings of *These Poor Hands*, the study of Coombes proved to be an object lesson in important scholarly virtues – a peculiar sort of tenacity and the necessity of holding initial conclusions lightly. This chapter represents my fifth (and final) reworking of the Coombes material. In retrospect I review the chase with something like amusement; in the living of it, there was a frequent sense of incredulity and exasperation at the slippery eel my quarry proved to be.

What is perhaps the most striking illustration of the fact that Coombes regarded his lived life as a highly malleable commodity, when it comes to autobiographical retelling, is found in his contribution to 'The Life We Want', a Liberal Party pamphlet published in 1944.[4] Lord Meston wrote the first part, giving a theoretical exposition of a desirable restructuring of society after the Second World War for the benefit of the working man. Coombes follows on, writing of the harsh experiences of a working man's life, and showing a shrewd awareness of how to interpret working-class experience sympathetically for the middle-class elements in his readership.

While, for the most part, we have to take what Coombes says at face value because there is no possibility of verification, what he tells us of his origins and early life until he leaves for the mines can be compared with independent records or with what he has written of that period in other times and different circumstances (in parentheses in what follows). The disparities are very striking. In this pamphlet, Coombes presents himself as having been born on a farm in Herefordshire forty-five years before and as growing up on the land. (Barbara Nield's article in *The Dictionary of Labour Biography* records that Coombes, the son of a grocer, was actually born in Wolverhampton in 1893 and was therefore fifty-one in 1944.[5]) He implies he has at least one sibling. (In his second, unpublished autobiography, 'Home on the Hill', Coombes indicates that he was a lonely only child (279).[6]) He describes his sense of growing 'bitterness', 'confused frustration and helplessness' (14) in his childhood and youth as the son of a tenant farmer, as he takes in the utter impossibility of making one's way through life on the land. (In old age, he writes in the *Neath Guardian* of childhood years spent in the industrial con-text of Treharris, where his father and uncles were miners, and of moving as late as the age of fourteen with his parents to take up the tenancy of a farm in Herefordshire, where he spent only 'a few years' on the land.[7]) He describes the hardships that 'drove' him from the countryside (15). (In 'Home on the Hill' Coombes presents himself from the age of sixteen to seventeen as being in a comfortable job as groom to a doctor, whence he leaves for the mines in search of excitement and danger (27–43).) The very epitome of an enterprising young man, Coombes indicates that he cycles the whole eighty miles from the country to the mining valleys (15). (In *These Poor Hands* and 'Home on the Hill' he presents himself as travelling by train and, in the former work, is accompanied by a tin trunk (18).) 'The Life We Want' indubitably reveals that Coombes was prepared to go to considerable lengths to adapt his actual life-story, to suit the single clear message he is trying to put across in auto-biographical mode.

Before embarking on a complicated story where the critic-as-sleuth attempts to unravel such matters as the publishing history of *These Poor Hands* and the ramifications of Coombes's various, conflicting autobio-graphical assertions, it seems necessary to focus, as I did with Rhys Davies, on the appropriate expectations of a particular text that a reader might legit-imately bring to a work quite clearly marketed as autobiography. Philippe Lejeune, in an essay referred to briefly already (p. 16), puts forward the idea of an implicit autobiographical pact made between writer and reader, which conditions the reader's approach to and expectations of an autobiographical text ('Pact', 29). (For example, the 'pact' encourages the reader to trust that he is reading an account of a lived life.) In an attempted definition of the genre Lejeune states: '[An autobiography] is a retrospective prose narrative written by a real person concerning his own existence, where the focus is his indi-vidual life, in particular the story of his personality' ('Pact', 4). He adds a little later: 'The *author*, the *narrator* and the *protagonist* must be identical.' In the same essay, he tackles the thorny question of autobiographical truth:

> As opposed to all forms of fiction, biography and autobiography are *referential* texts: exactly like scientific or historical discourse, they claim to provide information about a 'reality' exterior to the text, and so to submit to a test of *verification*. Their aim is not simple verisimilitude, but resemblance to the truth. ('Pact', 22)

He posits a referential pact with the reader, running alongside the autobiographical pact, in which the writer is undertaking to tell the whole truth, as it seems to him/her, in the area in which the contract applies. As we have already seen, Berry has made clear that he limits the contract by explicitly excluding his family life. The title Coombes gives to his work – *These Poor Hands: The Autobiography of a Miner Working in South Wales* – encourages the reader to read with the expectation of a factual account of the writer's working life. The author, narrator and protagonist are indeed one and the same: at the beginning of chapter 6, Coombes explicitly writes himself into his text when he describes hearing his new wife named as Mrs Coombes for the first time.

The Liberal Party pamphlet, which I identified and consulted midway through my researches, gives telling evidence of Coombes's cavalier attitude to autobiographical truth in 1944. The lengthy enquiry which culminated in this chapter has cast doubt on the referential status of *These Poor Hands*, too. As I embark on a consideration of the evolution of that work,[8] it is necessary briefly to introduce two of the leading players. John Lehmann, an editor-publisher, and Victor Gollancz, a publisher, were of key importance in creating a culture that made possible the meteoric success of *These Poor Hands*. Appalled by Europe's inexorable course towards war in the mid-1930s, as the Fascist threat increased, they both engaged in promoting literature which exemplified the effective brotherhood that existed between victims of oppression. Lehmann, to some degree, and Gollancz far more single-mindedly, right up to the Nazi–Soviet pact in 1939, saw an alignment with the Communist aspirations of the Soviet Union as the way forward in the fight against the certain evils of Fascism. Victor Gollancz helped to create a strong market for a particular sort of book with his Left Book Club imprint. While keenly interested in being published by the Left Book Club – he made a lengthy approach to Gollancz in February 1937 – Coombes initially committed his projected autobiography to Lehmann, presumably because Lehmann's response was the more enthusiastic.[9] When Lehmann ran into trouble with his publishers, Coombes returned with alacrity, with his just-completed book, to Gollancz.[10] It was, however, a further twenty months before the book was published as a Left Book Club choice, with guaranteed sales of nearly 50,000.

I first began to suspect that *These Poor Hands* might not be a conventionally straightforward autobiography when I read a letter from Coombes to Glyn Jones, written in 1939, now in the National Library of Wales. It declared: 'By the way, I had to alter the ending of the book as it was rather too drastic a criticism of the conditions and the last two chapters were written in great haste.'[11] This observation set me off on an extended period of burrowing in archives, where a range of finds opened up new vistas, necessitating several reshapings of my material. In late 1998, in the B. L. Coombes archive in the South Wales Coalfield Collection at the University of Wales Swansea, I explored a veritable treasure trove: two fragmentary drafts of *These Poor Hands*, including the two discarded chapters, the typescript of an unpublished second autobiography, 'Home on the Hill', and a scrapbook of letters and cuttings to do with *These Poor Hands* and early reviews of it.[12] Later I read the Ruth Dudley Edwards biography of Victor Gollancz. One source fed another but led me into a quagmire. I discovered that, as early as 1937, Victor Gollancz's record of tampering with texts submitted for publication in a 'good' (that is, pro-Communist) cause was striking.[13] Remembering that Coombes had declared that 'too drastic a criticism of the conditions' was the reason for change, I surmised that Gollancz had wished to suppress these chapters because they showed miners powerlessly conniving in an unjust legal process which went against their best interests. It seemed that Gollancz might have wished, rather, to enhance a public perception, since the 1926 miners' strike, of miners as the epitome of worker solidarity. Misled by Coombes's embellishment, I later came to own that this was a surmise too far.

The Dudley Edwards biography also disclosed the exciting information that, at least up to 1987, the firm of Gollancz had extensive archives from the Left Book Club period. However, by 1999, when I started making enquiries Gollancz had been taken over by Orion. After lengthy investigation I found myself talking to Mike Petty, the then publishing director of the Gollancz imprint of Orion Publishing, who had to tell me with regret that the entire Left Book Club archive was languishing in a warehouse in Poole, Dorset, completely closed to the world since the Orion takeover. An impasse, then, had been reached.

However, some six months later, in March 2000, the position changed. A decision had been made by Orion to move the entire archive. In the period when the warehouse was open but in a state of upheaval, Mike Petty, in an expedition worthy of his quarry, complete with torch and explorer's fervour, had edged his way around the fork-lift trucks and wrested the Coombes file from oblivion. He informed me with some pleasure that a folder, containing some fifty letters exchanged between the firm of Gollancz and Coombes, largely between 1937 and 1940, awaited me at the Orion offices. This proved, perhaps, the most important single find in an exciting period of discoveries. Most immediately, the rather banal reason for the discarding of the two chapters came to light: Gollancz had become very afraid of attracting a libel suit from a colliery official, a fireman, whom Coombes had portrayed as a bully, craven in the face of danger, in the two powerfully written chapters which described the death in a mining roof-fall of a friend of 'Coombes', 'Griff', and the subsequent inquest.

In an autobiography in which names and places had been changed and few dates given, these letters provided a golden opportunity for attempted verification of the autobiographical status of *These Poor Hands*, about which I was beginning to have substantial doubts. When a lawyer had started asking questions, Coombes had given a rough date for the accident, its approximate whereabouts and the name of the brutal colliery official.[14] I was driven to a lengthy attempt to verify this incident in the public record and local newspapers.[15] Next, in reading Adrian Wright's biography of John Lehmann,[16] I became aware that the Harry Ransom Humanities Research Centre at the University of Texas at Austin had a sizeable Lehmann archive. By 2001, letters exchanged between Coombes and Lehmann had been found to be there, and provided me with key pieces of the jigsaw.

It seems important to establish how Coombes presented his book to his publisher, and thus created expectations of it in the publisher and, subsequently, the reader, before making a judgement of it as autobiography. When Coombes approached the firm of Gollancz in February 1937, with ideas for a novel,[17] he was firmly told that his proposed book would have more chance of publication if it were factual – autobiography, for example.[18] The typescript Coombes submitted to that publisher had a prefatory note stating that, although he had changed names and places, 'All the things mentioned have occurred to the writer.'[19] The agreement he signed with Gollancz on 10 March 1938 undertakes that 'all statements purporting to be facts are truthful and accurate'. When, because of the perceived libel risk, a solicitor started asking questions about the roof-fall accident, Coombes declared:

> This is a true instance and the fireman is still alive. His name is Hopkins and I have called him Godfrey . . . As only three of us were concerned in this affair and

one is dead, there are only two of us left to give our version and apart from the altered name, the event is true in detail. The name of the deceased is also altered and it took place over four miles away from where I live . . . about five years ago.[20]

However, in a letter to Lehmann about the same incident, his story is rather different: 'It is more or less a true happening – and it does happen in the mines frequently.'[21] When the solicitor asks several further questions about minor libel risks, involving a range of people, Coombes responds, detail by detail, as though every word he has written is literally true.[22] On several occasions in writing to Gollancz and to Lehmann he refers to his work as autobiography.[23] The title-page of the book proclaims it as such. However, fascinatingly, in a letter to Lehmann, on 12 June 1937, while he is in the early stages of writing *These Poor Hands*, Coombes describes it as an autobiographical novel, and I will return to this point. Nevertheless, in all his dealings with his actual publisher, this work is presented as an autobiography.

The two abandoned chapters make engrossing reading. They contain a high number of elements of a horrifying generic accident which would have shocked and moved readers. There was persistent bullying by a mine official (with the threat of sacking) to make men work in dangerous conditions, with Griff's need to comply being all the stronger because of his many dependants. There was the vivid imaginative impact of someone being killed within inches of where Coombes was working; the trauma of observing the mutilated body; the pathos of carrying the body home through the dark and having to observe the distress of Griff's family. After this, there was the stress of having to testify at an inquest, without being able to do what would have been in a miner's best interest – to proclaim the dangerous conditions under which they had been forced to work – because this would have involved loss of insurance money for Griff's dependants.

With the information provided – approximate date, area, name of the fireman and Coombes as witness at the inquest – I scrutinized mining records (which proved less than fully informative) and also microfilm of the *Neath Guardian*, for a two-year period from April 1932 to March 1934, crosschecking with the *South Wales Evening Post* and the *Aberdare Leader*, where appropriate, for fuller accounts of inquests and funerals. I was not able to find any account that was even an approximate fit, even when allowing for Coombes's later assertion that two men were killed. This is not conclusive evidence: local newspapers are not comprehensive journals of record and no scrutineer is infallible. Nevertheless, this extensive trawl reinforced my feeling that, in spite of assurances to the contrary to Gollancz, the accident as related was a conflation of many Coombes had heard about or known as a worker and ambulanceman, rather than representing one episode of his lived experience.

One consequence, then, of the fear of major libel risk is that two chapters were dropped. Coombes knew he already had a buyer for the discarded portion in Lehmann, who had declared his admiration for the two final chapters in the draft he had read. Within a matter of months of the publication of *These Poor Hands* by Gollancz in June 1939, the two excised chapters appeared as the short story 'Twenty Tons of Coal' in the Christmas issue of Lehmann's *New Writing*. The protagonist is slightly (further?) fictionalized in being presented as a bachelor, and the inquest is omitted, but, after some trimming, eight key pages dealing with the behaviour of the fireman are transposed more or less verbatim from the 'autobiography'.[24] Yet Gollancz had emphasized to Coombes that ' "Libellous" remarks about people are quite as libellous if the people are disguised – provided they can be "spotted" ', so reassigning to a fictional mode was not necessarily any protection.[25] However, if Coombes knew that neither the bullying and cowardly fireman nor the events he was involved with bore any discernible resemblance to real life then there was no risk in repeating the story under the label of fiction. It seems probable that the months of delay and heart-searching by Gollancz over the 'libel risk' were all over an invented character who had been given particular dastardly attributes to emphasize class issues: twenty years later, Coombes writes of the accident: 'no one could really be blamed' ('Home on the Hill', 55).

Long sections of the concluding chapters in the published *These Poor Hands* are definitely fictitious, although they create a closely corresponding accident to one in the dropped chapters. Coombes deftly transposed the mine accident from south Wales to a colliery up north, having had two people he had presented earlier, Hutch and Billy Ward, Coombes's fellow workers on machine-cutting, move there in search of work. Billy returned to report, in a conversation which Coombes handled in a skilful and feeling way, the horror of the accident in which Hutch had been killed outright in a roof-fall (*These Poor Hands*, 245–57). One wonders whether, in Hutch's necessary demise, Coombes had killed off a character from the real world, for Hutch had been fully presented in earlier chapters. More probably, as with the characterization of Godfrey the fireman, Hutch, and possibly other people portrayed, were fictional creations.

When I returned to the drafts of *These Poor Hands* after work on the Gollancz archive, I discovered, to my dismay, that what I had found particularly moving in 1998, when I first read the published text, I now discovered to have been fictitious embellishments – or even a volte-face – to avoid the risk of a libel action. I felt exploited. From my own experience of disillusion, I observed how much an author's commitment to an autobiographical pact mattered. In the early draft Coombes had felt 'very bitter' about the behaviour of blackleg Bill Yardley who, weeks before the end of the strike, had been put in charge of machine-cutting, Coombes's job ('These Poor Hands 1st draft', 243). After a warning from Gollancz's solicitor that such a presentation could constitute libel, Coombes refers scornfully to Bill Yardley's total disappearance some years before in a midnight flit with his wife and 'gang of children', to escape many debts.[26] In the published work, the character is transformed into Billy Ward:

> Some weeks before the end of the stoppage I heard that Billy Ward had gone back to work. He was living in an isolated cottage on the mountainside, and the under-manager had been there persuading Billy that if he did not start he would have no chance of work when the stoppage was over. Billy did not have the support of other men living near, as we did. (*These Poor Hands*, 185)

The change has moved the incident closer to the normative types of socialist realism. The blackleg has become the redeemable worker, his aberrant behaviour explained by his physical isolation from worker support and solidarity. Coombes seems rapidly to have developed an ear for this sort of register – unsurprising, perhaps, in one as dedicated to reading Left Book Club publications as the letters to Gollancz reveal. When, in the fictional analogue to the roof-fall episode, Billy Ward returns to south Wales after the death of Hutch, Coombes writes of him with tenderness: 'I had the affection for Billy that every workman feels for a mate who had shared years at a dangerous job with him' (*These Poor Hands*, 246). In loyalty to and friendship for his 'old mate', he agrees to put himself out to try to help Billy get a job locally. If Bill Yardley/Billy Ward ever existed in the real world, the insincerity Coombes finally shows in reaction to him is disconcerting. 'Coombes' emerges as the loving, supportive co-worker of a man the writer seems actively to have disliked, in an episode that is pure fiction. This surely should give us pause over the numerous occasions Coombes represented himself as loyal, supportive, warm-hearted and generous.

In all this, an important, though now near-invisible, character in *These Poor Hands* is the spirit of the age. Coombes was well aware of the expectations of his target readership. That texts are written in *circumstances* for *purposes* needs to be borne in mind for all my subjects, but most pressingly for Coombes. Although he needed some further guidance from Lehmann before he achieved a fully 'spot-on' proletarian identity, in his first importuning letter to Gollancz he makes clear that he is aware of the particular parameters writing for the Left Book Club might require:

> I appeal to you to give me – one of the earliest to join the Left Book Club – the chance to let the world know what is hidden in the mines . . . Your help may result in the L.B.C. producing one of the proletarian writers the working class needs so badly, but I am aware that a book written on the lines the Club wants would be alarming to the ordinary publisher so that I would be writing for one chance of a market – and only one.[27]

The high degree of working-class identification that was highlighted in my earlier analysis can be attributed, in part, to a shrewd response to discerned market forces. There was undoubtedly a bias towards selecting events and characteristics that show the miner in the best light. Although, for example, an early conversation that Coombes has with his friend Jack's landlord shows the latter is obsessively interested in boxing (26), and he later mentions a manager who is fascinated in a similar way (155), there is no developed account of this collier passion. As we shall see, Berry, by contrast, delights in revealing the typical pugnacity of the miner, the sheer naked aggression which he undoubtedly shares and which can well up and be channelled into fights, with or without gloves. It is probable that Coombes's sense of an audience would deter him from highlighting anything that would encourage the middle classes to perceive the miner as Other. Undoubtedly, too, he is at pains to emphasize inter-class struggle throughout the work: the management class is always portrayed as reprehensibly exploitative. Coombes later shows that he has no compunction over assuming a role, particularly if that role places him centre-stage. In letters to John Lehmann, he describes being photographed as an 'out of work' miner and mentions writing an article in support of the pictures:

> Get 'Picture Post' for the New Year issue. Have an article there and also a series of pictures of myself as an unemployed miner – true at that [deleted] this time . . . Took several inside pictures of our little home and son Peter. Also some of the area and I was in most. Don't think I'm always so shabby – it was necessary to be so. Over a million weekly circulation with that paper so it should be a real boost.[28]

In a further letter, 9 January 1941, again to Lehmann, he regards himself as a symbol of his class, and is thoroughly unperturbed to declare that he personally is in no difficulty: 'Of course you will realise that the lack of mining work did not worry me unduly.' Readers of the *Picture Post* showered him with offers of work that he did not need!

Coombes's chance to become an admired and influential writer grew centrally out of the events of the troubled 1930s. Proletarian literature had an important exemplary and inspirational function in the publishing climate of the times. As Coombes wrote most of *These Poor Hands* believing Lehmann would be his publisher, a brief consideration of John Lehmann's likely publishing intentions seems called for. He was a thoroughgoing European who lived in Vienna for long periods between 1932 and 1938. From Vienna and Berlin, he became intimately aware of the Fascist movements afoot in Europe and realized that time was running out before a new world war.[29] In starting up *New Writing* – which gave Coombes his first chances of publication with his story 'The Flame' – he was attempting to bring together writers from many countries who held the same views on Fascism and war. Encouraged by its success, Lehmann had high hopes that, when his periodical moved to Lawrence and Wishart, official publishers of Communist literature, the new sponsors would publish a *New Writing* library of longer works by authors he had come across in his exploration for the magazine.[30] This was the situation in 1937, when the drafts of *These Poor Hands* were written. In 1936–7 there was an exhilarating feeling abroad of the new empowerment of workers, due to a powerful groundswell in parts of Europe in response to the despotic Fascist menace. In France, the Popular Front coalition of left and centre parties, united in opposition to Fascism, had swept to power in May 1936, bringing about working-class euphoria, which resulted in immediate strikes, involving two million people, in an attempt to win particular reforms from employers stunned by the election results. In Spain, the sense of dedication and courage shown by workers in defending gains brought about by a Popular Front government created a sense of the infinite possibilities of the ordinary working man. *These Poor Hands* seems to have been written and redrafted within the broad scope of the aspirations of the time. It is interesting to note how Coombes's work, as it evolves through its drafts, constructs a persona increasingly approaching the norms of socialist realism. As we shall see, individual idiosyncrasies disappear, partly under editorial directive, as this exemplary worker is constructed.

From the Lehmann archive, the element most interesting for the evolution of Coombes's autobiography is the letter of 26 July 1937, in which Lehmann comments on the draft of *These Poor Hands* he has just read. He encourages the inclusion of further tales of unemployment struggles and dramatic events of mining life. He suggests dropping themes that are peripheral to this, such as the author's experiences as a writer and musician, and recommends that

Coombes should not concern himself much with family life. Lehmann's purposes clearly require a stark sense of the travail of the working man. He offered Coombes undoubtedly sound advice, giving him hints on how to improve the forward narrative thrust of the book and encouraging him to conceptualize more so that each chapter had a unity. He had found chapter 12 in 'These Poor Hands 1st draft' 'rather too irrelevant' and wrote, in his idiosyncratic hand, on the draft itself: 'This chapter too discursive – misses the chance of describing 1926' ('These Poor Hands 1st draft', 229). Lehmann thus gives Coombes a sense of what will be of interest to his target readership, about which Coombes has, at times, had poor judgement. The heroic struggle of 1926, that year of the long miners' strike, is, in his draft, overlaid with banal tales which reveal cynicism and a rather crass sense of humour, as Coombes tells stories, for example, of how a doctor, barber and others make a fool of the local landlord ('These Poor Hands 1st draft', 233). He is much more scathing about people in this early draft. The disappearance in the published version of the anecdotes irrelevant to the main theme shows his improving conceptual grasp of what is needed. The ambient tone develops a more consistent seriousness and high-mindedness. Sometimes, too, the 'feeling' tone changes completely. The reasons Coombes gives for marrying become more loving. In the early draft, he had laboured some leaden anecdotes about how hopelessly he and his friend keep house in their bachelor days ('These Poor Hands 1st draft', 60). By the time of the published version, there is no sense that a strong reason for marrying was in order to improve his creature comforts: in fact, he explicitly declares that his bachelor lodgings 'were excellent' (*These Poor Hands*, 61).

Throughout the fragmentary 'These Poor Hands 1st draft' retained in the B. L. Coombes archive, there are marginalia and underlinings, some identifiable as by Lehmann but most of them probably by Coombes, following the principles Lehmann has enunciated, the majority of which result in changes in the published work. Coombes had considerable ability and quickly picked up a more nuanced sense of the agenda of the publishers he was working for. When considered cumulatively, the changes between 'These Poor Hands 1st draft', and the published work amount to a slightly altered presentation of Coombes as 'worker hero'. The narrative persona has mutated in a somewhat idealized direction. The miners, too, become conceptualized into something a little more admirable, as tales of their hard swearing and cruelty to pit ponies are reduced in both length and strength.

However, quite apart from editorial strictures, Coombes seems to enjoy nothing better than reinventing himself, as we have already seen in the Liberal Party pamphlet. At several different points in his writing life, he shows an ability, chameleon-like, to change colour according to the circumstances and purposes of an autobiographical assignment, the climate of the times or, perhaps, personal whim.

Constraints of space prevent detailed accounts of Coombes in the act of shape-shifting. The immensely evocative opening of *These Poor Hands* has Coombes, as a farm boy, suffering the chilly deprivations of that life and dreaming of a better future as he contemplates the warm industrial glow in the distant night sky. The reader accompanies him in his wondering initiation into the joys and hardship of this new life in a mining community. However, at a time of considerable personal significance – his Golden Wedding, a celebration of twenty-five years as a columnist for the *Neath Guardian* and a presentation by the South Wales Miners' Federation for his outstanding contribution to working-class literature – Coombes writes of the centrality of the *industrial* experience for him from childhood onward and, comparatively speaking, the marginal nature of his youthful experience on the land.[31] He now declares that, at the age of ten, he was living in Treharris, where his father and uncles were miners, and that it was not until the age of fourteen, when he accompanied his parents to take up the tenancy of a farm in Herefordshire, that he had any experience of the land, although he 'never regretted those few years in the country'.

Motives of political expediency would seem to explain Coombes's construction of an 'on-message' youth of hard rural struggle, with convenient omission of his petit bourgeois origins as the son of a grocer in Wolverhampton. Politically committed outlets were Coombes's only likely avenue to prominence as a writer, and so he crafted his life to fit. Making his story that of an oppressed agricultural worker moving in hope to what turn out to be the dangers and exploitations of the coalfield suggests a prioritizing of ideological suitability.

An equally striking self-disclosure by this erstwhile proletarian writer comes in his second, unpublished autobiography, 'Home on the Hill' (1959), where he divulges that, in the year before his departure for the south Wales coalfield, he had been employed as a groom by a local doctor, becoming 'almost a gentleman' in his regular uniform of bowler hat, kid gloves and totally waterproof mackintosh (23). The reasons he advances for moving on to the mines were that his way of life was making him 'slack' bodied and he wanted 'to shape the world up a bit', to go in search of excitement and danger (42). No longer writing for a politicized readership, and composing in 1959, in the very year *Cider with Rosie* was to win success in harking back with nostalgia to semi-feudal times in a rural area, Coombes, too, responds to the climate of the age. From an agricultural worker huddling in damp clothes he now metamorphoses into an expert controller of horses, a smooth operator, in bowler hat and waterproof raincoat; from escaping hardship and deprivation his motivation for moving on becomes a need for thrills. A slip, chosen at random from several placed in his bowler hat, replaces, as a precipitator of action, the magic, warmth and allure of the Bessemer works, most improbably visible against the night sky.

Further false claims in which Coombes indulged were to do with his need to idealize his own talent as a writer. An important aspect of the persona he constructs is that of a writer who gets things right, fast, through his own native wit. In fact, as his letters to Gollancz and Lehmann show, he constantly sought advice and acted on it. In 1963, at the time of the author's Golden Wedding, Clive John wrote a celebratory article which seems to have been based on a lengthy interview with Coombes and his wife. John declares:

> His 'These Poor Hands' was undoubtedly a masterpiece. Published by Victor Gollancz, it made a Left Book Club choice – but not one single word in the book was altered or deleted. Such was his ability to write the publishers couldn't find a thing wrong with it.[32]

Coombes needed to be seen as a particularly gifted writer, soaring effortlessly to the heights with his star-quality book. The advice, long-term encouragement and constructive criticism from Lehmann, the protracted hassle with the firm of Gollancz, culminating in the dropping of two chapters and rapid rewriting of new ones, are totally suppressed. In his radio documentary 'I Stayed a Miner' (1957) he gives an astonishing misrepresentation of the process of writing *These Poor Hands*, declaring: 'I did not revise one word, nor did anyone see it except myself until it arrived at the offices of one of the largest publishers in London' – Gollancz.[33] He declares there was a delighted unconditional acceptance within a month, Gollancz immediately conferring on it Left Book Club choice status. Lehmann's input, and twenty months of heartache for Coombes and constant chivvying of Gollancz, followed by extensive rewriting, are wiped out. The revealed truth of Coombes's writerly character, as the archives disclose it, is of quite different, striking traits: first, the obdurate determination to become a writer, and then extraordinary tenacity through endless delays and setbacks.

These Poor Hands was shaped by many powerful forces. By the time Coombes had revised his early draft in 1937, he had a clear idea what the market wanted and would take. It could be a 'make-or-break' experience for him as a writer, and his importuning letter to Gollancz of 18 February 1937 reveals the depth of his desire for recognition in this area. As with most people, his motivation in writing was a complex interweaving of many factors. His declared motivation was a desire to proclaim to the world the hardships and dangers of a miner's life, which had its source, he sometimes wrote, in the roof-fall accident which I have already considered at length: this was perhaps the personal myth he lived by, the way he saw himself ('Home on the Hill', 56). He observes that a further prompting had been a desire to redress a balance: 'No one class of people have been so misreported and slandered as the mining community' ('Home on the Hill', 42). *These Poor Hands* was written in an unheated bedroom on a £2 'junk' typewriter, often at the end of an exhausting period of manual labour. Part of Coombes's initial impulse, one has no reason to doubt, was powerful feeling, but this should not be seen as pure altruism.

The common writerly spurs of the desire for fame and fortune were in evidence in his case. Indubitably, Coombes wanted to write a book that would sell. When his manuscript moved to Gollancz, the possibility that his work might become a Left Book Club choice, with guaranteed sales of near 50,000, was a heady proposition. According to Coombes (*These Poor Hands*, 231), a miner's weekly wage in 1938 was £2.35 in present-day notation: from the Gollancz accounts he made £639 12s. 9d. (£639.63) in royalties in the first six months of sale. He would have needed to have been a saint not to have cared deeply about the financial implications of success, and Coombes was not one. Indeed, in one of his letters urging rapid publication he declares: 'Frankly, I need the money.'[34] The book as delivered to Gollancz was as appropriately 'on message' as he could make it. Further, it is clear from his preservation of letters from the great and good in his scrapbook that he enjoyed, after the event, the prominence and success that *These Poor Hands* brought him. A desire to maintain that status and esteem was some part of the impetus for his subsequent sustained efforts.

Yet the nature, strength and duration of the obsessive drive that kept him writing seem to go far beyond these impulses. In one of his assertively prodding letters to Gollancz over the delayed publication of *These Poor Hands*, he indicates that Gollancz has had the manuscript for over a year and that he feels he could have had a second or third book out by now (28 January 1939). He proposes sending a second autobiography, should publication be further postponed. That same autobiography is rejected by Gollancz in 1940, as Coombes records in a letter to Lehmann of 5 November 1940, and again between the years 1940 and 1945, although he has had two further documentary books published elsewhere during that time, it forms a constant theme in Coombes's letters to Lehmann as he submits it to him, accepts criticism, rewrites, revises and tries again, hoping against hope that Lehmann will bring the book out.[35] His view of himself as a writer, in a very basic sense, is revealed by his use of headed paper, proclaiming, in 1944, 'B. L. Coombes, Miner-Author, over 1,000,000 words published', amended, by 1947 to 'over 2,000,000 words published'. There seems to have been a deep personal drive in Coombes to be 'a writer' that goes beyond any explanation offered here: given the psychoanalytic thrust of this study, it is a matter of some regret that no more is known with certainty of his early life.

Coombes was a vivid storyteller. He had a capacity to produce in the reader a keen response to his lively representation of the experiences of miners and, especially, to the hazards of the coalmining industry. Verisimilitude and autobiographical veracity are, however, clearly different things. From general tendencies in Coombes I have been exploring and from evidence which it has been possible to check and where striking disparities have been found, one can hypothesize that, in *These Poor Hands*, Coombes regularly improved on life in his attempt both to write a dramatic and readable work that would sell, and to deliver a persuasive work that conformed to the ethos of the Left Book Club. The balance of probability is that *These Poor Hands* is, indeed, an autobiographical novel, based by Coombes on his own life, including composite or invented characters, with events of the sort that regularly happened to miners transposed into the narrative of his individual life. In the early stages of writing, Coombes describes his book as an autobiographical novel to Lehmann, who seems to have made no objection (12 June 1937) and, in a further letter, as 'the novel' (21 December 1937).[36] However, Coombes was very clearly aware that Gollancz required a factual approach. When his book moves to them, he behaves, right up to publication, as though, apart from changed names and places, the book is pure fact; and, packaged as autobiography, it goes out into the world to seek its fortune.

Coombes remains something of an enigma, displaying the most labile sense of self of any of the autobiographers studied here. In the early draft of *These Poor Hands*, his persona showed several less endearing characteristics – elements of cynicism and a rather crass and, at times, unkind sense of humour, for example – but by the published version, the main impression of his personality is of someone warm-hearted, long-suffering and unassertive. To experience, then, the aggressive, self-promoting and self-interested side of the author's character in his letters to Gollancz has been fascinating. In these, Coombes shows considerable persistence and tenacity, and, on one occasion, anger and downright rudeness (10 July 1938). The persona of the letters is much less gentle than that of *These Poor Hands*. The idea of Coombes as a naive proletarian eyewitness has sometimes seemed to suit people's preconceptions. The archival material has provided hard evidence of the inventiveness and, indeed, literary ability Coombes brought to the many constructed versions of his life story.

To move from Coombes to Berry is to invite energetic comparison. They are yoked together here because each was deeply influenced by the Welsh mining experience, but one would be hard put to it to find two autobiographers more different in intention, in temperament and in narrative style. Coombes's ostensible motivation is to act as the mediator and explicator to the world at large of the often maligned and misunderstood miner. He sees himself as a representative miner. In contrast, Berry's need is to record, in all its intensity, his unique human experience, and then to act as elegist for a vanished people and way of life. The energy sparks out from the page, sometimes threatening to short-circuit, communicating distress, puzzlement, some ferociously partisan judgements and much celebration. Rarely has there been an autobiographer more deeply fascinated by the differences in human beings or more prone to tease out the nature of his own identity through evaluation and implicit measuring against others.

History is What You Live was published in 1998, the year after Berry's death. Probably, from various datings in the text (most usefully and explicitly on p. 97), the writing and redrafting was spread over nearly a decade, the final one of his life, which saw the virtual demise of the coal industry in south Wales. This historical background contributes vitally to Berry's implicitly explored and hard-won value system. 'Everything passes', Berry seems to be saying, 'but let's celebrate what we have known.' The ground themes stated, modulated, recapitulated and built to a climax in the final pages are evanescence and loss.

Conceptually, the landscape around the village of Blaen-y-cwm in the Rhondda, particularly its mountains, is the organizing framework of the book. Berry's exact and vividly visual memory imbues that landscape with often poignant meaning: one feels his urgency to record what only he in his uniqueness can know, before the recalling, perceiving and connecting mind and feeling response that is Ron Berry is snuffed out. There is, too, a fervid eagerness and a baffled need to record, as tellingly as he knows how, what it feels like to be him. Olney posits, in his fascinating *Metaphors of Self*, that in the autobiographical process: 'One cannot hope . . . to capture with a straight-on look, or expect to transmit directly to another one's own sense of the self; at most one may be able to discover a similitude, a metaphor for the feeling of selfhood' (266–7). Berry's metaphors of self are often telling, sometimes revealing a sense of spiritual and emotional hunger amounting to starvation. There is a feeling that, whatever he knows himself to be – cranky, wilful, obdurate – it is because, with his genetic endowment, in his particular historic time and environment, he can be no other, if he is to assuage his voracious longing for genuine experience that may, in the end, feed him.

Berry wants us to understand and almost become part of the process of change and loss that he mourns. We accompany him to different spots in and around Blaen-y-cwm and its surrounding mountains, at different times in his growing up and adult life. We feel something of the inevitability of change, as he describes the petrified mussels dating, he declares, from 250,000,000 BC, which were found on the slag heap of Tŷ Draw colliery, now a grassed-over part of Graig y Ddelw (30). He interprets his habitat in an imaginative and loving way, so that we can see its value through his eyes. We come to understand the richness (and the violence) of the mining culture. As Berry lists the range of skills painstakingly imparted to children, the sense of the diversity of talents in the community is conveyed, as well as the affectionate involvement that the transmission of know-how represents: 'Learning takes time and time again' (46).

We experience the feelings and memories called forth in Berry by so much that is, at first sight, mundane in his environment and feel that he possesses the landscape through those memories. Follow any linear course and it will yield significance. There is the tunnel where Grandmother Berry's first husband was killed; the cutting beyond, where violets and early catkins could be found; the spot where the best willow twigs, for making whistles, grew; the hollow oak where early sexual adventures are remembered; the railway foot-bridge from which gentle and generous Percy Prior, one of Berry's early mining 'butties', committed suicide when suffering from one hundred per cent dust (40–1). Time and again Berry wanders in memory the mountain tops that hem in Blaen-y-cwm – Graig y Ddelw, Mynydd Tŷ Isaf, Cefn Nant y Gwair and Pen-pych – musing on their different delights. He trains us to see the meaning of different landmarks: what seems mountain is often grassed-over slag heap, 'herring-boned with huge drainage ditches since Aberfan's tragedy shook the bowels of absent experts' (30). He evokes the delight he felt as a boy on Pen-pych: 'Wheatear territory this, since time stood still' where one might also see 'planing skylarks' and 'mock-crippled pipits flopping between tussocks' (31). He mourns that his grandchildren will never experience these joys because of the environmental vandalism of the Forestry Commission, which has planted dark sitkas along all the tops – ousting such enduring life as 'hardwoods older than Cardiff city . . . whin-berry ledges, ivied buttresses' (29) . . . 'The leavings of prehistory sacrificed to Mammon masked as a quango' (31). His habitat is altered beyond recognition.

He recreates the feel of Blaen-y-cwm when the Rhondda was a single-industry, thriving valley, commemorating all that he knew of the suffering and endurance of the small but typical cross-section of the mining fraternity he worked with at the Graig level. As a secular requiem, he intones the names of many of the dead friends who worked with him there, and the nature of their dying: rheumatic fever, dust, accident, TB (41–3). He muses on what he learnt of the variousness of human nature as the junior in the close butty relationship: Sid, a stingy payer, who 'had the one-way mind of a ratting terrier and the twpness' (55); 'the most insular year of my life' with open-handed Percy Prior 'whose entire self was given to coal. Foolishness everything else . . . What I learned from him was *doing*' (62–3); sociable Jimmy Shanklin, fun to be with yet whose careless shoring caused Berry's first accident (56–7); on machine-cutting with club-footed Eddie Jones Cochyn, with whom he came 'near to feeling inseparable from mining for the rest of my bread-winning days . . . Native born slot fit . . . *Humanitas Jerboa*' (67–70). The macho code of the Rhondda inflicted extra hardships: 'For two years I carried a burning sore on the small of my back. Healing scabs were knocked off . . . Boys were not allowed to kneel in the Five Deep. Kneeling signified moral weakness' (55). He communicates vividly a sense of typical, everyday dangers, such as their headlong dash when the subterranean lake comes flooding into Five Deep 'and the black lake filled the district, dozens of stalls . . . supply roads, airways, water rising steadily up the Five Deep, drowning the toil of half a century' (65–6). By 1990, the whole colliery is gone: 'And now, since then, time has obliterated Graig level, the arched stonework blown in, the whole mountain's flank thick with conifers' (66). Indeed, by the time the autobiography is completed, 'King Coal is dead, sole reason for both Rhonddas, leaving twin valleys of commuters (20 per cent unemployment of course)' (30). The Methodist chapel has become a bus garage (30). Berry weaves in regular elegiac refrains: 'All gone now though, gone, Treorchy, Trealaw and chapel cemeteries' sempiternal harvest' (34); and, even there, winds and weather remove the names from the gravestones, as they have effaced all record of Grandfather Noah's last resting place (37).

As Berry worries away at what he is and why he is it, the reader becomes quickly aware of his certainty that one of his key endowments is the acute recording of sense impressions, particularly visual ones. By the end of *History is What You Live* one has a sense of a memory bank overflowing with intense recall, a human personality unusually endowed in recording, being nurtured by and finding meaning in, what he sees. As Berry is poignantly aware, with Philip Larkin, of 'The sure extinction that we travel to', his recording on paper of sights in particular, but also sense impressions in general, that have touched and changed him, many now passed away from the face of the earth, is his own personal stay against evanescence. He writes vividly of his earliest awareness of himself as a bundle of sensations:

> Smells, tastes, sounds, sights, sensations crowding my infant ganglia, confirming oneself as singular. A soul bud. Chopped mint, drops of blood, sand on the flagstone floor, the pure tugging of candle flame, bladders of air behind gulps of stingy-nettle pop, soapsuds burning eyes. (14)

There is a sense of recall of a time when the external world itself seemed a secure and tender nurturing place, reflecting a promise of sure sustenance: 'Loving-kindness shone from externals, from buttercup chains, Selsig minnows and loaches, jack-frosted windowpanes, woollen vests, hawthorn berries' (16). Sight imbues the autobiographer Berry with a sense of continuing wonder at the potential glory of the world. A poignant tracing in *History is What You Live* is that, while the receptivity remains, a sense of having a secure place in that world vanishes for ever, and vanishes early.

The fact of the aggression and dis-ease which he finds so basic a part of himself is something frequently recorded in *History is What You Live*. Certain it is that the deepest security Berry records in his adult life is in his male bonding. His macho Rhondda background has given him very particular models of male identity. We have already explored the range of 'butty' relationships Berry experienced before he was twenty, a very formative period in anyone's life, and the culminating one with Eddie Jones Cochyn, which was a close and trusting one. He recalls in impressive and minutely discerning detail all that he remembers of the individuating elements of a wide range of early peers, almost all male, and, in many cases, what later flowered and what withered in them. He remembers with warmth how he was saved by his comrades, being given the means to pay the fine incurred after assaulting the colliery manager, when inwardly he believed 'Prison seemed fitting . . . Cardiff or Swansea' (88): 'Very many of the colliers who chipped in have passed away. I knew them all by name' (88). His early relationship with cycling mate Vernon Rees, a fellow miner, taught him a great deal about himself: 'Cycle racing exposes limitations, reveals what's in the blood' (73). He writes about discovering what those limits were with great insight. The most detailed analysis of any in the book is of his relationship with Cliff Williams, tubercular from his teens from work underground, with whom he drifted and learnt harshly realistic life-values.

Aggression in the tough mining environment could be regarded almost as a necessary evolutionary adaptation for survival, yet Berry recognizes something pathological in his own inordinate aggression. From adolescence he is aware of a need to defuse himself: 'Innately vexed, equally liable to bouts of savagery and brightly meaningless standstill, sweaty bike rides depolarised some of my adolescent aggro' (68). In the workplace, he is aware that he 'hankered for conflict', leading him to challenge the 'heftiest bullying haulier in the Graig [to a] stand up fist fight' (70). His image of feeling like 'a solitary piranha among inedible weavers' (70) suggests how innately aggressive he feels, and yet how impossible it seems to find ways of channelling that aggression. Seeing his ego as 'intact like a blocked biro' (85) implies a recognition of his dysfunctionality – 'a chrysalis waiting for Cain heat' (72). The charting and detecting of pattern involved in writing this autobiography have helped the-man-who-held-the-pen to see how compulsively he has resisted all authority, from the regular mitching from Upper Rhondda Junior Technical school (20); through his hitting the colliery manager when refused any job except one in the silicosis-inducing hard heading (88); through threat of military detention for 'flout[ing] discipline' (114) by his refusal to salute officers, which results in his walking out on it all (114–6). At different times he is twice sent to psychiatrists and, though longing for help – there is positive envy of Chunks Lewis at a later time whose breakdown is 'classified, treated' (129) – he is unable to accept what is proffered. Typical exchanges with the psychiatrist run like this:

'Name, rank and number?'

'Yours in exchange for mine' . . .

'Why do you resent authority?'

'Why do you have authority?' . . .

. . . 'Are your parents alive?'

'Are yours?' (117–18)

Such intense resistance to authority often has its roots in early relationships with parents – as he seems to be well (and resentfully) aware – and later I will be exploring what can be deduced from what we are told of these relationships.

There is a tone amounting to awe as Berry sees with hindsight the tragic nature of the agonizing mental states he went through. He describes winter in a distant place doing a mindless menial job:

Against seepage of despair, I plugged bitty Cloud 9 aspirations. My worst flood
of depression arrived in Huntingdon. The universe turned grey. Total greyness
one Saturday night in a cinema, robots mouthing on the screen and hoar spreading
from within . . . Too sane for suicide, I got drunk. (127)

It is possible that Berry is aware that depression stems from anger and aggression being turned self-destructively inwards. Throughout this autobiography,
there is an appalled fascination with madness. Having described a mortuary
attendant at his place of work being carried off in a straitjacket, there seems
to be satisfaction, even triumph, in his observation: 'Most of us are blocked
off from insanity. We abide, we hold our ground' (132). Yet there is recognition from his end-of-life perspective that at times it has been a near thing. On
a long ramble on the mountain with Cliff Williams:

Like pilgrims we visited a dugout built towards the end of my squeezed escape
from the Merchant Navy. The turfed roof had collapsed . . . Had I tried to live in
this dugout, God knows what brute stuff would have surfaced. That secret, des-
perate hideaway in the hills, bizarre to the point of exit. (124)

As he catalogues what the world would judge as bungle after deliberate disaster, Berry would also seem to have been aware, on the fringes of his vision,
that there has been in him a determined failure to thrive. Although at or near
the top of his class at primary school (17), he fails the eleven-plus and regularly truants in his final years at his technical school (20). He strikes the colliery manager and is thenceforth *persona non grata* in local pits (88). It has to
be said that his resolute evasion of a second voyage in the merchant navy
seems a clear indication of perspective and sanity (101). He deserts from the
army (114). When offered government training, against all advice because of
his damaged knee he chooses carpentry, but does not complete the course
(119–21). He later completes another government carpentry course but exer-
cises the skill only briefly before selling his tools (134–6). When accepted for
a one-year course at Coleg Harlech, he gives up his study of history after two
terms (136–7). He is accepted as a mature student at teacher training college
and gives up on that (143). A regular image of how he is perceived by others
is 'waster' (102) and, by himself, a drifter:

Since birth I think I've been possessed, measured for twilight drift instead of
making a wage, the worst crime of all in chapel-hagged Wales. 'Him, that one,
he's like Uncle Dan', they used to say, my own kin passing judgement. Solitary
old Uncle Dan, tramp from youth to pension age, unkempt, . . . despised. (36)

There is a psychologically acceptable explanation of his self-thwarting behaviour that would be in keeping with the levels of emotional distress Berry sometimes describes. If experiencing strong emotional pain, it is clearly more tolerable if one is able to find good reason for this in one's everyday situation, rather than be driven to accept that it is fuelled from inner sources over which one has no control.

Berry's end-of-life, hard-won ability to value himself comprehends an ability to see in his past self a seriously troubled human being. Frequently he expresses a neediness in himself in terms of hunger, and sometimes that hunger is orally linked. He describes 'gorging [himself] on flora and fauna' (58). He identifies the obsessive thirty-mile cycle rides he and Vernon Rees undertake every evening for a period after a day in the pits, as a result of 'tap roots starving' (76). He declares that 'We find out what we are from hungering enough' (32) and that 'I've starved for other things than bread' (111). A very powerful image of frustrated oral aggression is the one already noted where he sees himself as a solitary piranha amongst inedible weaver fish. One of the most vibrant images of the whole book is to do with feeding. He describes succour after fear when, as a toddler, he has accidentally started a fire and is comforted, presumably by his mother, Mary Anne: 'Afterwards, snug as buddhas by firelight, we [he and his cousin] ate toast and jam' (15). He describes with pure love his perception of Mary Anne's brief period of untrammelled happiness in the early years of her marriage, as she sang songs such as 'Myfi sydd fachgen ieuanc ffôl': 'That pulsing old love song, her young-wife contentment, fulfilment of her days. Mary Anne's headaches came later when there were seven mouths to feed' (14). There is one lyrically expressed occasion of personal pride for Ron Berry, accompanied by a photograph in the text, when he clearly felt special to Mary Anne:

> On July 2nd 1927, Treherbert Hospital carnival. The Junior First Prize silver-plated cup was bigger than my head. I heard women on the pavement 'Well, yes, George's boy, him dressed up as a little costermonger, them pearl buttons, silk scarf and blancoed daps . . . Great idea mind. Trust Mary Anne, wonderful dress-maker she is.' (16)

The early ousting from the paradise of mother's special love has been tellingly described by Laurie Lee in *Cider with Rosie*. We can hypothesize a similar sort of deprivation for Berry – but coming about earlier than Lee's – from what we can read between the lines in Berry's narrative.

Berry's earliest memory is of a time when, a one-year-old 'still frocked and napkined, on Mary Anne's lap', he is 'lost and found next to my unborn sister Marian' (13). He is ousted at the breast by this child, who is further special in being given a merged version of her mother's name and quickly becomes special in other ways – 'From childhood, Marian blazed quick delight, energy' – but who dies before her twenty-first birthday (36). Through collating various pieces of factual information, we discover that this beloved child died at just the time when Berry's difficulties in communicating with his father, which he described as being 'hopelessly alienated' (68), moved into a period of stronger rejection by both parents.

> Familial values sundered between '41 and '43. In my case, eldest son found wanting, fallen far short of expectation . . . Villagers saw me as unsound, a young man of little account . . .
>
> It was a time I had to live through. (101–2)

In a section where Berry has been pondering grief in a mystified way, he observes: 'When Marian died the old man wept and wept. She was his favourite' (36). One can imagine the misery of being the eldest child 'found wanting' (101), out of work and drifting, when parents were grieving intensely for the seemingly preferred child. In such circumstances, the earlier displacement at a time of acute vulnerability would be bound to resonate.

Although there is always love and understanding in the way he writes of his parents, there is, too, a striking distancing in his use of his parents' first names, George and Mary Anne, throughout. Surely this is a most striking 'failing . . . to salute . . . officers' (114). Certainly some of the most traumatic events in the book are to do with his parents' rejection of their oldest child, sometimes recorded in a way that reveals the pain, sometimes set down noncommittally. When Berry abandons the army, he takes fifteen days to plod painfully home, his long-injured knee causing near agony. When, at last, he makes it to Blaen-y-cwm:

> Local coppers had already made enquiries. Greater than my father's, Mary Anne's rejection was absolute. I slept in a railway signal box . . . Ten days in military detention awaiting trial, ten days and nights of yet more delving inwards . . . Stress times, insomniac's end, a time of repair even as flags of faith disintegrated, as ramparts cultivated since infancy toppled. (116)

Those 'ramparts cultivated since infancy' seem to be to do with defences set up against awareness of a lack of love. He later records in turn his parents' lack of interest in or any sense of celebration of his success, at last, as a writer (33, 145).

From what he takes trouble to record, albeit in an unshaped and unfocused way, it seems probable that Berry was aware at some level that problems of mental distress often have their sources in early childhood, born crucially of early relationships with parents. What I have outlined of recalled rejection or coldness in later years would have had particular resonance for someone who had been unsure of the strength of parental attachment in his early childhood. He interprets most sympathetically the burdens of life for people like his parents: 'Working class parents had to be colossi of dedication and survival' (14). In most respects, Berry seems a 'native born slot fit' (67) in his Blaen-y-cwm environment, yet he clearly had ambivalent attitudes to his Welshness, in part related to his incompletely acknowledged anger with his parents, particularly with his mother. He comments appreciatively of his sculptor friend, Bob Thomas, that he 'creates realities more everlasting than any Welshman since matriarchy ruled. Funny inheritance, Welshness' (125). The fact that the Welsh language was used as a means of control by his Welsh-speaking mother has left feelings of resentment: 'Mary Anne spoke secrets in Welsh to George . . . Language used subversively leaves a legacy of mistrust' (26). But he seems totally accepting of his great aunt's (Granny the Farm) 'pidgin English' and of her grandchildren who 'were our playmates every August when we stayed at Ynystawe, Wynford and Nellie, giggling Welsh monoglots. No hassle at all about communication' (37). Measured against this model, the Rhondda seems a different country: 'This Wales wasn't Welsh. Some Blaenycwm families clung to Cymraeg with private hints, Janus-murmurs, hopelessly fragile against the ups and downs of Rhondda's coal klondike' (26). His evocation of his Valleys' idiolect rings true as a bell: 'Yes, aye, illustrious vocation' (70); his interspersing of characteristic 'Ach y fi' to indicate particular repugnance expressed by relations (145); his use of sobriquets, as in Eddie Jones Cochyn (79) (*cochyn* being a common Valleys appellation for a redhead), and Dai Lewis Short-Arm (44). He has been stirred by aspects of this culture, as when he records his small-child response to his mother's singing of Welsh love ballads (14) and his appreciation of Mari Lwyd nights (35). He tellingly evokes domestic habits of a south Wales mining community, when he describes 'gnarled Granny treading *pele*' (18) in clogs, creating and shaping combustible briquettes from coaldust. Unmistakably, his native scene exerts a strong pull. His essential moulding is the typical Welsh industrial experience, based on the geological given of coal seams mined in the valley, where industrial waste accumulates, but with the possibility of escape within moments of hard climbing to the beauty of the surrounding mountains. He writes pityingly of a fellow worker who was 'affable in the loud, meaningless way of townees deprived of privacy from childhood' (132).

While Berry gave short shrift to idealized or stereotyped notions of nation-hood or religion, he does show every sign of valuing very highly most aspects of his own particular patch of English-language Welsh native ground, with its particularities and idiosyncrasies.

Some of his resistance to strong Welsh identification is what he perceives as the 'chapel-hagged' nature of Wales (36). By the end of his life, Berry inhabits hard-won positions established from testing human experience. His exposure to religious narrowness and bigotry from early childhood onwards has revolted him. He presents searing examples of punitive fanaticism in the head of his own infants' school, who 'polluted innocence as surely as law and order comforts bigotry' (16) and there was 'Mr Minty for hate, Mr Elliott for Blood of the Lamb' (27). His merchant navy experience of appalling in-humanity and fecklessness, when added to his compassionate sense of the blighted lives of so many miners, has not given him any sense of God alive in his world. Resistant himself to bending the knee to any power or person, he is incredulous, when Stukas dive-bomb ships in Bone harbour, to see 'slum hardened Scousers huddled below begging protection from the Holy Mary' (99), and comments, 'Maybe man's a natural groveller'. He describes how, as a collier boy, he rejected 'everything that smacked of other-worldliness', for: 'Life's the clincher, inner and outer yeasting the matrix of YOU and ME. Christian adults preached cramp while trees, plants, fowls of the air and fishes in water, all things alive-O, alive-O gouted sap and spunk' (58). As his only models for religious experience seem to be intolerant institutional ones with 'Thou shalt not' writ large, he does not connect his own feelings of over-whelming awe and fusion with a life force with what others might classify as an experience of the numinous:

Once as a small boy, enraptured by swarming swifts in Wion gully, I felt universal, holier than ages, mightied by wonder. Another ecstasy a sunny morning before school, crawling over a hillock to watch a green woodpecker hammering its crimson-splashed head at the bole of an oak, yaffle and boy sounding alpha, alpha, alpha! (31–2)

The exposure of some of my subjects to the excesses of Welsh Nonconformity was so harsh that an experience which, say, R. S. Thomas would classify as reli-gious is not regarded in that light at all.

Berry, in what he signals from the title of his autobiography onwards, would seem to belong firmly to the group Paul John Eakin, in *Touching the World*, describes as: 'featur[ing] the active, conscious construction of the point of intersection between the individual's life and the larger movement of history of which it is a part' (144). Weintraub recognized Goethe as the first autobiographer to insist 'that his life would have been something entirely different had he been born ten years to either side' of his actual birth-date, in his case 1749 (quoted by Eakin in *Touching* [148]). Berry's coming to young manhood at the outbreak of war was crucially formative:

> The world I knew was a shambles, rags and tatters of pride, of convenience and shitten principles . . . Civilisation, I thought, was becoming extinct. Even my allocation of it, night shift behind the Longwall cutter in Graig level. (85)

Up until the time he lost his job to a younger, cheaper man, at a time when Bevin's Essential Works Order had given enormous powers to government control of workers, Berry seems to have seen himself as a typical hard-working, hard-playing miner, a good butty and a good mate. His image of his huge capacity to push himself to his limits cycling, experiencing the knock (delirium caused by fatigue and hunger) to such a degree that he briefly loses sight and feeling, establishes him as someone who has it in him to be totally, self-punishingly committed (77–8). Yet his more enduring image of himself over a longer span is as a 'meanderer' (138) and he hardly quarrels with others' view of him as a 'waster' (102). Bevin's Essential Works Order 'dry-rammed up the ring of personal choice and rang ding-dong knell on anyone cherishing him/herself as precious' (86). He loses a job that he does well on the cutter, and, at a time when he is made brutally aware of the health risks of any underground work as his friend, Cliff Williams, develops TB with haemorrhaging, is offered only work which everyone knew was a virtual death sentence on the silicosis-inducing hard heading: 'Miners were expendable in 1940. And *all* the men who worked that hard rock heading are in Treorchy cemetery' (87). As a result of striking the manager who will offer him no alternative work to this, he will never be offered another local pit job. In recreating from the present his mood at that time, he powerfully evokes an objective correlative to his remembered misery in the nature of the war events he chooses to list:

> After the court case, nothing much seemed to matter. Intimidation and fear, sanctimony and cant were everywhere. Fifth columns, pimps in office, Britain's aristocracy shipping their children overseas, ration cheating, MI5 round up of Rhondda Italians, the blitzing of towns, these were the slush of War. (88–9)

The searing clincher of what becomes a lifelong obsessive need to be his own person, required to defer to no one, was his experience in the merchant navy for which he volunteered 'to avoid wearing uniform' (98). With hindsight, he sees 'only the naive, bedevilled or frenetic' (98) joined the merchant navy in the winter of 1941. Berry's one and only trip was cataclysmic in its horror and in the way it modified his life attitudes permanently thereafter. He suffered constant, gut-wrenching seasickness. There was constant, at times wild, drunkenness in everyone, from the captain down; predatory, power-based sexual behaviour was indulged in; rations were stolen from the lifeboats; the bonded cargo was broken into, and food, drink and equipment intended for Monty's Desert Rats was sold; 'Big Mac' indulged his taste for north African child prostitutes and looted a motorbike, which travelled back to Britain with him (98–100). 'We were defending Western civilisation', Berry observes drily (99).

This experience seems to set in amber the utter distrust in Berry of following any sort of herd reaction and total resistance to knee-jerk responses to notions of honour or patriotism. His retrospective look at the feelings evoked in his child-self and in others by Remembrance Day is wondering and ironic:

And on Remembrance Day, Treherbert Brass Band glittering, bomping up to the Cenotaph like talkie extras . . . with a bugler fluting the Last Post up at Pen Pych, bared heads, stillness all over the country, my throat burning to the gristle, nape hairs crimped, prepared for reverence, ascent of the species via hallucination. (35)

Thereafter, as this backward look seems to understand, there can be no sense of serving King and country, and honour is a nonsense. As we have seen, in his attempt to give meaning to his whole life's mythic tale, Berry has identified himself as 'Since birth . . . measured for twilight drift' (36). Yet, until his service with the merchant navy, he was absorbable within the bounds of what society at the time would have regarded as normalcy. A brief summary of Berry's subsequent wartime experience establishes how it 'broke' him in conventional terms, while also consolidating within him an inalienable sense of his own fundamental selfhood. Through theft of the local library date-stamper, he is able to fend off, for a period, any further merchant navy postings, while still receiving food-ration coupons (101). After further drift, he ends up in the army, where he quickly reports that 'the shuffleboard of army life was breaking me', pushing him to 'unleash fatuity' (110) in an essay, causing increasingly harsh army crackdown. Buckling under the pressure, he goes absent without leave, is rejected by his parents; yet, in this hindsight record, he remembers this as 'a time of repair even as flags of faith disintegrated, as ramparts cultivated since infancy toppled . . . Clinically I was *out* of the mind one normally shares with other folks at all sorts of levels'

(116–17). Yet, even during the process of disintegration, the nadir of his life experience to that point, with hindsight he sees that at times he had felt 'profoundly warranted' (115), able to return to a censorious officer 'the only answer of my life: "I've starved for other things than bread" ' (111). The process of becoming a reject of society, as represented by the armed services in wartime, has given Berry some sense of the hard core of self, what he must be true to if he is to survive: 'At the centre, there's a core greening like bronze, a private memorial deckled with shrivelled blossoms. They glowed once, in the lost country of childhood' (113). One of Berry's final images of self is as an almost lifelong nonconformist, 'shaping the square peg of myself, escapee from round holes since before leaving school in 1935' (147).

Berry seems to perceive the historic times in which he lives as crucially moulding the potential embodied in his natural endowment and early nurture. As I have already posited, the anger with his parents, which was transformed into anger at, and resistance to, any authority figure, reached such levels of intensity when he was caught up in the power structures of wartime that the system's resultant crackdown almost broke him. He seems to see two wartime happenings as crucially formative. Fifty years after the event, he refers with venom to the harshness of Bevin's wartime Essential Works Order. During his brief service in the merchant navy, physical seasickness combined with a spiritual horror to bring about a subsequent tacit refusal to accept the state's decisions for his life. War gave him harsh perceptions of the nature of humankind, which he did not modify subsequently. Further, the time in which he lived, in which south Wales coal lost its traditional markets and the Rhondda valleys became largely a commuter dormitory, shaped and transformed his environment. Exceptional times created exceptional pressures. As Dai Smith's introduction points out, one of Berry's purposes is to 'witness and to refuse the suffocating custody of the comforting, herded tribe' (11).

History is What You Live is imbued with a sense of mortality, with memories of those now 'gone to clay' (100) and an awareness of how little of what has been thought worth human struggle endures. As Berry approaches the end of his own life, his final implicit perception is that a self that has written of itself has built a frail defence against the encroaching sea of annihilation. 'Foul hooked on language' (130) at one time in his life, he has won through to bear witness to what he and his community have lived through. Although in *History is What You Live* he has often identified himself with 'wasters', the sediment of society, his final image is a triumphant one: of himself, as a young man, scoring the penalty goal that won Fernhill soccer team the cup in 1937 and, as an old man, the last survivor of that team, he wins again in another way by making an enduring testimony of what he and his community have known. For all its shortcomings, the fact of *History is What You Live* – its complex structure, its glowing and loving evocation of a world now past, its linguistic bravura and Berry's final insight into his own complexities – stands in counterpoint to its record of failure. Berry wrote *History is What You Live* after he had won success as a writer. The self he explores there is the self which has part found, part created, a meaningful pattern, in and from the fragments of his lived life. The accomplishment in that patterning is a triumphant part of his perception of self.

5

You've Got to Laugh: Gwyn Thomas (1913–1981)

The subjects for this study have been chosen for a range of different reasons. In the case of Gwyn Thomas I have been impelled by a strong sense of challenge to penetrate the towering enigma that this one-time schoolmaster turned writer and television personality represents as an autobiographer. His talent for display in autobiographical or semi-autobiographical mode was as rich as any peacock's, finding outlet in his work on radio and television, in short stories, as critic and as notebook jotter in addition to his attested autobiography. However, in works intended for public consumption, defensive strategies, particularly humorous obfuscation, seemed to be far more prevalent than frankness or exegetical zeal. Gradually I came to see the spectacle as an elaborate fan-dance, concealing as much as it flaunted, tantalizingly obscuring, often through humour, deep-seated vulnerability and pain.

At first, it felt strangely difficult to take in the evidence of an initial analysis – that much of the humour characteristic of Gwyn Thomas might have its origin in anger or aggression. Theorists of humour, however, have no such hesitation. Joseph Boskin, in his essay included in *The Philosophy of Laughter and Humor*, underlines the aggressive roots of much humour, and quotes and comments on many authorities, including Freud:

> In Freud's analysis, humor gives pleasure by permitting a gratification of a forbidden desire. 'Humor is not resigned,' he observed of its energy, 'it is rebellious.' Hostility takes the form of 'tendentious humor', a veiled attack which satisfies an aggressive motive. For Freud, derogation – assault by joke – is socially acceptable hostility. When expressed through humor, the penalties for

aggression are diminished. Consequently, humor that is of hostile design often releases inner tension.[1]

The problem with laughter is that it disarms. It seems important, therefore, to reflect explicitly on my surprised coming to awareness of the aggression lurking beneath the often seemingly benevolent and high-spirited surface of Gwyn Thomas's writing, as in his story 'Arrayed like One of These'.[2] Here, anger and aggression are significantly, though obliquely, directed at his father, his sole surviving parent from the time he was six.

This is one of Gwyn Thomas's funniest stories, featuring a range of highly comic grotesques. Further humour is provided by his anarchic depiction of the dour sobriety of his chapel culture. There is a regular working-up to highly mannered set-pieces or maxims.

The reader is swept onwards on a surging crest of a comic wave; yet an analytic approach reveals a surprising undertow which the exuberant billows have masked. Gwyn Thomas sees that his father's 'tic of compassion' is always directed outwards, away from his own family. In the story, the writer's textual self is a sitting duck for the consequences of all the inappropriate acts of sympathy which his father directs at a range of unfortunates and inadequates in the tailoring trade. Early in the story, five-year-old Gwyn is to be clad in a shirt of hideous fabric bought by his father from a packman. 'He was delighted to see what a load he had taken off the packman's mind *even though he was now going to lift it on to mine*' (27–8, my italics in this and ensuing quotations). For a climax to the story, Gwyn Thomas dreams up a cringe-provoking situation so mortifying for his now-adult textual self and creates so baroque a grotesque in Aaron Phipps, that when one comes to analyse this section there is a sense of surprise that laughter kept erupting in the way it had. For the last and hardest hurdle of his educational career, his Final Schools at Oxford, Gwyn Thomas needs subfusc, an elegant dark suit to be worn for his exams with a white bow-tie and a gown. It is a life stage when one might legitimately expect to rely on the imaginative support of a parent but, characteristically, Thomas's father thinks only of benefits in trade for Aaron Phipps. As Thomas's suit materializes, Phipps's range of idiosyncrasies as a tailor is described with wild abandon, but then we get narrator comments like: 'I was wishing myself out in the light *and my father through the floorboards*' (32) and, later, 'As he saw the monstrous inaccuracies of Aaron Phipps twist my body into the likeness of Quasimodo *he did not show any depression*' (34) and, finally: '*But my father remained complacent about it to the very end*. He claimed it was my revulsion from the chapel tradition that made my limbs contract and twist at the touch of that heavy, sombre material' (35).

So much of the charge of the language of the story has been directed outwards in the grotesque comic effects that it takes an analysing approach to
pick up the anger in the situation. It is the grotesqueries that have been fore-
grounded, not the feeling. This story helps one to see that a comic drive may
be related to a need to displace anger. A further cover device seems to be in
use. It is almost as though Gwyn Thomas is denying that he is putting forward
the fictional father as his real father. How could he be? He has made a
grotesque of him. What is let through by having a denial available is a real
charge of feeling. Indeed, Thomas rarely, if ever, shoots directly at his
parental target, although oblique discharge can be telling. In an early version
of his autobiography, *A Few Selected Exits*,[3] indignant criticism of Thomas's
father, later deleted, comes as a sort of choric comment from one of his multiple narrators, Uncle Duncan, not in his own voice:

> Now your father . . . he never was anywhere near the target. All he's done on this
> earth is reproduce himself with unreasonable urgency [and] knock back ale . . .
> Such things as that and treating your mother to a quick, cheap burial . . . If it
> hadn't been for that fruit fly there, my brother, that fertile and futile buffoon she
> would have gone on . . . to fill the opera houses of the world.[4]

Getting a purchase on Gwyn Thomas, then, can be hard going. He regularly
tells his audience, usually with a broad and disarming grin, if it is a television
interview, or its verbal equivalent in writing, that he is a deeply anxious man.
The grin and the verbal humour are formidable defences. Further discussion
is discouraged because, the statement having been made, there is nothing further to say. Humorous juxtaposition prevents confessional statements being
taken too seriously: 'I have had more than one motherland. There was Wales
and, alongside it, Spain, irony, an overtowering sense of the past, and an anxiety neurosis roughly the size of the Eisteddfod Pavilion.'[5] He returns frequently, as we shall see in *A Few Selected Exits*, to the sense that anxiety is
his most powerful fuel. The clues for the misery this represented are widely
scattered, but cumulatively very telling, of a man who has taught 'Despair . . .
to sit up and grin at command' ('Gwyn Thomas', 72). The disparity between
the grey bleakness of interior day-to-day experiencing, as revealed, at times,
in Thomas's notebooks, and the façade of mirth and jollity surely requires
further probing.

Certainly, in important ways, Gwyn Thomas's childhood was harsh. He was
the twelfth child of an overburdened mother, who died when he was six, and
a feckless father, and so his early life seems to have provided little in the way

of nurturing care or protection. Of all the writers considered here, Gwyn
Thomas most repays a close study in terms of the branch of psychoanalytical
thinking known as attachment theory. John Bowlby, over the three volumes
and 1,500 pages of his *Attachment and Loss*, sets human early attachment
behaviour in the context of what twentieth-century studies in ethology have
shown about the behaviour of other primates in areas of dependency and vulnerability.[6] Attachment behaviour is any form of behaviour that results in a
person attaining or maintaining proximity to some other clearly identified
individual who is seen as better able to deal with the world, and is most obviously evident in early childhood. The biological function attributed to it is
protection, particularly, in evolutionary terms, from predators. A feature of
the greatest importance clinically, and one that must be properly registered in
an evaluation of Gwyn Thomas, is the intensity of emotion that accompanies
attachment behaviour.

Bowlby summarizes the three propositions central to his exploration of
attachment theory. The first is that when an individual is confident that an
attachment figure will be available to him whenever he needs it, that person
will be much less susceptible to intense or chronic fear than will an individual
who does not have this confidence. The second proposition postulates that
confidence in the availability of attachment figures, or a lack of it, is built
slowly during the years of immaturity and tends to persist thereafter, rela-
tively unchanged, throughout the rest of life. The third proposition posits that
the expectations of the accessibility and responsiveness of attachment figures
that different individuals develop during the years of immaturity are reasonably true reflections of the experiences those individuals have actually had
(*Attach2*, 235).

Gwyn Thomas, be it ever so humorously, regularly declares a state of anxiety
that is chronic and acute. Bowlby states that uncertainty about the availability
of attachment figures results in an increased susceptibility to responding with
fear, to such a wide range of situations that the person concerned is often
referred to as suffering from 'free-floating anxiety' (*Attach2*, 229).

In the wider world beyond his front door, as, originally, in his own family,
Gwyn Thomas found abundant reasons for insecurity, for distrusting any perception of the world as a solid place. Yet his own uneasy imagination often
transformed what was undoubtedly an unstable environment into something
cataclysmic, full of portents of doom. In *A Few Selected Exits* he describes:

> three . . . brutally recurrent dreams [. . . each with] its teeth and lips fixed around
> my thoughts with vampirical authority, leaving not even a muddy residue of
> calm. I plunge through the usual paraphernalia of unease: bogs . . . landslips,

she died [he was actually six] – and she was in her early forties, a woman of vast creative potential . . . I mean, here I was, the twelfth child, a totally unwanted child, and yet, you know, she had this faith in the world and the wind and the sky . . . and she would look at me, and she would almost forgive me at times for being there. Almost forgive me.[13]

The degree of idealization and the nature of the revelation in the Denis Mitchell interview strongly point to the possibility that Gwyn Thomas was anxiously, not securely, attached to his mother. Her death when he was only six would have significantly increased the anxiety with which he engaged with the world. The formidable amount of evidence Bowlby has accumulated includes substantial research data 'that events of later years, notably loss of mother before tenth or eleventh birthday, when combined with certain other conditions can play a causal role in the development of depressive disorders' (*Attach3*, 215). There is strong evidence for supposing that the results of this loss shadowed Gwyn Thomas's emotional life for the rest of his days. The general thrust of Bowlby's third volume, *Loss*, is that, for mourning to be healthily completed, the bereaved person, be they adult or child, must be supported while s/he takes on the full pain of loss and is buffeted by the powerful feeling of it. In a child, mourning is most likely to take a favourable course in the following conditions: that s/he should have enjoyed a reasonably secure relationship with her/his parents before her/his loss, that s/he should be allowed to ask questions and participate in family grieving at the loss and that s/he has the comforting presence of a surviving parent or substitute (*Attach3*, 320). From the accounts Gwyn Thomas gives, none of these features seems to have been present in his case.

For mourning to achieve a healthy outcome, then, children should be allowed to talk freely about their loss, ask questions and grieve openly. Again, in an early draft of *A Few Selected Exits*, Thomas writes:

I never once heard [my father] speak of my mother. I had the feeling that his thoughts about her were confused, inexpressible. There were things about her I would have wished to know. But no-one, except Uncle Duncan, ever spoke of her. It was as if we had each agreed to drop a meed [*sic*] of silence upon her. ('Drafts', 44 deleted, 32 substituted)

Bowlby's evidence suggests children value photographs highly, and that these are a particular help in the process of grieving (*Attach3*, 285). Dai Smith's *Writer's World* pictorial biography of Gwyn Thomas indicates that no photograph of Ziphorah Thomas survives (5).[14] Interestingly, Gwyn

Thomas has his narrator provide an explanation for such a lack in the story of a mother's ghost 'Not Even Then': 'My mother had died when I was two and of her I remembered nothing. There was no photograph of her in the house. My father, during the three years he survived, had destroyed them all to blunt the stab of recollection.'[15] A child must be helped to understand that death is final, that the body is in the ground or burnt and the beloved parent will never return (*Attach3*, 271); yearning and searching are a natural part of mourning and children need to be helped to incorporate the experience of loss, so that they can move on from it. Fascinatingly, in his play 'The Keep', the plot of which he describes as 'a kind of extension of autobiography' (*A Few Selected Exits*, 128), Gwyn Thomas has the daughter, who has been looking after a tribe of brothers for years after their mother's death in America, reveal what she has recently learnt – that their mother did not die in the train crash in America but escaped from it to a new and more satisfying life: 'Mam didn't die in that accident. She got out and kept heading west . . . because there were certain things of which she had had enough.'[16] It is certainly possible that Gwyn Thomas is here tuning in to an enduring hopeful fantasy from childhood.

In this beleaguered family, headed by feckless, improvident Walter Thomas, there simply was not enough sympathetic energy left to go round at the time of bereavement. There seems to have been no one who was emotionally responsive and available to the youngest child, Gwyn Thomas. He declares, variously and amusingly, that he was 'the strop for the tormented psyches of the family':

> When any pressure of anxiety among my elders needed to be relieved, standard practice was to take me to one side and belt me. And this often when I was in a mood of melting love for all my fellows. I got clobbered so insistently I could well have remained comatose into late middle age. ('Gwyn Thomas', 68–9)

There were further penalties, should he be unwise enough to draw attention to his own needs:

> There was also a tiny, lightless chamber beneath the stairs into which I was periodically thrown and I would spend an hour or so banging defiant fists against the door . . . During this period I saw no theme of logic in human life and often said so in terms which won me yet another cuffing and a spell in that little crypt. ('Gwyn Thomas', 69)

Bearing in mind the traumatic bereavement at a tender age, without the humour this would be recognized as an account of bleak deprivation.

Unsurprisingly in view of his early history, Gwyn Thomas seems to have had a lifelong need for strong attachment figures.[17] From his account in *A Few Selected Exits*, during his first year at county school his devotion to Walt, his elder brother, the first in the family to follow an academic route, fills an important need for him:

> During that period I was more devoted to Walt than any dog. (3) . . . During [his] last year at the school I served him as a sort of cut-rate djinn. I was there to serve. He studied right through every evening and never left the house. I wanted to match Walt's devotion to his books by my devotion to him . . . As long as he was at his table, I remained at my post of duty, which was exactly halfway up the stairs . . . Any word of command, any rustle of unease, and I was up the stairs like a whippet. (10)

The account suggests an urgent hunger in his boy-self for attachment, for proximity.

A tragic and enduring consequence of the lack of dependable early nurture can be the inability to move far away from what is perceived as a home base, because of compelling unconscious fears that whatever supplies of support and love that would otherwise be available might dry up. Thomas uses a most vivid image to suggest how the Rhondda took the place for him of the close maternal embrace that had regularly to be stimulated into action: 'My growing up place, the dark octopal gulches I never wished to leave, whose embrace, whenever it grew slack, I would stroke back into a pitiless rigidity' (*A Few Selected Exits*, 144). It seems probable that a major element in his deep unhappiness at Oxford was his inability, after the precariousness of his attachments in childhood, to adjust to being away from the only base he had known. Similarly, during the months in Spain during his second university year, his unease caused him to fashion a smaller and smaller cell for himself. First of all, Thomas withdrew from the course at the University of Madrid (69), and next he withdrew from meals at his *pension*. He took to reading books in English at boulevard cafés: 'But even from the boulevards I withdrew. I followed some kind of crypto-monastic urge that has flavoured a lot of my days . . . I have only to take a peck at any single experience and I begin to fall back' (*A Few Selected Exits*, 71). He calls his autobiography *A Few Selected Exits* and once explained, on the *Parkinson Show*, that he spent a lot of his life looking for the way out: escape routes really mattered.[18] His autobiography ends by making totally explicit his need for what he saw as his secure Rhondda base: 'I was home, at my earth's warm centre. The scared monkey was back in the branches of his best-loved tree. I've never had any truly passionate wish to be elsewhere' (*A Few Selected Exits*, 212). Attachment theory provides a more than sufficient tool for explicating his behaviour.

Where escape was not possible, defensive strategies were highly developed in this vulnerable man. He could control situations hilariously using his skill as a raconteur, where he was not expected to give turns. In the *Parkinson Show* interview (1971), he states that he could not be anywhere without reading, having a demented desire to isolate himself from awful threat. From his own account, his habitual and characteristic nervousness was considerably heightened when broadcasting, where he was, nevertheless, a bravura performer. A scrutiny of some of the remaining records of Gwyn Thomas in broadcasting mode produces some interesting insights.

From our vantage point of post-devolutionary political confidence, his assertions about Wales, often from platforms in England, seem ill-judged and sometimes offensive. Wynn Thomas, in a BBC television programme five years after Gwyn Thomas's death, *Gwyn Thomas: A Critical Reputation*, had this to say of the man as displayed in his occasional writings, TV appearances and radio broadcasts of his declining years:

> He could, at least on a bad day, sound to a Welsh speaker such as myself like a bizarre cross between Ian Paisley and Uncle Tom . . . Ian Paisley in the sense that he voiced, however wittily, the bigoted opinions of anti-Welsh-language sectarianism, and Uncle Tom, too, perhaps, because he seemed so keen, on the Michael Parkinson Show for example, to play up to an Englishman's expectation of what a picturesque Welshman should be and to play down the real thing . . . Towards the end, entertaining quips became Gwyn Thomas's fatal Cleopatra, for which the whole Welsh world was well lost at times.[19]

Transcripts of *Any Questions* helpfully indicate laughter and applause and its degree. The record for the programme on 5 June 1964 shows Gwyn Thomas in characteristic action.[20] In any individual programme, he typically elicits the greatest audience response of anyone on the panel. In this programme, broadcast from the University of Southampton, it is as though audience approval or amusement stimulates or goads him to further excesses. Seemingly playing to the preconceptions of his audience, Thomas relates with gusto a surely fictional tale of the appalled reaction of an African visitor to eighteen lugubrious renderings of the 'very lowering piece' 'The Martyr of the Arena' by male-voice choirs at an eisteddfod held in a disused wagon shed in Treorchy. Several people commented that, although he loved to make people laugh, it moved later into a kind of buffoonery – and, as Wynn Thomas indicates, often at the expense of Wales.[21] It may be productive, for reasons I shall be exploring, to interpret such behaviour as an attack on the 'mother' country.

The motivation for what seems to have been largely unconscious behaviour would appear to have been complex. As we have seen, from the time of his mother's death, his childish ploys for attention were severely rebuffed. What we do not get in early childhood often remains an unsatisfied craving. At last, with his live audiences and spellbound groups in the pub, Gwyn Thomas was getting the positive strokes he longed for. Playing to the gallery seems to have become second nature. Further, an antagonism to Welsh seems to have been built in to his childhood situation; a linguistic fault-line ran right down the middle of his family. Whereas his parents habitually communicated with each other in Welsh and the first six children had Welsh as their mother tongue, in response to the belief evolving at the start of the twentieth century that English would be the language of advancement in the world, children numbers seven to twelve in the Thomas family were explicitly taught no Welsh. Nevertheless, Gwyn was expected to attend a Welsh-language chapel; he testified to the boredom and frustration this evinced many times, perhaps most notably and entertainingly in a *Punch* article:

> We were thrust into a cosmos of moralizing and mourning conducted totally in Welsh. We were surrounded by people who seemed to have a mania for hustling the young on to public stages as bullets in the fight against joy . . . I became one of a troupe of lads on the didactic and propagandist side of the Sunday School and Band of Hope. We found no difficulty in learning the reams of Welsh and were no worse in our performance for not understanding a word of it.[22]

Exasperation and boredom over matters Welsh are therefore very understandable. However, Gwyn Thomas's feelings seem to run much deeper than this. We have already observed that the death of a mother figure before a child's tenth birthday can be a source of pathology in the future, and that none of the features which experts reckon may help a child healthily to complete mourning and move on seemed to be present in Gwyn Thomas's family. While anger at the desertion of the beloved dead person can be a feature of all mourning, Bowlby states: 'All are agreed that anger with the lost figure (often unconscious and directed elsewhere) plays a major role in pathological mourning' (*Attach3*, 28). It seems probable that Gwyn Thomas found it impossible to hold and express ambivalent feelings for his mother: as we have seen, he had a tendency to idealize her. Bowlby, exploring defence mechanisms, writes:

To direct anger away from the person who elicited it and towards some more or less irrelevant person [displacement], is so well known that little need be said about it. The term 'splitting' is also used in this connection when an ambivalent reaction is aroused with the loving component being directed towards one person and the angry component being redirected towards another. (*Attach3*, 68)

Thomas's mother, whom he at times both loved and hated, spoke Welsh for preference, a language which excluded him, and sang wondrously well. In the unconscious split that young Gwyn Thomas seems to have achieved – a split that lasted the whole of his life – his anger with his abandoning mother landed with full ferocity on her language of preference, Welsh. In all this, there was a kind of unconscious logic. He had experienced Welsh as the language of exclusion. Anger with the language therefore re-enacted his repressed feeling of being excluded by his mother before her death, by her death and from her grave. His love of her continued to find expression in his lifelong pleasure in singing and devotion to opera.

There were further deep-seated reasons, largely unconscious, for disparaging the Welsh language in later life. His widow, Lyn, explains in an interview with Michael Parnell: 'Gwyn increasingly found himself being less well treated by the BBC after the arrival of the new Welsh-speaking elements in the hierarchy; everything altered; going to the BBC began to be like going to a foreign country.'[23] Gwyn Thomas had most painful memories of exclusion, from his periods of incarceration in a cupboard under the stairs in the period of bleak deprivation after his mother's death; subsequent exclusion is likely to have been profoundly distressing to him.

Further, although he was later to become a teacher of Spanish, Thomas had a bemusing area of insensitivity to language. His teacher at Porth County School, Georges Rochat, testified to his being 'excellent at Spanish but he never fell in love with the language. He was not a natural linguist' ('NB', 6). He seems to have sensed none of the excitement that people who have a deep knowledge of more than one language experience, as they come to understand how uniquely and differently each language moulds the perception of the speaker. He seems to have felt no emotional response to language. Perhaps his phobic reaction to being vulnerably away from his home-base when abroad prevented him from ever really appreciating the degree to which language is a vehicle of culture: 'All around me were Spaniards and Spain and I had no real wish to know' (*A Few Selected Exits*, 71). His total insensitivity to the feelings of those who perceived the world and lived their lives through the medium of Welsh made him many enemies. In a radio conversation in 1979, he expresses astonishingly provocative views on the Welsh language, perhaps partly exercising his *enfant terrible* persona:

> I have never for one instant been tempted to compromise with my disapproval of the fact that Lazarus did not die. I think the language had been given its cue to leave the stage and I believe it would have been better for the health of the Welsh mind had it done so. Now this will outrage many people but it is adequately a truth as far as I'm concerned.[24]

In *A Few Selected Exits* he asserts: 'Anyone who struggles to revive a language that is dying gracefully and without pain is guilty of a most harmful treason' (59). It is certainly tempting to interpret such combative views, from someone who was regularly fielded as a representative Welshman by the British media, as a mixture of insensitivity to the issues involved and powerful unconscious drives.

One further area of autobiographical enactment, his notebooks, needs to be explicitly considered before I turn to what his American editor describes as 'An Autobiography of Sorts', *A Few Selected Exits*. Although the notebooks pose serious problems for the academic researcher, in a study such as this, which is attempting to discern how Gwyn Thomas perceived himself, such evidence of characteristic mental states is of some importance. There is no reason to doubt that Lyn Thomas carried out her declared intention of destroying the notebooks.[25] The extracts which are now available for scrutiny have thus been mediated through others. I have made use of selections typed by Lyn Thomas (and it seems safe to assume that she preserved only sections she believed her husband had composed, not items culled and copied from other sources) and a substantial collection of extracts which Michael Parnell transcribed because they were of interest to him.[26] Parnell records that, for the later journals in particular, Lyn Thomas exercised a ferocious censorship, destroying as much as two-thirds of one notebook before allowing her husband's biographer to see it (*MP*, Notebook 36, 25 May 1973). There are further problems of provenance. Against many of the extracts, Parnell has written 'GT' – which may be a transcription of Gwyn Thomas's note to himself that particular aphorisms and bons mots were indeed his and not jottings culled from elsewhere, to guard against inadvertent plagiarism. However, from internal evidence, many entries which are not so initialled seem indeed to have been composed by Gwyn Thomas. Presumably, in some of the deeply personal (and sexual) outpourings, he felt himself in no danger of unwittingly publishing as his own extracts absorbed from the works of another.

A characteristic theme of the jottings, particularly of the later notebooks, is the timorousness with which Thomas perceives himself as having engaged with life and the bleakness and meaninglessness of the whole experience:

> There are so many areas of life I have refused to touch through a secret revulsion or fear the final portrait of myself now emerging is of a single eye glaring from a fragmentary womb. The whole post-natal experience has been so partial, so evasive, my death certificate when it comes will be a frivolously unnecessary document. [Initialled GT] (*MP*, Notebook 18, 22 February 1969, 138)

As we have seen, Thomas's early life experience would have made him very vulnerable to depression as an adult: his notebooks, which were the receptacles of the unguarded expression of his raw feelings of the moment, offer convincing evidence of long-term depressive states.[27] A further, perturbing feature of the notebooks – the regular, intense nature of the sexual focus – needs some consideration here. While it seems near certain that Gwyn Thomas intended his notebooks for no eye but his own, transcripts of large sections are now in the public domain in the National Library of Wales. It seems important to attempt an interpretation which may be helpful to an overall understanding of Gwyn Thomas's work, while seeking to avoid being officiously intrusive.

In the course of discussion, general and specific, with people who knew Gwyn Thomas – people who were taught by him, lived in his neighbourhood, knew him at summer schools – there has been no suggestion that Gwyn Thomas was anything but devotedly monogamous in practice. Michael Parnell seems implicitly to have reached a similar conclusion (*Laughter from the Dark*, 111). Particular specialist expertise has been helpful at this stage – that of an analytical psychotherapist and a consultant urologist – who have helped considerably to clarify the issues. In his notebooks, Gwyn Thomas frequently and enthusiastically expatiates on the zealous masturbation of his adolescence. Of several possible psychoanalytical explanations of his regular dwelling on the sexual act in his notebooks, what seems most convincing is that it performed the function of a sort of cerebral masturbation, the intensity of which lifted his mood from black to grey: it was a defence against the deepest depression. In the mid-1960s, Gwyn Thomas became diabetic. At that time and later, there are several allusions to and explorations of impotence in the notebooks and discussions of the close relationship between sexual potency and creative ability. Urologists have confirmed that impotence is a not-infrequent consequence of diabetes.[28] Gwyn Thomas's obsessional preoccupation with sexual imaginings can surely be sympathized with, when they are perceived as an attempted defence against depressive dwellings on death and disintegration. The public persona of a happy clown is very much at variance with the perceived self of the journals at that time.

Writing straight autobiography proved to be immensely difficult for Gwyn Thomas. An entry in his notebook in 1970 – whether his own composition or culled from another – seems to capture retrospectively his feelings about writing in the genre: 'For the humorous writer, the fantasist, writing straight autobiography is a cyanide trip. He serves up the living guts of his raw material to the visiting condors' (*MP*, Notebook 21, 31 March 1970, 7). He spent the best part of a year on his first attempts at sustained autobiography. We can build up a sense of what Thomas's early work on *A Few Selected Exits* was like from the loose-leaf fragments that remain ('Drafts').[29] Early versions include rambling rather inconsequential accounts of his father, his brothers Dil, Emlyn and Walt and of a seemingly fictitious Uncle Duncan, with some long-running digressions. The autobiography had been commissioned in 1965, and simultaneous publication in Britain with Hutchinson and America with Little, Brown had been planned. Both editors were personally known to Gwyn Thomas. Letters in response to readings of the manuscript he submitted are encouraging and tactful but make absolutely clear that the work as it stands is absolutely unpublishable. Harold Harris of Hutchinson, in a letter of 28 June 1967, comments that all that the reader might like to know about Gwyn Thomas 'is in danger of being swamped beneath the eccentricities of everybody else he ever met, lost in a maze of digressional convolution and blown to smithereens by a succession of exploding images'.[30] He quotes extensively from a reader's report on the MS:

> Possibly we all differ in our definition of what an autobiography should be. I believe that, although people famous or infamous can add to its value, the author's life should take precedence and should be described through the events which have shaped it. And his views should be clearly stated so that he himself emerges as the dominant personality.
>
> His rumbustious, rhetorical style frequently defeats his purpose. He forgets that hyperbolic writing can result not only in repetition . . . but also in a farcical exaggeration of incidents and of characters which produces total unreality. All his people are blown up to bursting point; he ignores lapse of time, dates and sequence and these evasions increase the confusion . . . The whole book is a chaotic *non sequitur*.[31]

Harris confesses to having read the MS with editorial pencil in hand, and proposes an early meeting in Cardiff to discuss revision. Pencilled marks with 'stet' written beside them on sections of the typescript in the archive high-light characters and incidents he seems to have wanted preserved.[32] A large cast of characters subsequently disappears, and characters such as Mr Denning and Mr Metcalf gain a prominence they did not have in the original work, when part of a larger chorus.

A letter from Harry Sions of Little, Brown emphasizes his agreement with all the points made by Hutchinson and adds a few of his own: '[The book] really doesn't end, it somehow stops as though you had simply tired of the whole business or run out of typewriter ribbon . . .'[33] He finds it inexplicable that the autobiography should end at the point Gwyn Thomas leaves teaching and asks firmly for further work to include his experiences as a dramatist and television personality.

The conclusions that may be drawn from these comments are that Gwyn Thomas found it difficult to reflect on his life, even to the degree of giving his autobiography some discernible structure. Sions considers Thomas had diffi-culty expressing his feelings; to the end, in spite of three specific requests, he refuses to expand on his scant and cursory references to his wife. And in his own autobiography, outgoing showman Thomas found it difficult to fore-ground himself. It seems probable that an attempt to write an autobiography had brought Thomas much too close to unconscious material that had been repressed because it was too painful to contemplate. In an undated draft let-ter of reply to Harold Harris's criticism, he owns: 'The book was chiselled out of vast unwillingness. The literal facts of my life are so loathsome to my mind I get a withering shock right up my arm whenever I set them down.'[34] Thomas seems to have made a second attempt at an opening chapter.[35] In this, his first and concluding sections are verbatim recyclings of two articles he had written for *Punch*.[36] The first, which deals with his regular incarceration in the cupboard under the stairs, has a jocularity about it, understandable per-haps, given its original audience, which signals in this context a determin-ation not to engage with genuine reactions to experience. In his interview with Denis Mitchell, he describes comedy as an 'act of weeping'. Here, it seems an act of self-protection.

This chapter, too, was abandoned. The British version of *A Few Selected Exits*, published by Hutchinson, starts with Thomas on the point of departure for Oxford. Harry Sions, however, urgently asks for a fresh lead-in for the American edition.[37] What Thomas provided as a 'new' opening proves to be a verbatim recycling of an article, 'The Incomparable Cradle', which he seems to have published in the London *Evening Standard* of 13 February 1965.[38] He uses this for a third time when asked for an autobiographical sketch for Meic Stephens's *Artists in Wales*. This piece, while written with

Thomas's usual comic exaggeration, does deal with important life events, such as the death of his mother, and his perception of himself as deeply anxious, even neurotic. Where Thomas does manage to achieve significant self-disclosure, it is often in what he would perceive as an ephemeral medium – as in this piece, written first for a newspaper, and as in the Denis Mitchell television interview. Thomas states elsewhere, with what appears to be real conviction: 'The limits of one's activity as a writer are fixed by the imaginative antics of boyhood.'[39] A sensitive, detailed appraisal of that boyhood, therefore, would have been of great interest to the reader. But Thomas could not do it.

For the study of autobiographical works by Gwyn Thomas, the researcher is helped by the availability for scrutiny of extensive material assembled by his biographer. The Parnell archive is particularly rich in records of interviews with people who knew Thomas in many different capacities. Accounts of how other people perceived him in some cases add further definition to his proclaimed sense of self, in some cases run counter to it, and sometimes provide insights into areas which Thomas has consciously or unconsciously repressed. To produce a marketable autobiography, he needed some tough-minded help. In the version of *A Few Selected Exits* published by Hutchinson, we have a reasonably reader-friendly text, produced with two editors and a reader having flown formation on the author. Thomas finally structures his material into five chapters: the first deals with his departure for Oxford, with some digressionary swirls into his secondary schooldays and his account of local characters, which gives some sense of the environment which produced him; the second records his university experiences in Oxford and Madrid, including one notable long vacation; the third gives his impressions of colleagues in his years as a teacher; the fourth is an account of his doomed forays into playwriting; and in the fifth he presents himself as a media personality.

As we have seen, Thomas seemed unable to engage with his most deeply formative experiences, such as his childhood and his marriage. The most evasive and the least interesting chapter of *A Few Selected Exits* is, arguably, the third, which ostensibly deals with his time in teaching. His 'Autobiography of Sorts' was written in 1966–7, just a few years after he had quit the classroom after twenty years as a schoolmaster; teaching had been the focus of most of his adult life. His evaluation of this period consists of an account of an eccentric colleague, Mr Walford, described in such outrageously exaggerated terms that there is little danger of a reader believing that this is an exact portrait of anyone who ever lived. One can trace some of the models for the character. In his foreword to *Old Barry in Photographs*, Thomas pays tribute to 'the sparkle of unique character' in the many notable personalities with whom he had taught at Barry County School for Boys, and describes some of their most striking attributes, some instantly recognizable as traits bequeathed to Mr Walford.[40] Clearly D. J. P. Richards, 'the fanatical athlete circling the field in a ten-mile training walk after school, his razor-thin body covered only by a flimsy, bikini-type pair of shorts', is part of this composite portrait. Another is David Walters, 'who lived in a reverie of regret for the fields and streams of Cardiganshire. He taught Chemistry and hated it.' In this foreword, Gwyn Thomas asserts that he once found him in the staffroom fashioning a primitive sort of broom from twigs and a length of wire. To present a composite picture of the antics of his most eccentric colleagues as a monument to his entire professional life is bizarre, even for Gwyn Thomas, and surely needs further investigation.

A strong motivation, as ever, for this particular approach would be the comfort, security and ease of recycling what had already found an enthusiastic audience. 'Mr Walford' had already been a success in a radio play and *Punch* articles (*Laughter from the Dark*, 134–5, 188). But there would seem to be more significant reasons.

In spite of his huge abilities, Thomas, an undisciplined maverick, seems to have been an indifferent teacher of languages[41] although many pay tribute to his innate abilities.[42] During rehearsals for his play, 'Sap', at the Sherman Theatre in 1974, there was an interview session, in which both Thomas and Keith Baxter, who played a leading part in the play, took part.[43] Baxter, a former pupil of Barry County School, explained that, while he believed Gwyn Thomas had 'a very extraordinary influence' on pupils at the school, his practice as a teacher was highly unusual. As Barry County had no library to accommodate those with free periods, these pupils had to sit at the back of lessons in progress.

> I don't know how proficient his students became at learning Spanish. He was marvellously easy to sidetrack always and that's why his lessons were always crowded. I mean, given the right cue at the right time by somebody that perhaps hadn't prepared a Spanish essay, he could be diverted into a talk about the growth of the cinema in the Rhondda Valley or the effect on people of Greta Garbo.

To be taught by Thomas was an exciting experience – he certainly expanded his pupils' horizons – but it could be argued that the exercising of his skills as a raconteur did not advance his pupils' modern-language skills a jot. Reg George described laughing so much in Thomas's lessons that he felt ill ('NB', 89). In his television interview with Denis Mitchell, Thomas revealed how

alluring a temptation making people laugh might be: 'That would create a
laugh, you see, and laughter passes the time on in teaching; you don't have to
teach when they're convulsed' (*Private Lives*). It is probable that at the level
of conscious strategy Gwyn Thomas ensured that his practice as a teacher did
not deplete his energy too much. His unfailing routine was to write for several
hours on returning home, and this seems to have been the most deeply important part of his day. Genuine autobiography encourages a reflective backward look which discerns patterns in one's life. If Thomas acknowledged to
himself and the world that for twenty-odd years he had punched substantially
below his weight as a teacher, might that not force him – and, importantly,
cause his readers – to examine other parts of his personal myth, however
uncomfortable such an exercise might be? 'Mr Walford', standing for his
teaching experience, could be an effective blocking strategy on further potentially uncomfortable rumination for Thomas and detection of dissonance by
his readers, who might note, for example, how rarely his political convictions
had been translated into action with any cost (the one notable exception being
his support of Howard Fast, recorded by Parnell (*Laughter from the Dark*,
123) and fully explored and documented by Victor Golightly[44]).

Earlier, I traced the writer's neurotic need to withdraw from the world into
smaller and smaller spaces both at Oxford and in Madrid: Thomas was aware
of this trait in himself, but saw it as only part of the story of his life away from
home. An important element of the tale he told himself about his unhappiness
at Oxford was his righteous anger at the High Tory positions of fellow
students. He believed that his withdrawing from college life, existing on
transport café pies to avoid ever having to eat with his uncongenial fellow
students, was largely motivated by the moral fire of his political position:
meals had been 'ideological thickets through which [he] trudged in solitude'
(54). Similarly in Madrid, he advances political reasons for withdrawing
from meals at the *pension* (70). This seems to have been a necessary defence for
him, giving him a tangible reason for his deep misery and reclusive withdrawal.

One suspects that a major cause of his unhappiness at Oxford was a willed
resistance to what life there had to offer, a determined malfunctioning:

> Had I planned my honours course a little more wisely my troubles with [my
> tutor] might have been fewer . . . My aptitude for wrong decisions has never
> flagged. From every choice I have made a doom dangles. I recalled that E.T. [his
> headmaster at Porth County School] had warned me against taking up with the
> Middle Ages, so I chose the Middle Ages. E.T. felt I would not make a good
> medievalist. My tutor knew so and said so in some of the hardest Spanish I have
> ever heard. He detested the Middle Ages. (58)

Oxford represented, for him, a quite terrifyingly open door. Gwyn Thomas, through inadequate parenting, tragically lacked the internalized security for any of the take-off points Oxford had to offer. As Dai Smith inimitably puts it, 'The ladders of escape were there. The career marked "Exit" was available. But all the doors for Gwyn were revolving ones' ('A Critical Reputation').

Possibly the then recent death of his one friend at Oxford, Wynne Roberts, caused some painful reflection at the time when Thomas was writing *A Few Selected Exits*. Wynne Roberts, also of Porth County School, had been a year ahead of Gwyn Thomas, on a scholarship at Magdalen College reading Italian. The warmth of Thomas's tribute to him, the only time in the entire autobiography he risks communicating strong affection for anyone, could have been inspired in part by stirrings of guilt. Certainly, his tribute to Wynne causes him to reflect on his own lacks:

> I will never cease to be grateful to him, utterly different from him as I was, for I was in every regard so other from what I would have wished to be. I was clumsy at kindness, gifted at turning away, cursed with an imperfect sense of community, while denying myself the gains these ghastly qualities might have brought me in. (*A Few Selected Exits*, 82)

A study of the trajectory of Wynne Roberts's time at Oxford throws into relief the limitations of Gwyn Thomas's own awareness of self – his lack of political commitment, for example. Parnell's notebook records fascinating interviews with Nansi Roberts, widow of Wynne ('NB', 42–67, 150–61). From her account, Wynne was 'greatly enjoying Oxford' ('NB', 45), until Gwyn Thomas arrived with 'a huge chip on his shoulder' and 'in a sense corrupted Wynne out of his liking for Oxford' ('NB', 46). 'Why was [Gwyn] always so miserable?' she asks rhetorically. Thomas took Wynne Roberts to Communist Party meetings. 'He pushed Wynne in but stayed out himself' ('NB', 45). 'Gwyn Thomas didn't join the Communist Party but Wynne did and Wynne's family thought that all Wynne's troubles began with his friendship with Gwyn Thomas' ('NB', 150). Wynne was subsequently frequently out of work as a result of his Communist Party allegiance. In *A Few Selected Exits* Thomas seems to have misrepresented the circumstances of Wynne Roberts's poor degree – he got a Third – and his feelings about that evaluation, Thomas possibly finding anger with authority more tolerable than self-censure. According to Nansi Roberts, her husband had switched from Modern Languages to English, wishing, it seems, to do something more socially useful but leaving inadequate time to get on top of the heavily linguistic aspects of the course ('NB', 150). His Third therefore seems quite

understandable. She insists: 'Wynne did forgive Oxford for giving him a
Third, unlike what Gwyn Thomas says in *A Few Selected Exits*' ('NB', 44).
In his account, Thomas declares:

> Wynne Roberts went down with a degree of low value, an evaluation that reflect-
> ed absolutely nothing of his real talent, but that, I suppose, is the true function of
> degree giving. Intelligence of the more passionate kind is its own joy and fulfil-
> ment. Its assessment by people smugly dull enough to be assessors is hardly ever
> relevant . . . He never really forgave his judges. Nor should he have. (*A Few
> Selected Exits*, 82)

Nansi believed that 'Gwyn Thomas's spirit was sometimes rebuked by
Wynne's conscience (as Antony's was by Caesar)' ('NB', 54).

At rare times and in particular moods Gwyn Thomas did take private stock
and draw conclusions about his own shortcomings. An early notebook entry
reads:

> I am the root and flower of turpitude. I give people the impression that they are
> shortly to [be] led forth. I have that sultry, prophetic urgency about me when I
> speak to any number that causes to crack in their brain the glorious, apocalyptic
> thought that the way has broken open above their heads . . . Yes, I get a lot of
> people that way. In certain moments I have a certain type of eloquence, sharp,
> pointed and flickering with flame that melts the tortured question mark and
> hammers it into rigid statement – an exclamation of certain optimism in the
> immediate future of our species. Then I turn my back on them and take myself
> forth into a cinema, or pub, the marriage bed or any site whatever where I may
> forget all the conceivable terms of the hideous verb 'to be'. (*MP*, transcribed
> from exercise book carrying the County School, Cardigan label)[45]

The business of actually writing autobiography for publication was, for
Gwyn Thomas, only a limited means of coming to self-knowledge, because
of areas he excluded, deliberately or unconsciously. His declaration of how
'loathsome' the exercise of recalling the facts of his life was to him suggests
he was heavily blocked from exploring explicitly the realities of such elements as his parenting and childhood.[46] There are, however, areas in which *A
Few Selected Exits* communicates with zest and authenticity a sense of what
it was like to be Gwyn Thomas.

He had an unparalleled ability to encapsulate his sense of self in vivid
images, most of all his sense of 'spinning alienation' (81) from much of life. In
recalling a time when he was used as a theatrical extra, he most entertainingly

fixes in the reader's mind an idea of himself as a perpetual outsider looking in, always carrying with him a penumbra of doom and disaster:

> I . . . appeared as a passing stranger who peers through the window, a kind of omen of the doom that was surely on the way, and as doom was constantly on the way in the plays we performed, I was always somewhere near the window, leering. (142)

Not surprisingly, then, the title of his autobiography shows a constant need to exit, rather than engage with, situations in the world. In this heavily constructed autobiography, he crafts an entire chapter, where he features himself as a doomed playwright, to reveal his sense of predestined ill-luck as production after production nosedives, for reasons quite beyond his control. Similarly, at the end of his first year at Oxford he observes: 'I did not know that the sensation of falling off cliffs and going headlong over stretched ropes in the dark was going to be a fixed feature of my being' (88). His overwhelming sense of being an outsider amongst the superior band of sophisticates and attested superintelligences on the *Brains Trust* is inimitably communicated: 'In that company, you need to be as cool as an arctic seal not to feel like sending home for your leper's bell and hood' (170-1). An utterly characteristic sensation for Thomas was: 'of being a bee, buzzing with willingness but outside the wrong hive and stung by my leader for being laden with the wrong pollen' (151). The talent for appropriate encapsulating images is as much a characteristic feature of the style that is Gwyn Thomas as is his great appetite for meanders, lengthy digressional saunters through territory far distant from the main thoroughfare of his narrative. Thomas's characteristic discursive style resembles nothing so much as landscape gardening: serpentine paths which lead to different vistas, giving a sense of spacious territory, which is really the result of judicious planting and building. As we have seen, Thomas finds the idea of linear autobiographical narrative very threatening: it might lead him into territory that hasn't been tamed by him, perhaps to unexpected views where his defensive skills have no relevance. Almost certainly, Thomas found the possibility of having to readjust his personal myth in the light of newly gained insights painful, even threatening. His editors accomplished some rigorous pruning but substantial meanders remained, recognized as the essential style and expression of the self that was Gwyn Thomas.

At his best, Thomas genuinely persuades the visiting reader that the landscape that they are in, while blatantly improved, is both amusing and true to nature. The digressions, as in the first chapter of *A Few Selected Exits*, often perform a marvellous function by revealing the hinterland of relationships or put out tentacles that draw the reader deep into a community. The story of the first chapter – the bare narrative line in time and space – can be summarized succinctly: 'Gwyn Thomas, on the verge of leaving home for Oxford, is given a trunk and £5 for an overcoat by Mr Metcalf, a local shopkeeper. Now viewed as a prize pupil, he is invited to tea by his headmaster, E.T.' The patterning of the discourse, however, takes one through bravura digressive loops festooned around Thomas's brother Walt, Mr Metcalf and E.T.

What makes parts of *A Few Selected Exits* outstanding as autobiography is the convincing way Thomas enters into or recreates the states of mind of particular stages: in the first chapter, his own adolescent self. The digressive convolutions that spiral round E.T. are as good as anything Gwyn Thomas has done. He considers the ebbs and flows of his relationship with his headmaster over time. Now a prize pupil, he merits the use of the family silver when he is invited to tea. However, he recalls his earlier scapegrace relationship with E.T., before he caught the infection of academic ambition and dedication from his brother Walt. There is a wonderful and hilarious sense of the loitering, observing boy self of Gwyn Thomas on his way to school, noting all the fantastical ways in which the excess of water that poured into the narrow Rhondda valley from the hillside could be harnessed as excuses for not appearing in lessons: floods which could not be avoided, or drenchings which merited steaming gently in the cellar by the big boiler for many satisfying hours (28–32). There is a vivid sense of how, even as a boy, Thomas took the raw materials of life and twisted them into fantastical and fulfilling shapes. The sequence where Thomas describes the subculture of the bad boys, smoking and verbally exploring adolescent sexuality in the dark, clustered around the boiler, communicates vividly the security he derived from that contained, womb-like place, where the intense exercise of oral needs through smoking and holding forth to an appreciative audience were freely allowed (32–7). The first chapter of *A Few Selected Exits* is generously peopled with Thomas's grotesques, portrayed with a combination of humour, appalled awareness of mutilating life-circumstances and tenderness. The school cellar is the domain of Mr Williams and it is here that Thomas encounters Nemesis in the form of E.T., fetched by Mr Williams in time to hear the end of a bawdy story told by the chain-smoking Thomas:

> The caretaker was a man who could have stepped with ease into any mythology . . .
> He had been a miner for a long time before moving up into this comparatively
> smooth, new employment. As a miner, he had been so prone to accidents he had
> won a lot of sympathy. If a stretch of roof lapsed it seemed to insist on having

Mr Williams beneath to make the landing less brusque and brutal . . . By most of
the lads he was called Pluto. His type of slow gait always disquiets, then impresses
boys . . . The sight of him descending slowly into the cellar, with his hat and
brush, and even more slowly ascending, suggested a small divinity keeping in
touch with his private domain, conjoint thunderbolt and cleanser, King of the
Shadows, product of mutilating ironies: Pluto. [Later, the miscreants in
the cellar are discovered in flagrante delicto.] Mr Williams stood at the side of
E.T. . . . He looked like a medieval executioner in the service of a king or judge.
I heard a voice behind me whisper that Mr Williams was going to fell us systematically as we climbed the steps. (32–7)

Here there is a mixture of tuning in to adolescent imaginative mythologizing,
with its sense of impending retribution, and memorable characterization
accomplished by more than a little caricature.

Thomas, as an autobiographer, is often at his best when recreating states of
being of adolescence and young manhood. His communication of a sense of
ineffable disquiet over barely understood aspects of human sexuality is deli-
cately portrayed in his account of the enduring impact on his consciousness
of Mrs Metcalf, part fragrant goddess, part drunken nymphomaniac:

Mrs Metcalf has rarely left my mind. The dichotomy of her being, the daily
swing from a resplendent presence of loveliness to untouchable disgrace and
exile jolted for all time my view of other people . . . In the gallery of all my
bemusements and terrors her signature is on virtually every article. (15)

What Thomas's understanding of his own sexuality contributed to his
bemused view of self is too complex a topic to be dealt with properly here.

One sees what one brings, and an important tool in this study has been the
insights of psychoanalysis. How much of what has been discovered here
about his various autobiographical utterances did Thomas himself explicitly
perceive? Although, in his analysis of the poet W. H. Davies, for example, he
seems to have understood the power of unconscious drives, he shows little
preparedness to apply them consciously to his own life.[47] He is clear that his
characteristic ways of responding to situations, particularly through reclusive
retreat, are thoroughly self-defeating, but he is not sure why:

The other members of the committee looked at me as if they had already marked
me down as one of the few people who had a State Scholarship and the reflexes
of an imbecile. They were right. Whatever lumbered me with my present set of
reflexes is a half-read mystery. (A Few Selected Exits, 56)

Thomas typically evokes guffaws of laughter in the reader as he describes his continuing colossal anxiety, surely as a defence against our registering this as the torment it in fact was: 'I never undo my seatbelt once I have secured it. One day I will carry this phobia to a point where I will arrive at the hotel of my destination city dragging the plane behind me' (202). He understands that the extremes of misery and depression experienced in his young manhood and as he was writing *Sorrow for thy Sons* were biochemically induced, dealt with to some degree by an operation on his thyroid gland (102). Very obliquely, he indicates his awareness of the vast uncharted ground of what he might feel about his mother and her early death (9).

After ultimata from his editors, the final version of *A Few Selected Exits* is highly constructed, often to highlight absurdity and anticlimax. His first chapter ends with a magnificent send-off as he is launched for Oxford 'feeling like an emperor' and accompanied by a considerable village procession, including two of his brothers bearing Mr Metcalf's splendid trunk as if 'it were the covenanted ark', launched on what turns out to be the most grimly unhappy period of his life. In the opening sentences of the second chapter Thomas declares, anticlimactically: 'Had I been a Venusian I would not have made smaller contact with the place' (49). In chapter 4, each section ends with the production of a new play of his biting the dust, each for different reasons. This flamboyant wordsmith concludes the whole chapter with: 'Myself, a lust for silence welling up from every part of me, looked up Trappists in the directory' (165). His chapter on himself as media personality is constructed to accentuate absurdity, with himself in the role of buffoon. One section ends, not untypically, where, a film he has been involved with having been presented with a certificate of merit at a lugubrious party at the Czech Embassy, Thomas has to be prised off the newly varnished china cabinet by a reporter and junior Embassy attaché (193). Every aspect of the crafting of the autobiography – chapter divisions, juxtapositions, climaxes, images, language – seems intended to illuminate the force of a key observation by Thomas: 'I seek in every circumstance a bloom of absurdity and the bloom is delivered on the dot' (*A Few Selected Exits*, 135).

In conclusion, it seems important to return to a perception with which this chapter opened. Humour is not necessarily high-spirited, good-natured, innocuous: humour can perform an aggressive function, be socially accepted hostility, be a sign of unease. In a notebook jotting Thomas avers: 'Humour is a nervous condition. Listen to laughter. It has a strange, sinister sound: the yelping of an uneasy pack' (*MP* 2, Notebook 16, 20 August 1968, initialled GT). Unusually, at one point, Thomas drops all his masks and thunders out an utterly bleak perception, which seems to be the true baseline for him:

> The onset of what most of us call wisdom is little more than a rusting over of parts of the brain made wet by tears of angry protest shed soon and violently . . . After thirty, we are cooling fools. Too much blood has gone out with the compassion and we hear rumours that anaemia kills. Beliefs that had attained a tentative firmness liquesce and are lost . . . Nothing matters: nothing changes. Crime and idiocy remain constant in every generation. (*A Few Selected Exits*, 172–3)

Sometimes he has choric figures utter important thoughts. For example, the despised assistant headmaster, Mr Denning, articulates observations that Thomas seemed not to have been able to express publicly in his own voice: 'Of course you were small when your mother died, so you'd never have a chance to know what your feelings about her really were' (9). Yet one of his earliest notebook jottings had shown a private grasp of his own dis-ease: 'I was born in July of a dying and unhappy woman. The heat and rage of that occasion became the abiding core of my own self' (*MP*, transcribed from exercise book labelled Cardigan County School. Initialled GT). That 'abiding core' of self could not be probed directly, however, with the exploratory scalpel of the autobiographer. Similarly, Thomas leaves it to Mr Metcalf to declare: 'And there's no forgiveness for a man who goes through life empty and does nothing to fill the gap' (18).

The thrust of this chapter has been to uncover and analyse the void at the heart of this writer's autobiographical utterance. Thomas jotted a bleak aphorism in his notebook, which he recycled in his autobiography (*A Few Selected Exits*, 164), in a context that gave it a less desolating effect than in the original observation: 'And in the middle of my life, a mountain of all the things that never made any sense' (*LT*, 5). His extreme pessimism and sense of 'spinning alienation' (*A Few Selected Exits*, 81) grew from his lack of early nurture, an emptiness he lacked the strength and will to explore. Thomas was an inhibited and fearful autobiographer, writing to a commission rather than from a genuine desire to scrutinize his life. To accomplish what was for him the most painful and challenging of writing assignments, he brought into play a range of defensive weapons from an arsenal of humorous techniques that he had spent a lifetime honing. His often virtuoso and hilarious performance was indeed a masterly enactment of a self – the deeply defended public self of Gwyn Thomas.

6

Buried to be Dug Up:
R. S. Thomas (1913–2000)

While academic impersonality is often cherished as a self-evident good, there can be benefits to a researcher's coming out from behind the screen. A sense of the struggle involved in coming to an understanding of a work may be a helpful part of the enacting of the meaning discovered. I feel I had and have a very special relationship with the textual R. S. Thomas, as revealed teasingly in his only book-length autobiography in English, the prose/poetry collection *The Echoes Return Slow*.[1] His was the first – and certainly the most challenging – autobiography I studied in depth for what was to become the present work: for nine extraordinary months in 1995, when writing an academic thesis, I lived with and through *The Echoes Return Slow*, reading the slim volume through almost daily, steeping myself in it, leaving it to mull in my unconscious, to have unexpected connections pop up when my mind was at rest. Given pertinacity in the reader, it is a singularly revealing autobiography, but R. S. Thomas saw to it that understanding would not be lightly won. 'Difficult', 'cryptic', 'beautiful', 'brave' are all words I would use of this elusive autobiography. Thomas worked to exacting standards of honesty in his self-disclosure, but an important index of the privacy of his nature was the tortuous route he sometimes took to self-revelation. At times he demanded as reader a zealot who would follow by scent and by slot into the furthest reaches of trackless wilderness: my family were conscripted as readers when extensive ramifications of important (and very coded) allusions led me into a multiplicity of texts that threatened to bog me down.[2] Further, a knowledge of the poet's prose autobiography *Neb*[3] (*No-one*), written in Welsh, is essential to a full understanding of *The Echoes Return Slow*, and an acquaintance with his *Blwyddyn yn Llŷn*[4] (*A Year in Llŷn*), structured in journal form, is distinctly helpful. As neither had been translated into English at that time, and as R. S. Thomas's correct and rather academic Welsh prose-style proved beyond the penetration of my Valleys demotic, my early labours included translating these two texts.[5] So rich and compressed a work did *The Echoes Return Slow* finally prove to be that there is space here to trace in detail only a few of the thematic strands Thomas pursues in his search for self. A summary, therefore, of some of the striking features of this lovely work seems a necessary starting point.

What then is *The Echoes Return Slow*? We are presented with a collection of sixty linked pairs of highly wrought prose pieces and lyric poems on facing pages, each pair dealing with an event, relationship or stage in the life of R. S. Thomas and giving, on the most superficial level, a chronological account of that life. The image conjured by the title is of a sonar scan – a scan comprehending the whole universe, including its black holes – through which Thomas built up a three-dimensional picture of reality over a lifetime.

This autobiographer is breathtakingly original in the way he makes language behave. He can make words shift before your very eyes until you discern deeper undertows of meaning. A striking characteristic of *The Echoes Return Slow* is its extreme condensation, yet Thomas creates a spaciousness within that. His exploiting of polysemantic meaning for which 'punning' seems too slight a word, and the remarkable resourcefulness of his deliberately indeterminate use of language, make several meanings possible at any one time. An emblematic 'scrubbed doorstep', for example, represents both the gleaming frontier to a secure, respectable home and its opposite: in servicemen's slangy usage, a home that is eliminated when war breaks out. (Mrs Thomas and her small child have no permanent base for four years, as they move about the country to wherever her merchant navy husband is next expected into port.) Indeed, new blossomings of meaning came when repeated readings brought the awareness of how richly Thomas had harnessed the emblem tradition, including its allegorical frame of mind, beloved of such seventeenth-century poets as Herbert and Vaughan.[6] We experience the boy Thomas's childishly domestic view of the First World War as he lived through it, in the phrase 'as though war were cricket matches and jam tarts' (6), but the emblem deepens to an implied comment on the moral plane, by the adult pacifist Thomas, on the naivety of any view that war can be played by gentlemen's rules, like cricket, or that any nation stealing a tart (Belgium), as did the Knave of Hearts (Germany), can be brought righteously to book by chastisement and made to surrender what has been purloined. Thomas's verbal formulations can often have the fluidity, unexpectedness, disconcerting depth and beauty of a hologram. Sensitive to the acoustic properties of words, man-of-the-cloth Thomas can humorously recreate a sense of the antiphonal chant from which he is escaping in a snatched beach walk (56).

In *The Echoes Return Slow*, Thomas is at times the detached observer of his banal human story, at times an intensely involved protagonist in a cosmic encounter. In the sequence, he is both Everyman and the unique being, Ronald Stuart Thomas. At times he is the epitome of existential loneliness, portraying himself in his long spiritual quest as vulnerably adrift in a bleak, hostile universe. And yet he can, at some of the most deeply moving moments in his poetry, affirm the power of love as an overwhelming reality. In a poem which celebrates his sense of homecoming on arrival at what was to be his final living at Aberdaron, tentativeness gives way to luminous resolution:

> . . . He lifted
>
> > the chalice, that crystal in
> > which love questioning is love
> > blinded with excess of light.
> >   (69)

Unconventional Christian though he is, through his intense experience of how the narrow wedge of human consciousness can be fleetingly illuminated with a sense of overwhelming transcendent love, he knows at times that, even in his time-bound existence, he is part of an eternal scheme of things. Yet, for Thomas, no ground is permanently won: daily the quest is renewed as though nothing had already been established.

The Echoes Return Slow, then, is a deeply unusual and original autobiography, crafted in a way that reveals the idiosyncrasies of Thomas's mind and personality. The marrying of manner and matter is interestingly revealed in his depiction of how he experiences his sense of self. Unsurprisingly in one who has entitled one of his autobiographies *Neb* (*No-one*), Thomas seems to have had a weak and fitful sense of his own selfhood. In his explicit account of himself in *Neb*, Thomas returns several times to his inability to have any clear sense of who he is. While at university, he says that he heard people asking unkindly about him, 'Who does he think he is?' His inward reply was 'But he did not know who he was. He was no-one. Sometimes during a dance he went out and looked through the window at the happy crowd within and saw the whole thing as totally unreal' (*Neb*, 22).[7] On hearing that he will soon become a father, he asks, 'How can no-one be a father to someone?' (*Neb*, 48). In seeing his shadow fall on rocks a thousand million years old at Braich-y-Pwll,

Llŷn, 'he asks the same old question as before: "Who am I?" and the reply comes more emphatically than ever "No-one" ' (*Neb*, 87). Interestingly, evidence that a writer's weak sense of self has been strengthened through the very act of writing, both autobiographically and imaginatively, gives insight into possible gains R. S. Thomas may have experienced in writing in this way.[8]

While in its very structure *The Echoes Return Slow*, a sequence of sixty prose pieces and sixty poems, appears fragmentary as the story of a life, the text, in its discontinuity, may give an appropriate feeling of Thomas's lack of an achieved core of being. Thomas's seems, much more, a fleetingly intuited self expressed through metaphor. The dynamic interaction of prose and poetry on facing pages, and the indeterminacy of polysemantic words (where several meanings exist in a single word) produce a 'shimmer' effect remarkably appropriate for suggesting a nebulous sense of self. Only a quarter of *The Echoes Return Slow* passages come from the authority of an 'I' position (while *Neb* is written entirely in the third person, with Thomas using his role or status in life at any particular time to focus his sense of who he is). He declares that 'sometimes his shadow seemed more substantial than himself' (86), as though it took the evidence of his shadow-shape before him to convince Thomas he existed. The third poem of this work (7), considered below, is a trope of overwhelming experience, imaging Thomas's first understanding of terror: it suggests how vulnerable selfhood may be, how easily swamped. Again, when readings in theology and philosophy change Thomas's world view, he embodies the very nebulousness he is experiencing in the self by allowing the poem itself to drift spatially:

> In a dissolving
> world what certainties
> for the self, whose identity
> is its performance?
>   (33)

He describes being constantly ambushed by his looking-glass (108), as though he cannot reconcile what he sees there with any sense of what it feels like to be him. He uses highly evocative images (25) to make concrete his feelings of hollowness, fear and spiritual aridity when he describes himself as an apprehensive young vicar 'shrinking back' from parishioners, depicting the needs they confront him with as deep, empty wells that could suck him in.

For someone with a weak sense of self, the contemplation of his individual extinction may be all the more terrifying because of the known vulnerability of the flickering sense of identity. In a poem describing a period of near-despair

(49), Thomas enacts with great sensitivity his fear of annihilation. As he confronts complex philosophical and existential questions, his highly developed ability to make the ineffable tangible seems to answer a deep need in him to get a grip on nothingness, to tame it in some way, through creating images that reify alarming sensations and, in so doing, draw him away from the pull of non-being. The intense loneliness of his situation is corrosive: 'There was a hope / he was outside of, with no-one / to ask him in' (49). One can imagine how, in recurrent periods of anguish, creating images for this state gave Thomas some sort of purchase on it.

Yet there are rare moments when, for both the reader and the poet, Thomas's self may be discerned in the power of its living presence. Perhaps the most telling realization comes where a characteristic mental process in Thomas is enacted, with considerable psychological verisimilitude, by a prose/poem counterpoint (58–9). First Thomas evokes his vibrant delight in his surroundings in his second living, Eglwys-fach, where 'otters swam in the dykes' and 'wild geese and wild swans came to winter in the rush-growing meadows'. Then, on the facing page (59), he undertakes a ferocious act of self-castigation, finding himself weak, easily browbeaten, irrevocably domestic in his concerns and self-righteous. The pairing suggests how, for Thomas, surges of self-loathing erupt to blight the loveliest day and seem to be firmly part of what continuing sense of self he has.

For Thomas, then, autobiographical writing can be seen as an aid to consolidation of a self. In *Fictions in Autobiography*, Paul John Eakin suggests that this very function lies at the core of the autobiographical act: 'This is to understand the writing of autobiography not merely as the passive, transparent record of an already completed self but rather as an integral and often decisive phase of the drama of self-definition' (226). One suspects that, in translating a myriad transient sensations into specific powerful images, Thomas is arriving at very necessary moments of self-definition, fleeting times when he assembles his sense of self most completely.

Indeed, in considering what theorists have to say about the place of metaphor in autobiography, one can arrive at some sense of what *The Echoes Return Slow* achieves over and above other autobiographical acts by Thomas. James Olney, for instance, finds metaphor to be the essential exploratory tool of the genre.

> [Metaphors] are something known and of our making, or at least, of our choosing, that we put to stand for, and so to help us understand, something unknown and not of our making; they are that by which the lonely, subjective consciousness gives order not only to itself but to as much of objective reality as it is capable of formalizing and controlling.[9]

Metaphor would seem to be the ultimate means of perceiving, and of exploring what we perceive.

Further, where theorists are eager to emphasize the key importance of unconscious processes in creating powerful autobiography, they are often alive to the crucial role metaphor has to play in communicating total psychic life. In a penetrating chapter on Jung's autobiography, Olney emphasizes the point that the western world grossly overvalues ego-consciousness. He explains:

> Those like Jung (poets, for example) who are engaged with the more-than-rational, with the intellectually or cognitively inexplicable, with the experiences of the total psyche and the total man, necessarily have recourse to the language of the psyche itself, that is, to myth and metaphor.[10]

In the potent image-making of *The Echoes Return Slow* we feel that Thomas is very fully in touch with the life of the whole psyche in a way that he cannot be in the more discursive *Neb*.

Moreover, the more one senses that the images of the mind and one's whole personal past are in a state of constant flux, the stronger will be the need to 'fix' a past and an identity. It is fascinating to see how Thomas, in *The Echoes Return Slow*, bodies out fleeting feelings or mental states by giving them a firm narrative line. Describing his desolation at the sense of void left by the loss of religious vision in the modern world, and relating this to tourists bent on ephemeral pleasures, Thomas writes a negative parable of the feeding of the five thousand (51), ending with the fusing of the narrative and the demotic in a paradoxically climactic yet bathetic line, 'The picnic is over'. Ephemeral feelings and states take on a tangible identity and gain imaginative foothold in his own mythic tale.

Thomas has written, surely of himself, in his poem 'A Life':

> Lived long; much fear, less
> courage. Bottom in love's school
> of his class; time's reasons
> too far back to be known.[11]

It is surely of interest to attempt to explore what those 'time's reasons' might be, to try to understand the deep inner rift in Thomas, of which his frequent self-loathing and misogynistic tendencies are symptoms. As, in *The Echoes Return Slow*, Thomas seeks to discover who he is and what has shaped him, he portrays himself in a range of defining roles, amongst which his representations of his relationships with his mother and his wife seem particularly significant. Indeed Thomas, writing of his own experience in *Neb*, emphasizes that 'the relationship between mother and son is a strange one, and, perhaps, crucial' (93). Through the compelling images Thomas generates in *The Echoes Return Slow* in attempting to understand and evaluate his bond with his mother, it is likely that both he and the reader learn much that is new about that troubled relationship. For the images in *The Echoes Return Slow* to emerge most persuasively and intelligibly, it is necessary briefly to extend the focus beyond that work.

Thomas's problematic relationship with womankind has been highlighted by several critics. Tony Brown has charted a regular recurrence of images of females as constrainers of freedom and subverters of male selfhood.[12] M. Wynn Thomas concludes a carefully documented analysis of the nationalistic poems with the compelling argument that 'at the very bottom of his conversion to cultural nationalism is a hatred of his snobbishly anti-Welsh mother and an obsessive desire "to accuse the womb / That bore me" '.[13]

What we can discern of the history of Thomas's mother provides strong evidence for her being a very needy woman emotionally:

> Her parents died when she was six and she was brought up by relations who soon sent her to boarding school. She felt, thus, that she had been deprived of love and this did not add to the good of the home. And as his father was a sailor and often away from home, his mother played the key part in R.S.'s upbringing. (*Neb*, 92)

As psychological literature reveals, a very usual result of this sort of lack is that when such children grow up and have children in their turn, the child becomes the means whereby the mother unconsciously tries to have her long-dormant childish feelings taken care of.[14] The child's own needs frequently have to be suppressed to answer the mother's.

Circumstances conspired to increase the risk for the young Thomas. The First World War came, his father was at sea and 'he was followed from port to port by his young wife' (*Neb*, 7). Thomas's infancy and early childhood years were spent in utter dependence on his mother, in an insecure and frequently changing home environment. It was only when he was six, when his father started work on the ferries to Ireland and the family settled in Holyhead, that Mrs Thomas and her son achieved any sort of permanent home. Even then, Thomas, as an only child whose father's job necessitated frequent absences from home, was in danger of being required to be his mother's main emotional support. Most interestingly, we discover that Thomas did not start school, even at the age of six. 'I was supposed to be delicate. I had a reprieve from school on condition I was taught at home. I learned to copy marks which was supposed to be a lesson in writing.'[15] In *Neb* he expands: 'He failed to go to school because of some undefined illness again . . . and within a year or two he was ready to go to the sort of school where genteel people sent their children' (10).[16] This seems to suggest that Thomas did not start school until the age of seven or possibly even eight. From his wry tone of telling, Thomas seems to doubt whether his delicate condition went much beyond his mother's imagination.

In *Attachment and Loss*, John Bowlby, analysing anxious attachment patterns, offers an explanation for 'school refusal':

> A family pattern in which a mother or father suffers from anxiety over attachment figures and retains the child at home to be a companion is now widely recognised . . . More often, a mother is unaware or only partly aware, of the pressure she is putting on her child and believes, more or less sincerely, that she is doing everything possible for his benefit. In some cases, the train of events begins when the child contracts some minor ailment, and the mother treats the condition as of much more consequence than it really is. The child is kept at home, ostensibly to convalesce, but is gradually presented with a picture of himself as being unfitted for the rough world of school . . . Whenever a family pattern of this kind is present, the parent concerned is found to be intensely anxious about the availability of her own attachment figures and unconsciously to be inverting the normal parent–child relationship by requiring the child to be the parent figure and adopting the role of child herself . . . As a rule, the inversion is camouflaged.[17]

In *Neb*, Thomas describes his mother as 'nervous and anxious' (*Neb*, 13); the emotional tension aroused in such a mother by her only son's leaving home to go to university may be considerable, and Thomas describes the emotionally fraught atmosphere of the home on the night before his departure. Returning to the house, he hears loud crying upstairs and his father trying to silence his wife. Many hours later, Thomas awakes from sleep to discover his mother is kissing him over and over (*Neb*, 19–20), surely a gross invasion of the space of a nineteen-year-old. Moreover, his mother insists on accompanying him to college the next day, making him feel like 'the little baby arriving with its nurse' (*Neb*, 19). It would seem that the mother's over-possessive ruling and controlling of her son ('*orfeddiannwyd ganddi*', *Neb*, 20) stemmed from a compulsive need in her. Further, in the light of what has already been established concerning Thomas's weak sense of self, it is interesting to note the succinct statement that psychotherapist Alice Miller makes to summarize what she sees as an important general principle (using case histories outlined by others):

> Several of [the children] seemed to have developed scarcely any feeling of self. This can be seen as a reflection of the attitude of the parents who did not regard their child as an autonomous person but entirely in relation to the gratification of their own needs.[18]

An awareness of this background might encourage a more sympathetic understanding of Thomas's consistent unease, amounting at times to ferocity, in his handling of the female.[19]

Thomas's mother first appears in *The Echoes Return Slow* in the poet's disturbing description of his birth. In the first poem, he sees himself as 'time's changeling' (3), as though in origin he did not feel himself to be his parents' child. He understands something of the enigma of motherhood, the love that endures through pain: 'Her face rises / over me and sets; / I am shone on / through tears' (3). By the second poem, his very early experience of meningitis has taught Thomas the limitations of loving motherhood, which cannot protect him from pain, and also that love's doting aspect, where the photograph of a babe 'only half sane' is framed and treasured.[20] The 'scrubbed doorstep' of the second passage (4) represents both the frontier of a secure, respectable home, presided over by house-proud Mrs Thomas, and its opposite, a home that will be eliminated (in the idiomatic, serviceman use of 'scrubbed') as Mrs Thomas follows her husband from port to port after war breaks out. The third prose/poem pair (6–7) is a key one, so complex its intense images, so meaningful on many different levels that it seems reductive to tease them out:

As though war were cricket matches and jam tarts. The figure in white flannels occasionally had gold braid. The syrens wailed from the berthed steamers. I lay in a bunk while they feasted, turning and turning the glossed pages. The cockroaches should have been a reminder. The shadows from which they crawled were as dark as those where the submarines lurked.

And beyond those silk curtains the weed sways that is Salome dancing before a salt

throne, asking only, when the dance is complete, the head of the twice-baptised on the sand's platter.

The chief feeling Thomas apparently seeks to communicate is that of his first experience of terror and betrayal. He has been left in his father's cabin while his parents 'feast' elsewhere. Cockroaches emerge and terrify him. In *Neb* (8) he describes this as an experience of '*arswyd*', terror). Through that vivid and overwhelming experience of fear, he comes at some level to understand what wartime death might be like for any sailor, but more particularly his father: drowning, after submarine action, entangled in weed which will not let him surface. At another level, the poem shows a strong awareness of his mother's sexuality. Salome, in the version developed by Wilde and in the Strauss opera, dances the immensely erotic dance of the seven veils, incestuously arousing her stepfather (and uncle) Herod. The infant Thomas, his mother's little man, at the Oedipal stage of development intensely bonded to his mother, has been abandoned to fear while his mother goes off, in preference, to 'feast' (as did Salome) with that stranger, his father. Doubtless the boy is also aware of the sexual charge between his parents that excludes him. The Salome dance image sees the danger in sexuality, for Thomas has earlier written 'My father was a passionate man, / Wrecked after leaving the sea / In her love's shallows'.[21] In this prose/poem pair, the ship's 'syren', spelt with an archaic 'y', reminds us of the seductive maidens who lured sailors to their deaths on the rocks. Through the weed image, there is simultaneously an understanding of the pain and betrayal experienced in infant Oedipal sexuality, a feeling of the terrifying power of women and a sense of being submerged and over-whelmed.

The next prose/poem pair (8–9) describes the father's domestication. In a most intelligently crafted passage, we see Thomas's father, 'who had tra-velled around the world several times under sail' (*Neb*, 10), becoming trapped, as breadwinner, by humdrum shifts of merely crossing the Irish Sea, losing a sense of the mystery and magic of the sea as the young boy gains it:

> After 'the hostilities were over', the return to cross-channel. So many hours at sea, so many more on shore. The salt waters were spat into from Welsh mouths. Dreams were laid at the roots of a boy's curls. The sea-horses were ridden by dark riders (8).

The sense of time being segmented into boring units is admirably conveyed and reinforced by rhyme: 'So many hours at sea, so many more on shore.' As life closes down for his father, we feel it opening up for the young Thomas as the passage moves onwards from three controlling passive constructions to express lively movement through sibilant soughing alliteration in its final sentence: 'Watching steamers was more exciting than watching trains, though sometimes the harbour was a forest of masts where *sh*ips of *s*ail *s*ought *sh*elter from the *s*torm' (8, my italics). 'The salt waters were spat into from Welsh mouths' suggests, beyond the primary meaning of nautical tobacco-chewing, the dislike Mrs Thomas felt for the proper sea faring life which her husband is being made to abandon. 'Dreams were laid at the roots of a boy's curls' is one of the cleverest lines in the whole work, revealing what the future would hold for each member of the family triad. 'Lay' is a word very rich in polysemantic meanings, allowing the poet to indicate obliquely many of the processes that were set in motion by the move to Holyhead. Possible meanings in order of consideration are: to put below the horizon by sailing away (nautical); to relinquish; to bury; to produce and deposit an egg; to deposit. The passive sentence structure allows indeterminacy as to the doer of the action: each family member in turn enacts the laying of dreams. The father's aspirations are lost sight of as he surrenders a fulfilling career at sea to provide a secure home for his son. Expectations of happy family life are relinquished, even buried, as he comes home to what quickly becomes an unhappy marriage. 'He [Thomas] remembered the troubles there had always been between his father and [mother]' (*Neb*, 91–2). There is a further possible implication that the son replaced the father as the primary object of the mother's love. In her turn, like a great hen laying, Thomas's mother builds grandiose hopes on her pretty boy. It is she, for example, who later sets her sights on the Church as a career for her son. 'As I reached the top-form, there were background debates as to what I was to do . . . My mother, early orphaned and brought up by a half-brother who was a vicar, fancied the Church. Shy as I was, I offered no resistance.'[22] Revelling in Holyhead's island position, the boy himself becomes totally absorbed imaginatively by the sea. 'Dreams were laid at the roots of a boy's curls': the sentence shimmers, expands and takes on new shapes as the construing mind of the reader changes its focus; it has all the disconcerting depth of a hologram.

Sometimes images are contextualized in the pages which follow a poem: it does not become clear until p. 12 that the poem on p. 11 is about the poet's mother:

> With cash in the one,
> no harm in the other,
> they persuaded all
> but the child, who knew
>
> with a child's roguery
> whichever he touched
> of the hands held out
> would always be empty.

One possible reading is that of the mother withholding on her child emotionally, 'playing games' and teasing. In one sense, the child's 'roguery' would involve his dissenting from the 'game' being played by running away and becoming a 'rogue', a loner apart from the herd, and perhaps here Thomas is hinting at the source of a basic mistrust in him. The next passage shows him

escaping. 'No muscle. All legs. His cleverness was in running away' to college where 'He tasted freedom in a parent's absence' (12).

The last poem (77) dealing with Thomas's mother describes her death and
the ambivalent feelings he continues to experience to the very end of her life:

> She came to us with her appeal
> to die, and we made her live
> on, not out of our affection
> for her, but from a dislike
> of death . . .

In the first four lines, the breaks repeatedly fracture expectation in a shocking
way, keeping at least two possible meanings before the reader, the one
expected and the one that is delivered. An appeal in a judicial sense is often
for the appellant to be allowed to live, but his mother wants to die. 'We made
her live' sounds miraculous, although the compulsion in 'made' is evident,
but 'on' modifies it all as it becomes clear that the living for which they have
preserved her will be a dreary, pain-wracked existence. 'Not out of our affection / for her but from a dislike' powerfully links a negated 'affection' with
'dislike', making unmistakable the strong undercurrents of animosity the
poet continues to feel for his mother. We then move on to 'dislike / of death'
where 'dislike' is so inappropriately mild a word that one becomes aware of
a deep level of dissociation in Thomas in his inability to confront death in this
context. They are saved from this:

> . . . The ambulance came
> to rescue us from the issues
> of her body; she was delivered
> from the incompetence of
> our conscience into the hospital's
> cleanlier care.

The harsh 's' sounds in the second line suggest tortured feeling and 'issues',
packing densely multiple meanings, reveals both the son's sense that his
mother has become an insoluble problem, and his sense of appalled insufficiency before her body's dissolution, involving, possibly, haemorrhaging and
incontinence. 'The incompetence of our conscience' is a marvellous phrase,
where 'incompetence' in a medical sense is understood to be something like
the inability of a valve to function correctly and allow the passage of liquid,
and 'conscience' is understood in the obsolete sense of 'heart'. Their care is

'incompetent' because the horror of what they are having to experience inhibits the flow of tender feeling. The final image of the poet taking his mother's hand and forming 'a tight-rope / of our fingers for the mis-shapen / feelings to keep their balance on', movingly suggests some sense of coming through and holding in the midst of much honestly acknowledged dislike and distaste. From the strength of feeling revealed here, this was an important relationship for Thomas; it is likely to have been crucially formative.

In 'Eve's Ruse', Tony Brown surmises that 'given the temperament and attitudes we have been considering, marriage is going to be a relationship fraught with potential difficulties' (246). The poet's discussion of his relationship with his wife in *The Echoes Return Slow* is rich, complex and, finally, profoundly moving: it is given added poignancy by the fact that the sequence is being written in the knowledge that his wife is dying and also in the assurance that she has, after all, loved him. The poet's exploration of this central relationship in his life is, while frequently oblique to the point of obscurity, unsparing in the way it confronts the emotional and sexual currents of a long marriage.

His wife first becomes the focus of a poem in the context of her wish to have a child (35). In *Neb*, Thomas had recorded: 'As hopes developed that the war would not last long, the rector's wife made clear her desire to have a child. He had not seriously thought of the possibility' (*Neb*, 47–8). In a parallel prose passage in *The Echoes Return Slow* (34) we are told:

> With the lifting of a cloud on the horizon, the desire of a woman re-asserted itself for someone to cherish beside the beloved. Close as they were, her soliloquies were too soft. He re-interpreted them with a poet's licence.

The decision for parenthood seems to have been a unilateral one by his wife. 'Poet's licence' suggests licentiousness, and tolerated freedom. Looking back to the time before they become a family, he composes, with his 'poet's licence', the soliloquy he wishes she might have spoken. He imagines his wife feeling pleasure in her coming motherhood, but delighting too in memory of

> that time we lay
> all night, side by side,
> the moon virginal,
> his sword naked between.
>
>   (35)

In the first stanza, Thomas has been referred to as 'he' and in classical literature the moon is always female. Thus we imagine the poet cheerfully and fondly remembering erotic love-play that fell short of intercourse ('the moon virginal') in the early days of their marriage, the sensuality of which was something he believed they had both enjoyed.[23] The child is born and there is a sense, reinforced in other poems, that Thomas has been moved from centre-stage, that the child is now 'the apple of the mother's eye' (40): 'Where two / were company, he the unwanted / third'.[24]

The next allusions to his wife are elaborately coded. Again, briefly, one needs to move beyond *The Echoes Return Slow* to 'Nuptials', a poem in the collection dedicated to the memory of his wife.[25] Here he celebrates the early joy in marriage and then observes the change:

> . . . Once the whole loaf:
> flesh white, breasts risen
> to his first kneading;
> a slice after, the appetite
> whetted for the more
> not to be; the fast
> upon fast to be broken
> only in love's absence
> by the crumb of a kiss.

Given the collection's dedication, it can be surmised that the poem has autobiographical resonance.

In *The Echoes Return Slow* (56–7) Thomas appears to return to this theme. Escaping briefly from his church duties, he walks on the beach and tries 'to evacuate the ear of the echoes of cloying Amens'. With humorous assonance, he suggests the antiphonal chant from which he is escaping: 'He *walk*ed on the sh*ore* again to *cau*terise his nostrils with *raw* s*alt*' (my italics). Then the prose lilts into liveliness as he manages 'to refresh his ears with the white waves tumbling thunder'. The passage continues: 'Others walked there, too; women figures like those of Troy, gathered to watch the tilting of innumerable riders. Like Graves before him, his eye fastened on one woman.' Thomas is drawing attention to a nexus of ideas: the pounding surf as sexual consummation (a generally recognized media cliché); the Trojan story, in a later version than the *Iliad*, as the medieval 'tilting of innumerable riders' is referred to; and Robert Graves's focus on one woman. Robert Graves's obsession with Laura Riding ('riders' being a near pun) was a literary wonder of the 1930s when, in an attempt to resolve a *ménage à quatre*, Laura attempted suicide by leaping from a high window and Robert jumped after her from a lower one, on the second floor.[26] One of the most remarkable features of their long relationship was that Laura withdrew her sexual favours very early on, a situation Robert managed to tolerate.[27] Laura later became very jealous of Robert's great success with his *I, Claudius* sequence and declared she would write a historical novel to show the world how such things should be done.[28] *A Trojan Ending* was the result, a self-glorifying work of quite remarkable banality and failure to grip, published only as a result of Robert's influence with his publisher. In the work, Laura herself is Cressida, Robert Graves a combination of Troilus and Diomedes. Cressida, too, makes it clear that hers is a spirit too rare to be involved in carnal engagements. Just before she leaves Troy for the Greek camp, Troilus observes in exasperation:

> It is not Troy that Cressida is betraying. She is betraying me, her pledges of love to me . . . her going is an act of spite against me. Why? Because I grew tired of her lofty pose and demanded that she treat me as a man instead of as a companion in intellectual ecstasies.[29]

Diomedes, too, has to accept that there will be no sexual union with Cressida but the authorial tone invests his position with heroic fortitude and dignity.[30] Thomas seems to be obliquely alluding to a parallel situation in his own marriage.

In the poem facing the prose Troy/Graves/Riding allusion, Thomas is reacting with misogynistic hostility to 'one of James' women' (57), to what he sees as a posturing and aloof woman, one prone to reject men, rather like Isabel Archer in *The Portrait of a Lady*, who had resisted marriage to Warburton and Goodwood before her unhappy alliance with Osmond. Thomas sees her as 'having her splendid / moments staring with all her sex's / wistfulness at the robust / sea'.[31] As he approaches her, he discovers she is neither hostile nor stand-offish,

> but driven to the extremity
> of herself by the forces which
> she resisted; a woman formed for
> desire, but repudiating even the velleities of it.
>
> (57)

In this prose/poetry interaction, Thomas seemed to fictionalize a very painful personal situation. He has, perhaps, come to understand that a woman's absolute hostility to sex, 'repudiating even the velleities of it', might not be a rejection of a particular man but might be a state provoked by tormenting tensions which have driven her 'to the extremity / of herself'.

As though by stream-of-consciousness association, the next poem (59), in self-castigating mood, reveals the dangers to male selfhood under female influence: that caritas becomes too domestic, valour too prudential. However, as this long sequence moves into its closing stages, the redeeming effect of the poet's wife's love is what shines through. In the sequence, Thomas has wanted to set before us the joy of the physicality of his young love, very indirectly, his suffering from the sexual withdrawal and, finally, the serene depths of the spiritual love of old age.

Thomas himself sees personality as a constant process of becoming: 'Character is built up / by the application of uncountable / brushstrokes' (93). From a time well beyond the finality of his mother's death, he attempts to symbolize – through the image of being overwhelmed (7), through the sense of emotion having been withheld from a child (11) – how that relationship had felt and how it had moulded him. He seems to reach an important conclusion in his statement: 'His cleverness was in running away' (12). He further takes a long-perspective view of his relationship with his wife and, from the tenderness of the present moment and the knowledge of the coming parting, reviews previous events, particularly those which caused his sense of sexual rejection, and sees them in a new light. Through his poetic evocations of the feel of these two key relationships, Thomas is revealing their innermost private significance to him as he moves into the final phase of his life.

Present needs, then, influence the way in which we retrieve, reconstruct and interpret memory. Thomas's personal confronting of the imminence of death for his wife and, ultimately, for himself, is set in a context of a more general anguished and prophetic awareness of what the possible outcome of the reckless exploitation of scientific discoveries might be in terms of world destruction. Published in 1988, the year before the Berlin Wall crumbled and glasnost took a real grip, *The Echoes Return Slow* is shaped by its time and place of composition. Thomas was actively involved in the Campaign for Nuclear Disarmament in the 1980s. At Easter 1986, he had taken part in a national demonstration at Carmarthen, focused on a nuclear bunker, which had culminated with thousands of people 'playing dead' at a given time to simulate the results of nuclear attack.[32] Then, in April 1986, the Chernobyl nuclear disaster caused widespread radioactive fallout over many countries. Snowdonia, beloved and familiar backdrop to R. S. Thomas's boyhood rambles, became seriously polluted by radioactive dust. The idea of death in a personal sense and the possibility of global annihilation impinged with force on his consciousness.

An examination of some of the metaphoric ordering, in Olney's sense, that Thomas chose to give the situations and events of the past during this period offers illuminating insight into his sombre perception, at that time, of the world in which he lived. For him, the myths of Genesis speak profound truth about the human condition. In a period of 'dark thoughts', he senses the potentially savage and vengeful nature of God for whom 'the forbidden tree flourishes / in his garden and he waters it / with his own blood' (39). It is a truism of the typological connections important to earlier times that the Tree of Knowledge and the cross are intimately connected: because of Adam and Eve's disobedient stealing of fruit from the Tree of Knowledge, the redemptive power of Christ's blood on the cross was necessary. Thus God, in some perverse way, is fertilizing with his own blood the Tree of Knowledge which will ultimately prove man's undoing. Thomas feels scientists are impiously tampering with dangerous knowledge beyond man's right to know and, as 'the combination is yielding', he has a premonition of apocalypse in his dread of 'what will come forth / to wreak its vengeance on us / for the disturbance' (39). Thomas sees the tree of science as an analogue of the original Tree of Knowledge (as it is etymologically) (89) and the scientist is the equivalent of the guileful serpent which promised 'Ye shall be as gods'.[33] Through the power of the image, Thomas is able to suggest that the blandishments of science have diverted human beings from God's intended purpose for them, repeating, in a sense, Adam's first sin, perhaps with equally disastrous results. Almost despairing of God's continuing concern for the sceptical world of the late twentieth century which has engaged in thoughtless devastation of his creation, Thomas fuses the dove of Genesis, which returned with a token of hope to Noah's ark, with the spirit of God descending as a dove to inspire Jesus, as he implores, in lines in which the strength of the stresses reflects the urgency of the need:

> . . . Dove of God,
> self-powered, return
> to this wrecked ark, though it be
> with radiation in your bill.

(111)

The Genesis images have an integrating effect, placing the world of the late second millennium AD firmly in the context of ancient mythic truths about human nature. By setting his own autobiographical preoccupations with flaw, loss and death in the context of that of wider humanity, Thomas is, in Erikson's sense, 'accepting some definition as to who he is'.[34]

Within such a comprehensive frame of reference, other prophetic images resonate with singular potency. In other autobiographical writing, Thomas's descriptions of early morning forays in childhood for mushrooms are recorded with delight, zest and wonder: 'those early mornings were full of magic. Have you ever touched cold mushrooms, wet with dew, smelt their freshness, and tasted them?'[35] In *The Echoes Return Slow*, looking back from a vantage point shadowed by death and global pollution, Thomas has a perspective on that earlier world which is forbiddingly different:

> White skulls, oily with dew in the late moonlight. Rising before dawn, he peered into a field as into a cemetery of white grave-stones. His feet rustling in the wet grass, he moved from one to another like an angel, not to raise but to gather them in a meshed basket. Forty years later he did so again, the sun on his hand. Nature was still bountiful, but man was erecting, beautiful and poisonous, the mushroom-shaped cloud. (74)

By fusing an evocation of simple beauty, purity and natural beneficence in the milk-white, smooth, compact mushroom, appearing like manna in the dawn (10, 74–5), with the mushroom-shaped cloud that could yet destroy life on earth (34, 74), Thomas engages us with both his Song of Innocence and his bleaker Song of Experience.

Such ponderings on Armageddon, while revealing something very characteristic about Thomas's mental cast, are also important metaphoric intensifiers of his recording of his personal encounters with death. A delicate pattern of further allusion adds increased texture to this autobiography. The references to dancing are particularly intriguing. In the late Middle Ages, epidemic outbreaks of the Black Death, war and famine in Europe caused the medieval mind to fix in fascination and horror on the grislier aspects of death, from which the lasting iconography of the *danse macabre* was born. Thomas, numbingly aware of the possibility of global catastrophe after the Chernobyl disaster and, personally and painfully, ever more conscious of his wife's increasing debility, envisions his own memento mori. The Dance of Death motif appears in *The Echoes Return Slow* as a flickeringly recurrent image rather than a clear and constant focus. It seems to adumbrate the poet's recognition of his lifelong nagging but diffuse fear of death, a fear which he had not, perhaps, fully confronted and owned until the writing of this poetic sequence.

Thomas, of course, would have been acquainted with the *danse macabre* through artistic and ecclesiastical tradition; more particularly, he had read

Huizinga's *The Waning of the Middle Ages*, where a powerful chapter, 'A Vision of Death', traces the obsession of the Middle Ages with thoughts of death, putrefaction and hideous memento mori of various kinds.[36] The chapter gives an account of the evolution of the Dance of Death, describing the notable mural which adorned the walls of the cloisters of the Church of the Holy Innocents in Paris. This representation depicted each individual in a hierarchically organized procession being seized and dragged into a dance by a decomposing corpse, the living man as he would soon be, in graphic reminder of the imminence of death.

The dancers in *The Echoes Return Slow*, too, are moving inexorably towards death. The poet observes of his student self: 'He studied, he danced' (12) and in the next prose/poem pair (14–15) he is traumatically confronted with his first experience of death. Later, in a vivid depiction of the dance of all created things to the music of 'the thin-lipped piper' (99), the poet declares:

> . . . I only
>
> look at him as I dance,
> shaming him with the operation
> on the intelligence of
> a creature without anaesthetic.

The unspecified 'operation on the intelligence' that Thomas deplores seems to be that only human beings have to live with the consciousness that they must die: for that awareness you need an opiate. Besides the specific dancer references, there are other echoes of the *danse macabre*. Thomas is 'ordained to conduct death' (16), in one meaning becoming Death's familiar and guide in his regular role as officiator at burials. In the poem 'Entered for life' (21) Thomas refuses to follow the lead of his *danse macabre* double by becoming a corpse in the Second World War, when volunteers are called for 'to play death's part' in the grisly masque of death that engagement will become. He mentions memento mori explicitly (44). There is frequent focusing on death, funerals and graves. But perhaps the most powerful effect of this at times shadowy motif is in the way it subtly links the poet, as he becomes increasingly aware of his fear of death, with an age when such a preoccupation bulked obsessively large in the mind of man, and gives an understated hint of the possible dimensions of the dread Thomas may at times have experienced. Thomas enacts his own encounters with death within the resonances set up by these echoes, a tracing which needs now to be followed chronologically.

The skirmish with death begins for Thomas at the point of birth. In the opening of *The Echoes Return Slow*, it is plain that Thomas is aware that his very coming to existence could have been life-threatening for his mother. As Thomas explicitly denied that he had been born by Caesarean section,[37] his disquietingly stark description of the process of his birth – 'the woman was opened and sewed up' (2) – has, apparently, even more disconcerting meaning, blazoning what is normally very private obstetrical detail, in a way which colours the reading of the ensuing sentence too. 'Time would have its work cut out in smoothing the birth-marks in the flesh' (2) fuses a domestic and violent image: that of Time as a cosy old woman busily trying to massage away the scars of birth and, more literally, Time having its work cut out as Thomas, the large baby, during a difficult birth, was possibly forcibly extracted from his mother by episiotomy slit and forceps, a usual technique even in 1913 for expediting a protracted labour. Traumatic births leave a legacy: Thomas's continuing psychic memory of 'coming to the crack too narrow to squeeze through'. The Salome/weed image (7) of overwhelming experience associated with his first exposure to terror expresses, at one level, a strongly felt understanding of the danger his father ran of death by drowning when in the merchant navy during the First World War. The 'twice-baptized' is a drowned man.

As Thomas moves through the carefree life of a student, 'He studied, he danced' (12) is double-edged, representing his insouciance and his dancing towards his first experience of death. He fails 'the less / gentlemanly examination / of death' when 'Eileen', whom he seems to have loved, dies and he is made aware of 'the rift in time / he was powerless to repair' (15), a sense of something utterly irrevocable for which he is quite unprepared. Dismayed by his desolation in the face of death, Thomas is perversely drawn into the very calling that will constantly expose him to it. He describes himself, as priest, at the grave's head, a conductor of 'a shabby orchestra of sniffs and tears' (16), revealing through the conceit an agonized sense of distancing himself from what is painful and reacting with distaste to overt signs of feeling with which he cannot cope. On the facing page, there is an image of the tender memory of bereft parents, as though Thomas is seeking to highlight through contrast his own inability to channel feeling appropriately where death is concerned.

In the Second World War sequences, sensitivity to death becomes more complex. Opposite the prose passage mirroring the terrifying build-up to the slaughter of war there is placed an image of Thomas and his wife, while living at Tallarn Green, looking up towards the red night sky over blazing Merseyside:

> . . . He learned fear,
> the instinctive fear
>
> of the animal that finds
> the foliage about its den
> disarranged and comes to know
> it can never go there again.
>
> (19)

In 'Autobiographical Essay' he makes clear it was the effects of the bombing raids which generated what he saw as 'a cowardly wish to get away from this in a place where I did not belong' (9), a wish that encouraged him to learn Welsh as a means of returning to where he perceived his roots to be. A depth of self-contempt seems to be based on the belief that he was, through deep pacifist conviction, simultaneously a non-combatant in wartime and acutely frightened of death as high explosive rained from the air. On the next page he begins, 'Others were brave' (20). It is significant that he declares he preferred to be 'prompter than prompted' when volunteers were called to play death's part (that is, to become corpses in the *danse macabre*) and in a later poem he describes himself as 'one of life's conjurors' (59), intending a subsidiary meaning to be 'one who solemnly charges or entreats'. Thomas is part of a Church structure that urges others to do what he is conscientiously opposed to doing, but which he also fears he would be too frightened to do.

Gradually, however, a sense of reconciliation grows. In the wartime sequences, he had shown a tortured awareness that there is regeneration beyond dissolution as he pondered on flowers growing in the graveyard (23). He later sees himself as a priest planting bodies in burial for coming up at the resurrection, a macabre image which is possibly intended to shock (42). On the facing page, however, there is a most beautiful image of time effacing the works of man, as on a book-shaped gravestone where:

> . . . The weather
> has worn the words
> smooth

but nevertheless redeeming by causing new growth, as

> . . . moss brightens
> the spread pages, wings
>
> of a dove daily
> returning from its journey

over the dark waters
with green in its bill.
(43)

The sense of fading away is beautifully suggested by the liquid flow of the
repeated initial semi-vowel 'w' and the long diphthong of 'smooth'; gradual
regeneration is evoked – through a delicate interplay of continuing semi-
vowels in 'wings' and 'water' – by tauter, containing sounds such as, in
'brightened', the firm plosive 'b' and the trim, light 't', and the emphatic
alliteration of 'dove daily' and 'dark'. Beyond death, Thomas begins to see
renewal and resurrection. He moves through meditations on possible contamination and death in a global context (74–5) to a searingly honest attempt
to record his complex feelings on his mother's death, in the poem already dis-
cussed (77). The next, lovely, poem in the sequence (79) – where, supporting
images of great stillness, every word is given its full weight rhythmically and
the considerable harmony of the assonance is regularly interwoven with the
beauty of the liquid 'l' and fricative 'f' – may be read as the poet's realization
that his mother's death has brought him peace. Slowly, his great antipathy to
death is dissolving. A later prose/poem sequence on death achieves a miracle
of resolution. Thomas starts with his usual distaste for and discomfort over
the overt grief displayed at funerals, in the acerbic phrasing of 'women
blubbed for him' and the poem's comments on 'the cheap mourning' and
'expensive, competitive flowers'. Then:

. . . A petal blown
From time's wreath, the barn owl
came drifting. In the vicarage

hard-by on the frayed
curtains, as the lights
came on, the shadow of two
faces drew near and kissed.
(91)

The barn owl (which we know from *Blwyddyn yn Llŷn* actually roosted near
the rectory) is both factual and symbolic, being 'a petal . . . from time's
wreath' both for the millions of years it has taken for its feathers to evolve
their totally noiseless flight (a source of wonder to Thomas in *Blwyddyn yn
Llŷn*, 92) and from the frequent appearance of owls in legend. Doubtless
Thomas is thinking of Blodeuwedd, a woman created out of flowers but

changed into an owl for her betrayal of her husband, Lleu Llaw Gyffes. But from a view of shallow, undignified love and of love's betrayal, Thomas moves to an image of two faces kissing at the window of the vicarage just above the graveyard, surely a symbol of love continuing in the face of death.

The next sequence (92–3) explores the poet's increasing sensitivity to the power of love: self-despising Thomas comes to realize that he is no longer afraid of death, and discovers that, after all, he has courage. He knows now that there will not 'be mutiny / at the day's end'. He is ready to face death:

> . . . The spirit

> retains its poise
> ready any time now
> for walking the bone's
> plank over the dark waters.
>   (95)

It is a triumph of no mean dimension, integrally connected to his new understanding of love.

Continuing, he acknowledges that all created things move in the dance towards death (99) and speaks with affectionate acceptance of the puzzlement of each stage in life (101), understanding that he will not now learn the answers to the questions 'Life? Love? Truth?' He reaches gentle acceptance that in dying one becomes part of a continuing cycle of growth and decay:

> . . . And 'Grey-beard'
> earth said in anticipation of
>   its bone meal, 'you have been
> up too long. It is time for bed.'

The sequence moves into a serene consummation as Thomas comes to understand that love transcends death and is able to contemplate his wife's approaching end with equanimity. Earlier (92) he has recognized his own insufficiency in loving: 'Everywhere he went, despite his round collar and his licence, he was there to learn rather than teach love.' As he reaches the climax of his autobiographic search (120–1), he finally grasps intuitively that, just as his passionate love of the sea has in no way depended on a rational, factual understanding of its nature, he can accept the enigma of his marriage relationship, the depths of which he has never fully sounded:

Both female. Both luring us on, staring crystal-eyed over their unstable fathoms. After a life-time's apprenticeship in navigating their surface, nothing to hope for but that for the love of both of them he would be forgiven.

The mannered reference to the mesmeric power of the beloved objects, the sea and his wife, 'luring us on' seems to be a shy cover for the depth of feeling that has been released in him by his new understanding of the mutual love within his marriage. In his awareness of the depth and scope of his love for his wife and of the sea, he hopes he will reach a final equipoise: that his sins of commission and omission, particularly in love, recorded in the Book of Life, his metaphorical balance-sheet, will be wiped out.

In the first stanza of the concluding poem (121), ruminatively aware of his wife framed against the sea, he contrasts the transient with the timeless: against the aeons of existence of the sea, his snowy-haired wife, frail and dying, is all too obviously subject to time. Then love becomes a visible miracle as he observes something like a chemical change being wrought in her through the strange power that their mutual love engenders:

> Am I catalyst of her mettle that,
> at my approach, her grimace of pain
> turns to a smile?

Known, valued and defined by the love of his wife, Thomas seems finally to perceive, at the point of laying down his pen, that death has lost its sting.

Thomas's autobiography is characterized by the virtuosity with which he communicates his unique way of experiencing the world. A central feature, certainly, of his inner process is his ability to make sense of inner and outer life through images which well up from deep within. Indeed, a salient feature of his perceptual base, which Thomas is at pains to emphasize early in *The Echoes Return Slow*, is that he is deeply introverted. (Jung describes an introvert as someone who derives his main energy and refreshment from inner withdrawal and communing, as opposed to an extravert, who is re-energized by other people and the world.[38]) In a prose/poetry pairing, Thomas meditates on action in wartime (20–1). The prose passage explores the acute problem of being a deeply reflective man of pacifist inclination when the whole world seems to be moving into unhesitating action to take up arms. In a paragraph that repeats 'brave' four times, he mulls over his inability to believe in certain sorts of action and winces at what he sees as his cowardice. The facing poem describes what he sees as his essential, introverted self:

> Entered for life, failing
> to qualify; understudied
> for his persona, became identical
> with his twin. Confronted
> as the other, knew credit
> was his for the triumph
> of an imposture. Slipped easily
> into the role for which
> his double was cast, bowing
> as low as he to appropriate
> the applause. When volunteers
> were called for to play
> death's part, stood modestly
> in the wings, preferring rather
> to be prompter than prompted.
>
> (21)

'Entered for life' suggests both that others signed him up for life without his agreement and that it feels like a long sentence. The introverted essential personality 'failing / to qualify' in any participant sense, Thomas creates a persona which people take to be the real man. This seems to deal adequately with the outside world, leading him to university and into the Church, where he takes on given standards of what a vicar should be doing. The persona plays the role and takes the applause but is barely integrated at all with the underlying true personality. The persona, responding to the standards of the world, might have led the true Thomas into danger as an army chaplain, where 'double' and 'death's part' make clear that he could have ended up as a corpse in the 'danse macabre'. At that point the real personality, with the deeply considered pacifist values of the inner Thomas, digs in its heels, although 'preferring rather / to be prompter than prompted' shows his self-contempt and distress at being priest in a Church which is encouraging other young men to fight. This interesting poem is an extended attempt to describe what dealing with the outside world can feel like for someone who is very deeply introverted, to the degree that his 'real' self feels utterly dissociated from the parts that are active in the world.

Thus for someone of Thomas's reflective, inward personality, arriving at a considered position can take time and agonized self-scrutiny, as the piling-up of questions in reflecting on his wartime experiences suggests (20). In a phrase in which you can hear the drumbeat, he describes the men who 'went forth to the war, as their fellows had done hundreds of years' (20), the ease of the rhythms suggesting his view of the spontaneous straightforwardness of such immediate extravert action. By contrast, the tortured convolutions of 'An unwillingness by some to recognise war as the lesser of two evils exposed at the tribunals to the satisfaction of whom?' (22) gives a sense of the agony of trying to put into inadequate words, end-products of the intelligence, a conviction which has been arrived at by the whole being. We see Thomas mulling over the treacherousness of language which can rouse men to act in response to, and to die for, such slogans as 'The war to end all wars' (8) or to believe in the factual truth of lurid atrocity propaganda (22). In *The Echoes Return Slow*, from the wartime period onwards, the reader registers a profound awareness in Thomas of the flawed nature of language, its unreliability and the impossibility of trusting in any inevitable connection between signified and signifier, a perception he constantly explores through polysemy. His evolving perceptual base has him distrust any formulations of language as inciters to action.

The Echoes Return Slow reveals Thomas's psychological process in a fascinating way. While his pacifist position may well have grown stronger in the post-war nuclear age, his characteristic self-contempt, here over the belief that if forced to fight he would have been afraid, is not likely to have diminished either. One of the weakest poems in the collection – it is electric with malevolence – is also one of the most interesting psychologically for what it shows of what touched Thomas on the raw (47). The man pilloried, Major General Lewis Pugh of Cymerau, Eglwys-fach, one of Thomas's parishioners, was the poet's near opposite as an extraverted (but intelligent) man of action. Son of a DSO crippled in the Great War, he was awarded the DSO three times himself and returned to some prominence in the late 1970s, when one of his wartime operations was celebrated in a book and then a film (with Gregory Peck playing Pugh).[39] In this poem, in his retrospective surge of loathing, it is likely that Thomas experienced Pugh simultaneously as a reproach and as a hated embodiment of the establishment militaristic values that his own conscience could not accept.

Successful autobiography expresses far more than the author ever consciously adumbrates. The production of images from deep in the unconscious can sometimes bypass habitual repression mechanisms and can offer to the reader truths about the writer of which he may himself be unaware. Part of the fascination of autobiography is the reader's cumulative awareness of blind spots in the writer, the sense that s/he sometimes has of unreliable narration, as in the undue harshness with which Thomas often views his motivations and actions in *The Echoes Return Slow*, or in his portrait of Pugh.

For a factual narrative of the events of the life of R. S. Thomas, some of the dates, the personalities, the places and the broad sweep of his commitment to

Welsh language, ornithological and environmental concerns – for self-written biography in fact – one would certainly turn to *Neb*; but throughout that work one is aware of a personality held at arm's length. Yet, from *The Echoes Return Slow*, obliquely, within the framework of highly wrought prose passages which epitomize the poet's life story and poems set in counterpoint to these, we gain a most revealing sense of a unique personality embodied and enacted in its most characteristic and most telling mode of expression, the lyric poem. We are further able to trace the poet's exploration of some of the forces that moulded his identity. We take in, often through illuminating image, something of the inwardness of his experience of his own sense of self. We come to appreciate his habitual ways of perceiving and understanding, often intuitively through metaphor and symbol. We encounter within the work a constantly evolving personality which has paused at one particular point in its unfolding '[to draw] all the significant past up into the focus of the present', thus discovering 'through the glass of memory, a meaning in his experience which was not there before and which exists now only as a present creation'.[40] Given perseverance in the reader, *The Echoes Return Slow* can be seen to be autobiography of the most searching sort.

Yet one also has to acknowledge that it is, at times, a cryptic, difficult work where ambiguity and indeterminacy are cultivated in deliberate and purposive ways, both to achieve multivalent meanings and to avoid explicit statement, a feature crucial in making possible the level of self-disclosure Thomas in fact achieves in this work. Thomas is not being convoluted or obscure from malicious scorn of the reader but because, at a very deep level, the protection by deniability of what he has seemed to have said is essential to him. From the lonely depths of his introverted identity, his poetry is a sure bridge that he builds with the outside world.

> A pen appeared, and the god said:
> 'Write what it is to be
> man.' And my hand hovered
> long over the bare page,
>
> until there, like footprints
> of the lost traveller, letters
> took shape on the page's
> blankness, and I spelled out
>
> the word 'lonely'.[41]

The Echoes Return Slow is born not of any impulse to confess, nor even, primarily, of a desire to be finally understood by his readers. Thomas's chief need has been to explore and understand himself: to have a construct outside himself that enacts both the shaping of that self and its achieved form at a particular time. He has fashioned in the world an artefact that represents a unique identity which can reflect back to the lonely, uncertain self some sense of who he is. Ultimately, through such processes, 'Narcissus' may become less 'tortured / by the whisperers behind / the mirror'.[42]

7

Hacking her Way Out: Lorna Sage (1943–2001)

Bad Blood, Lorna Sage's bravura account of her unusual growing-up in the rural Border backwater of Hanmer, in the then Flintshire Maelor, in the 1940s and 1950s, is an exciting book with which to end this consideration of twentieth-century Welsh autobiography in English.[1] As a professor of English, a literary scholar, Sage was heavily involved in her working life with theoretical perspectives which emphasized the constructed nature of individual worlds, so the story of her own life comes to be told in the terms of a late twentieth-century academic and critic, with considerable use of postmodernist insights and techniques. Writing from a consciousness that there is no ultimate reality, she is particularly acute in her re-creation of codes or conventions that structured life in the 1940s and 1950s, showing how what appeared self-evidently proper and natural was in fact a result of a human creation of meaning in a particular time and place. She establishes how devastatingly transitory meanings, regarded at the time as absolutes, impinged on her life. She is playful, too, as she teases the reader by drawing attention to the constructed nature of her life story – this is no holding of a mirror up to nature – and creates pastiches of styles. She takes us vividly into the subjective world of each of her key characters, conjuring up a very convincing version of the world each inhabited, what their operant ideas might have been shaped by and the sometimes insane logic which seemed to have stimulated particular sorts of self-defeating behaviour. Seven years in the writing and published when its author was fifty-seven, *Bad Blood* takes a retrospective view of the first twenty-one years of Sage's life. One of the most striking aspects of the sense of self she reveals is a seemingly innate propensity towards being analytic.

Her cast of significant figures is vividly and skilfully individualized. Church in Wales vicar of Hanmer (R. S. Thomas had been one of his curates), her grandfather was a boozy philanderer but cast an enduring spell on his granddaughter through his bookishness. He was Lorna's early minder: 'I was like a baby goose, imprinted by the first mother-figure it sees' (4). He had a facial scar 'which Grandma had done with the carving knife, one of the many times he had come home pissed and incapable' (3). Grandma, from Tonypandy in the Rhondda, a real world of shop windows, trams, tea-shops and cinemas, spends her time loathing Grandpa, 'the old devil' (7), and regressively mourning her paradise lost where she had lived a thoroughly posh life in the family-run Hereford Stores, 'lounging around upstairs, nibbling at the stock' (33).

Their daughter, Lorna's mother, is their wartime domestic drudge, increasing in ineptitude after the post-war shift to a council house, even managing to forget how to ride a bike. Sage's accounts of her mother's domestic incompetence as she redistributes the dirt – 'wringing out a floorcloth with conviction was the sign of a coarse-grained nature' (120) – and battles to the death with food, while they reveal the author's sharp eye for human foibles, are always firmly underpinned by Sage's adult understanding of and compassion for the events that had defeated her able mother young. Sage's workaholic father, having risen to officer status from the ranks, is permanently prisoner-of-war to the experiences of that time, never able to understand the insubordinate other ranks – his family and his workforce – who will not 'Look Sharp!' and 'Jump to It!' (116).

A naive view of the resources on which autobiography draws might posit that memory is the all-important and perhaps only essential ingredient. Good academic that she is, in her attempts to make the imaginative leap into the constructed world of her significant others Lorna Sage draws on artefacts of various sorts for her work of creative reconstruction and interpretation. The most important documents considered are two diaries kept by her grandfather, for 1933 and 1934, which came Sage's way after her mother's death in 1989 and were crucial in reshaping Sage's personal myth. Equally importantly, they provided incontrovertible evidence of the shallow draught of Grandpa's inner life, which Sage had previously romanticized:

The sinner I was expecting was guilty of pride, lust and spiritual despair, not merely of sloth and ineptitude. This was the diary of a nobody. So I nearly censored January to June 1933 in the interests of Grandpa's glamour as a Gothic personage. (47)

Particular works are exemplary in suggesting the immense influence of the world of books in shaping the perceptions of the family's obsessive readers, Sage and her grandfather, linked at a deep level by a 'bookish complicity' (51). A novel from her grandfather's library, *Lorna Doone*, provided Sage with both her Christian name and her understanding of her grandfather's scorn for his daughter's cross-class marriage. Books mould Lorna Sage's perception of the real world, with catastrophic consequences. At sixteen, she is appalled, mystified and outraged when told that she is pregnant. Partly by analogy with Amber in *Forever Amber* and Lady Chatterley in her A level text, she had 'absorbed the notion that real sex was some kind of visionary initiation involving the whole of you. It seemed until that moment Amber had only been half alive . . . That's why I was so sure I hadn't done it' (239). She clearly shows how ideas absorbed from books can become prisms through which individuals' views of reality are refracted.

As well as written documents, photographs presented in the text offer at times a particular sort of evidence. For example, in *Bad Blood*, Lorna Sage enacts the way in which her early flowering sexuality caused problems in her life and was a constant source of heated family remonstrance. A photograph of herself at fourteen, a nubile, sexually attractive young woman, endorses her account of herself at that age.

Two trunks which 'held the compacted residue of her lifetime's squirrelling' come to light after Grandma's death and appear as the autobiographical text of hoarder Grandma (44–5). They contain the incriminating diaries which enable Grandma to blackmail her husband (and which are supported evidentially by an account containing £500 which came to light in Grandma's lifetime) and love-letters from the time when 'a juvenile Grandpa and an even younger Grandma met and married and inaugurated hell' (38). A lifetime's accumulation of paper bags folded within paper bags, with banknotes slipped between, reveal Grandma's typical obsessions, and bars of scented soap, never used in the vicarage life of 'secret squalor' (36), her continuing yearning for the 'posh' urban life she had left behind.

Sage sees herself as shaped by a particular time and place. Her earliest sense of identity was fashioned in part by the long-standing social pattern of the Border area, which had persisted since the establishment of Marcher lordships after the Norman Conquest, but in her childhood was on the cusp of change. Hanmer, though undoubtedly in Wales, was an untypically Welsh village, because there was no chapel, as the Hanmers would not lease land to Nonconformists. Hierarchical social gradations were tangibly part of her early scheme of things. The churchyard as play area was within Sage's gift as vicarage child, and it seemed totally normal that Kenyons and Hanmers had family vaults, while the relations of the children who played with her were consigned to unmarked, untended, tussocky ground after death (25–8). Life felt very feudal with so many families living in tied cottages. The social status quo was preserved at the primary school by what Sage terms the 'muck shovellers' curriculum' (250), which virtually institutionalized illiteracy and where homework was set to three people only, on a basis of social class (20). In spite of Grandpa's reputation as a boozer and philanderer, while she is vicarage child Sage's status is assured, because vicars are gentlemen. That status is seriously diminished after the move to the council house, neither their families nor the village approving of her parents' cross-class marriage (112). In the wider Border context, Maelor Flint is hardly revered. In adolescence, when she and her friend Gail are bused across the border to Whitchurch High School, Whitchurch girls would hold 'our Hanmerness against us . . . being bused across the border . . . accounted [in part] for the slackness of our grip on the real world' (201). Further, 'None of us spoke Welsh, but we had broader Shropshire accents than Whitchurch people, marking us out' (146). The 'backwoods' sense of Hanmer is exacerbated by the traffic across the border on Sundays, ferrying drinkers from dry Wales: 'Then the same blue bus that I caught to school turned into a drinkers' shuttle, ferrying thirsty Maelorites over the border into England' (145–6), leaving the bus reeking of Wem ales and Woodbines on a Monday morning. Whitchurch disparaged backwoods Maelor Flint, setting a quota for high school places for girls from the sticks. When Sage moves to live in Whitchurch at the age of fourteen, the complacent self-regard of that small town, coming after her early nurture in the sleepy Maelor district, provides considerable incentive to succeed academically in order to get away to somewhere more aspirational. Sage, in her retrospective look, sees this detached part of Flintshire which ran only to villages as 'more and more islanded in time' (5) as the years go by.

This, then, is the world in which Sage perceived herself coming to consciousness. Her considerable skill as an autobiographer comprehends an ability to show distinctive ways of looking at people and events at different stages in her life – to communicate a sense of the experiencing self in the immediacy of childhood encounter and the reconstellating of particular experiences with the new vantage points provided by maturity, striking new information and the wisdom of hindsight.

For the child Lorna, Grandpa is her early minder whom she loves. From him she acquires a lifelong orientation, a recognizing of the central importance, magic and refuge of the world of books She becomes a member of the church choir very young, becoming deeply aware of Grandpa's 'shamanistic glamour' (56). Grandma impinges much less powerfully in Lorna's infancy, remembered as a largely nocturnal being in a permanent rage at being deprived in this 'dead-alive dump' (6) of her real dimension, the urban ecstasies of Tonypandy. The mutual loathing between her grandparents created an atmosphere in the vicarage that was 'pungent and all-pervading' (7). During the time the vicarage was home, Sage remembers her own mother only as a nebulous 'shy, slender wraith' (8) whom the grandparents had turned into a maid-of-all-work.

In her vivid characterization of her immediate family, Sage preserves, then, a sense of the different stages of her awareness of them. The understanding imparted by the diaries becomes part of Sage's adult sense of how much of Grandma's rage was born of an infantilism which refused to recognize the adult human realities of sexuality and childbirth: this caused her to project on to Grandpa the entire responsibility for her misery: 'It was as though he'd invented sex and pain and want . . . That is, he was making it up as he went along, to spite her *and with no higher Authority to back him up*' (39). The adult autobiographer perspicaciously places Grandma in the context of her family of origin, now seeing how her obsessive hoarding tendencies come out even more bizarrely in her brother Stan 'who'd had a colossal breakdown and was never quite right again' (34). As a Rhondda shopkeeper in the years of the Depression, he had taken as pledges such things as bicycle wheels and piano keys, part of expensive and treasured objects, in the absence of which the original objects would be of no use to their owners. When they were not redeemed, Stan continued to hoard these sacks of junk, 'as excited and pleased as if he'd invented his own currency and was a secret millionaire in it' (41). These hoarding tendencies would certainly suggest an entire sibling cohort fixated at the anal stage. Sage is impressively astute in reconstructing the notional universe inhabited by her grandmother. The annual return to the Hereford Stores in the Rhondda was a going back to where 'Life was unfallen, prelapsarian, as though paying for things hadn't yet been invented' (33). Grandma's lifelong sense of entitlement was assuaged only in the Rhondda visits. There it was understood that cooking, cleaning and washing-up were properly the duties of a skivvy (35) and as there was not one, it did not get done. There is an implicit authorial marvelling at the lengths to which people will go to keep their personal myth intact, at how unchanging the stories they tell themselves about who they are can be in totally new circumstances.

Thus Grandma's sense of being a considerable cut above the Hanmer peasantry came from her shaping in the Rhondda:

Her sense of what class amounted to was remarkably pure and precise, in its South Wales way. Owning a business in a community where virtually everyone else went down the pit for wages *would* have seemed, in her youth, thoroughly posh. And the simple fact of *not working* when all around you were either slaving away or – worse – out of work would have been sufficient to mark you out as a 'lady'. (33)

Grandma, a woman 'of nearly no brains at all' (38), remained in thrall to the values of her early home until her dying day: 'She stayed furious all the days of her life – so sure of her ground, so successfully spoiled, that she was impervious to the social pressures and propaganda that made most women settle down to play the part of wife' (39). For Sage, Grandma constituted an awful warning, a life model to be avoided at all costs: 'She scared me a lot, in truth, because she represented the prospect of never growing up' (43). Child and adult valuations are juxtaposed, without losing their discrete identity, so that we have a clear sense both of the experiencing child and of the adult overview.

Later perspectives modified Sage's childhood apotheosis of her beloved Grandpa, too. His diaries for 1933 and 1934,

> turned out to be a bit like eavesdropping on the beginning of my world . . . how life in the vicarage got its Gothic savour, how we became so isolated from respectability, how the money started not to make sense and (above all) how my grandfather took on the character of theatrical martyrdom that set him apart. (46)

Two affairs are recorded in detail, one with the district nurse, which starts virtually from the moment of his arriving in Hanmer in advance of his family, and, more shockingly, one with Marj, the closest friend of Sage's then sixteen-year-old mother, propelling Sage into a compassionate understanding, sadly after her mother's death, of how she believed her mother came to be as she was. The diaries are singularly revealing of character: her grandfather's own autobiographical utterance prevents Sage from fabricating a more heroic inner world for him as she reads of 'a pottering, Pooterish, almost farcically domesticated life' (47). Grandpa was seen to drift, in terms of taking the pleasantest line of least resistance in taking any delights that life seemed to offer, with little attempt to take stock or reflect on his behaviour. The manner of reconstellating her view of Grandpa in the light cast by some of the diary recordings is worth considering in detail, as it demonstrates, in generous measure, through the accomplished panache of the literary critic, an important area of Sage's established identity. In her attempts to understand – and have the reader understand – an appropriate way of reading Grandpa's relationship with the district nurse, she frames it in a range of different ways, seeming to take a playful delight in the possible different ways of apprehending the affair. She is virtually there as an eyewitness, as she evokes in lavish detail a likely scenario for their illicit coupling (they 'hug and knead each other among the mallows and Queen Anne's lace' [54]). She even imagines the contraceptive techniques they might have engaged in and recalls the restrictive social codes of the time which would have prevented a nurse marrying and keeping her job. Denied the chance of making Grandpa a Gothic figure, she finds it: 'inviting to picture this love affair – the Vicar and the Nurse – in the style of a Hogarth etching of carnival appetite on the rampage. Flesh triumphs over Spirit. An allegory of hypocrisy' (56). Finally she looks at the scene in 'less moralising transformation', imagining the couple remade by Arcimboldo in fruit and vegetables (56). While highlighting the ludicrous elements in the situation, through imaginative play she sets the acts of an individual life within the flow of archetypal human behaviour across time, thereby, perhaps, reducing for her the uniqueness of the pain. Her postmodernist pastiches are in keeping with the fictional style of the period in which she is writing, the last decade of the twentieth century, and, of course, are very revealing of one aspect of her world – her interests as a literary academic and critic. As she ponders on suitable ways of presenting and framing the activities (or antics) of a progenitor, her autobiography becomes a story about storytelling.

The second affair detailed in the diaries is one whose shock effects have considerable impact on Sage's own life long after the event. Sage discovers that one of Grandpa's affairs had been with his sixteen-year-old daughter's closest friend, and that he had made his own daughter a cover for the relationship. Sage sees her mother's resulting alienation from her own father, to whom she had been very close, as having a profound effect on the rest of her life. She turned away from everything he represented, including the world of books. She became 'shy, fearful . . . saw herself apologetically as inept, unable to cope with life. She wouldn't talk about intimacies of almost any kind' (75). This impinged dramatically on Lorna Sage's own sense of who she was. The mother's fierce censoriousness about her daughter's sexuality grew from the terror of the rampant power of the unfettered libido she had learnt from her father: 'You're just like your grandfather, my mother had said when we rowed over clothes or make-up but now [when Lorna becomes pregnant at sixteen] it was almost too blatant to need saying' (240). A further serious consequence of Grandpa's betrayal of his daughter, given that Grandma had no interest in mothering, is that Sage perceives her mother as being incapable of surrendering her own daughter role. Of the vicarage family at the time of the arrival in Hanmer in 1933, Sage writes: 'This family, though, is dangerously fissile, falling apart, orphaned since nobody wants to play the part of parent' (72). Her mother regularly put herself in debt to a certain Mrs Smith who ran a nearly-new clothes shop. The adult Sage, reflecting, concludes: 'It was my mother's need to feel mothered that drew her back to be fussed over and flattered by Mrs Smith . . . For it seemed that nobody inside our family wanted to be mother, everyone was a daughter in perpetuity' (161). Such conclusions have serious implications for the sort of adult self Lorna Sage is prepared to contemplate for herself. The diaries help Sage – and with her, the reader – trace cause and effect through the generations right up to the moment of writing.

The high level of self-knowledge achieved in this autobiography includes a real understanding of the process of the writer's own functioning. The very nuanced sense she communicates of her own individuality suggests a reflective more than an interactive temperament. Sage's considerable emphasis on the great importance of defended space for her own sense of self strongly suggests that she is an introvert, centrally aware of her need for withdrawal and privacy for effective functioning. She reinforces structurally the importance she feels that living space has had in her life by dividing her autobiography into three parts, each dealing with a distinct phase of her growing-up and each section, for the most part, being centred on one of her three childhood homes – the vicarage, the council house and Sunnyside.

In spite of the permanently poisonous atmosphere engendered by her locked-in-loathing grandparents, the vicarage was most deeply home. Grandpa was her principal attachment figure, while his role as vicar conferred some status and extended the territory – the graveyard, the church, the vestry – that she could regard as home-ground. She could 'curr[y] favour with the pack' (25) by offering play benefits, and 'even managed – on some blissful days – to feel accepted, a member of the child world of Hanmer' (28). Grandpa was centrally important in that early sense of self: 'He was the source of my sense of having an inner topography, a sort of vicarage soul' (92). Sage remembers her early entry into school playground rituals as 'hell' because of her lack of demarcated territory: 'I think that we all forget the pain of being a child at school for the first time, the sheer ineptitude, as though you'll never learn to mark out your own space' (22). The move with near strangers to open-plan council-house living, where individual private space is abolished, seems cataclysmic:

Even being locked down the horrible cellar by Grandma for being naughty, although terrifying, was not so threatening as the return of my father from the army and the birth of my brother when I was six. My real family didn't seem congenial to me at all. (88–9)

She found nuclear family living emotionally claustrophobic – 'no-one had enough private space' (110) – and felt very much an interloper, more comfortable roaming the countryside, ever the outsider looking in: 'Everything about our situation felt exposed, it was somehow safer outside. And although very soon the council put up concrete posts and a chain-link fence to mark our garden, it wasn't a boundary you could believe in' (102). Within a year, another sort of demarcation of space becomes an issue, when she travels to the high school daily by bus, where 'an elaborate unspoken seating plan' (146) proved a minefield for a nervous child (147). After five years, when the open-plan council house is bursting with the frustration of family members, they move to Sunnyside, 'a shady, reclusive house with lots of solidly separate rooms' (223). Sage has the reader feeling that, for her, an unassailable sense of self can be preserved only within secure territorial parameters.

In a sense, this act of writing an autobiography has been for Sage a retrospective demarcating of self in the world. By academic orientation she is deeply interested in other sorts of demarcation: she has a panoramic view of the multiplicity of codes through which humankind has structured its reality and, in this postmodernist autobiography, she has implicitly analysed several of them. Paul John Eakin in *Touching the World* refers to the argument by the French autobiographical theorist Philippe Lejeune that: 'The private speech of the individual engaged in the autobiographical act is derived . . . from public discourse structured by class, code and convention.'[2] Sage has an impressively subtle awareness of the assumptions of her cast of characters in all of these areas.

We have already seen how Grandma was immovable in the class and code assumptions of a petit bourgeois shopkeeper in a mining area with a grafted-on awareness of the establishment position of the vicarage family. When Lorna is found to have headlice at primary school, Grandma declares that they cannot be seen buying the necessary lotion in any local towns where they are known (28), so Lorna is left infested and infesting others for several years until, with maximum humiliation for her, they are again discovered in her first year at high school. Sage is deeply aware of the codes covering choice of mate amongst the yeoman farmers of the area. She writes: 'Hanmer still lived in the era when most engagements were really contracted between legacies and land, abutting acres, second cousins twice removed or, at least a tied cottage and a tea service' (112). When playing mixed doubles with rather older Young Farmers, she sees her attractive friend Gail's 'glamour dwindle. Her mother's history and her family's plentiful lack of land were entirely anti-aphrodisiac for them cancelling out the way her thigh muscles were moulded' (208). Both she and her boyfriend, Victor Sage, know they have to do well at school, and Lorna had further picked up a sense that in the Rhondda there was a real enthusiasm for scholarly success, which was a means to getting on (44). However, in this complacent farming area, 'trying too hard was in Whitchurch a sign that you were an outsider and socially shifty' (230).

It is, however, in Sage's analysis of the codes dealing with the nature and position of women in the 1950s and 1960s that anger and distress breaks through. From her position at the time of writing of being a most able and successful critic and literary academic, the sense of how near she was to missing any opportunity of higher education is chilling. Her life story seems to exemplify Rowbotham's assertion about the situation of women:

> A woman cannot . . . experience herself as an entirely unique entity because she is always aware of how she is being defined *as woman*, that is, as a member of a group whose identity has been defined by the dominant male culture . . . Her mirror is the reflecting surface of cultural representation into which a woman stares to form an identity . . . That mirror does not reflect back a unique individual identity to each living woman; it projects an image of WOMAN, a category that is supposed to define the living woman's identity.[3]

From what one can piece together from her account, Lorna Sage went through the high school with an excellent academic record, usually being at the top of her class. A different sort of education seems to have been thought proper for girls, and science was not on offer at examination level in any form: for that you had to go to the boys' grammar school in the sixth form. She becomes pregnant at sixteen in her A level year. Her parents' first plan is that she should go to a church home for unmarried mothers, from which her baby would be adopted and 'from now on you could count yourself lucky if they let you learn shorthand and typing' (237). As the months pass, the young couple successfully apply pressure within their families and are allowed to marry, but have to leave school. The male GP assures Lorna and her mother that her immediate future is taken care of, as it was well known that, as pregnancy advanced, 'you became absorbed by it, serene, preoccupied, reconciled, round' (244). Nevertheless, Lorna determines to take her A levels, which would be just about possible if the baby arrived on time at the end of May. Her headmistress tries to discourage her from entering the school, the

local 'open centre', to take her exams (269). She has missed French dictation
and oral while giving birth but otherwise does spectacularly well in her A
levels, in spite of the hormonal changes of parturition and having undergone
a difficult 'breech' labour. She ends up a few marks short of what is needed
for a state scholarship, because of the reduced French score, and is then
denied a discretionary county award because she is married, although her
husband would have been allowed one. She has earlier explained:

> You were supposed to choose between boys and books, because for girls sex was
> entirely preoccupying, your sex was *more of you* than a boy's appendage, you
> *were* your sex, so you had to do without if you were to have enough energy, self-
> possession and brains left over to do anything else. (232)

She goes to the doctor for advice about contraception and he refuses her any
help:

> What he was saying . . . was that he wouldn't aid and abet me in acquiring any
> control over my own fertility. In any case he must have thought . . . I was some
> sort of nymphomaniac and shouldn't be allowed to have my cake and eat it. (270)

In terror of further pregnancies, she and Vic continue a pattern of abstinence
from sexual intercourse. The afterword to the autobiography proper reveals
that they are divorced within a decade of graduating from Durham, where
they have both achieved first-class honours in English. The publicity their
success generates, including their photograph with their daughter in the *Daily
Mail*, produces a letter from a young woman who had had her first baby in the
bed beside Lorna in the maternity hospital four years before. Living in a tiny
house on a smallholding, she now has five children, including two sets of
twins. Sage does not explicitly comment from her turn-of-the-century perspective: the interpreting mind of the reader is left to form its own stunned
judgement at the construction of female reality that was the norm in the 1950s
and early 1960s.

Sage is adept at revealing the sometimes ludicrous yet malign nature of
particular constructed worlds. Crosshouses, the specialist maternity hospital
to which she is sent because obstetric complications are expected, is deep in
the countryside, having no public telephone, short visiting hours and no bus
service, giving full scope for the exercise of repressive power. In this isolated
spot, 'the ward was the world' (261). Sage experiences it as a sort of prison:
'Breast feeding . . . had suddenly become the rule and created many more
minor offences to do with having too much milk or not enough, or the wrong

sort of nipples' (261). It is within this isolated environment, whose changing codes (evolved from current medical theory) are imposed with oppressive zeal, that she experiences a sort of epiphany. She has an embattled encounter with the Day Sister in her attempt to get herself released in time for her exams: 'I was shocked and elated. I'd never had a row as savage as that with anyone outside my family, in public' (264). It produces the desired effect and she is discharged:

> Crosshouses was grim, but the fact that they were so much better at moral hygiene than the other kind had taught me a lot. From now on I was making my way against most people's assumptions, I'd have to count my friends and fight back. (265–6)

She has come to see conventions and systems of rules of the external world as harshly coercive but surmountable; as a result, she becomes more entirely inner directed. Entering Whitchurch High to do her A levels feels like crossing a sort of Rubicon. When the headmistress appears at the gate and tries to deter her: 'I walked around her as if she were a mere personification of prudery . . . The lines she drew had lost their power, you could just step over them' (269). Indeed, the process of her own mythic reconstruction had started from early pregnancy. From their marriage and exclusion from school, working together in embattled intimacy, the young couple 'from cellmates . . . turned into soulmates' (243). Inventing a story for themselves that 'soon took on a life of its own . . . patch[ing] together a new mutant myth out of poems and stories and sheer necessity. Our brainchild. In it we grew up overnight and cast off the mind-forged manacles of Hanmer and Whitchurch' (243–4). There is a sense of rapid reconstruction of personal myth in ways that will give two beleaguered young people the strength to survive, aided and abetted by the social changes which heralded the swinging Sixties.

Yet, in spite of her triumph towards the end of the book at stepping over the lines her headmistress drew, there is a preoccupation throughout the auto-biography with boundaries, for Lorna's mother was particularly bad at drawing them and trusting in them. Although Sage's description of her mother's efforts as a cook make hilarious reading, they are imbued with Sage's adult awareness of the pathology of her mother's fear of food:

> All meat had to be made safe by boiling . . . even then it was dangerously full of knots of choking gristle and shards and spikes of bone . . . And, if anything, she thought vegetables even more dangerous and difficult to subdue. They had to be cooked all morning, particularly green ones like sprouts, which got very salty

and stuck to the pan as their water boiled away, and came out in yellow mush (120–1) . . . She simply could not take food or leave it at all, for it was a sign of a larger unfocused fear (123) . . . Her fear of food, which was a fear of the outside getting in, was a key to her character as a wife. (123)

Sage gives a powerful sense of a mother who was not really there: 'The absent and amorphous aspect of her daily self – "miles away" she'd say innocently, not apologising' (126). For Sage, the move to the uncongenial nuclear family based in the unappealing council house coincided with the death of her grandfather, which left her in a 'disbelieving and desolate state' (91). In this new environment she could not trust the material boundaries between her house and the rest of the world and, as the momentum of her life carried her inexorably on to that first entry into Whitchurch High, she cultivated experiences which brought about a diminishing of the sense of self: 'In the spring, the ground sucked at your feet; with every step you could savour the pull of the mud . . . You could hypnotise yourself with it . . . This way you could lose yourself until you slowed to a dazed standstill' (104–5). A fundamental insecurity for Sage seems to arise from the fact that the 'child wife' cannot demarcate boundaries: 'My mother's timidity and her dread of confrontation meant that it was horribly easy to defy her and bully her and so we [Grandma, Clive, Lorna's brother, Lorna] did' (164). Until adolescence, Sage herself is regularly put across his knee and spanked by her father, 'until I say I'm sorry, I won't do it again' and 'howl and writhe with humiliation' (165). Thus Sage's father is regularly invoked to impose what seem to be the only clear boundaries in her world, possibly boundaries which Sage unconsciously craved.

As a child Sage looked with wonder and admiration at Mrs Edge, her friend Valerie's mother, who:

lived in her [council house] with style, not only were her net curtains whiter than white, but the whole space and the whole shape of the day, had an elaborate decorum. She changed her wellies on the back step for carpet slippers with fake fur around the tops, or hid her curlers under her turban, or combed out her hair and put her lipstick on to a regular, reassuring rhythm. (107)

The sense of the security of someone discovering a regular pattern to a day seems to be a modelling Sage longed for from the 'blatant shambles' (119) of her own home; such feelings are possibly the source of her highly developed adult sense of how 'codes' order life.

In retrospect, she conceptualizes the nature of the family myth and the dysfunctional needs on which it was based. '[My parents'] obsessions had met, fallen in love and married' (186). The mother's domain was Fancy and indoors was her department (125); '[her] acquired ineptitude fitted [the] post-war pattern'. Sage's father sees himself as the practical realist (126), although the adult Sage is caustically aware of his limitations in this area. The sense of self each parent needs depends on a collusive role assignment, however far short of their imagined fulfilment of role the actual qualities of each may fall.

Trips in the family car, and one particular disaster, become a potent metaphor for how Sage feels about family life and its insecurities within the parental claustrophobic closeness and the very flimsy family boundaries provided by the imagined world of her parents:

> They left *no room*. Family life was the open-plan living-room, the family car. It was like a nightmare council house on wheels. (186) Clive and I in the back seat . . . were made to know our place. We were the passengers, they were in charge. Except that it was all tied together with string. (185)

After one family trip, returning home through the dark, mother comments on the pretty patterns of the headlights flickering on the hedgerows. With horror, the father realizes the engine is on fire, and leaving the family standing 'in the circle of firelight and watch[ing] the car burn' (185) races off to find a garage. A passing motorist shoos them away because of the imminent danger of explosion:

> The-car-that-went-on-fire became a family story in which somehow my mother's fey remark supplied the comic point, not my father's sketchiness as a mechanic and definitely not our escape from being barbecued. Our family life may have been a fragile construct, my parents may have been making it up as they went along, but they were good at improvising – at least as far as their story went. They always closed ranks and pretended everything was solid, normal and natural. (185–6)

The chasm between family myth and observed reality for this sensitive, highly intelligent girl was a source of powerful insecurity.

Sage, in this retrospective interpretation, ascribes her mother's ineptitude and loss of faith in herself to the rampant transgression of boundaries represented by her own father's behaviour with her friend Marj. Beside the betrayal of his loving daughter that such a relationship implied, Sage comments in pondering on the diaries on 'the sheer moral untidiness of the breaking down of boundaries between generations and classes (Marj being neither respectable nor safely an outsider)' (74). Reflecting on the confident, outgoing girl she believed her mother to have been at sixteen, she concludes:

> [Grandpa] certainly scarred his daughter's sensibility horribly . . . She became fiercely censorious about bodies and their wants, so much so that it always seemed a bit of a miracle that she'd managed to make an exception for my father. (75)

The resonance of the title *Bad Blood* is experienced at many levels. It blazons the hostile relationships within and between generations of Sage's family. It further suggests that Sage sees herself with some ambivalence as her grand-father's heir, as transgressor of boundaries. It captures the overall sweep of the book, Sage's somewhat ironic sense of how far back she could trace ele-ments of dysfunctionality in her family. 'Bad blood' is a labelling given to Lorna by her mother for her early flowering sexuality and, most of all, for her pregnancy at the age of sixteen. She is perceived as Grandpa's creature long after his death. The degree of inhibition Sage's early pregnancy brought in her subsequent sexual relationship is perceived partly, too, as a legacy of her grandfather's priapic tendencies and her mother's resultant very timorous inhabiting of her sexual identity. The 'bad blood' of the title further suggests Lorna Sage's rage at being trapped by the fertility of her body after the onset of menstruation, of how the mere fact of being female can slam the door on possibilities: 'I wanted my body back . . . Pregnant I was my own prison' (245). Through this pregnancy 'My treacherous body had somehow delivered me into other people's hands . . . If they were outraged, *so was I*' (236–8). From the vantage point of the much greater sexual liberty of the end of the century, the degree of isolation and suffering Sage experienced as a result of this pregnancy is dismaying, as is the sense of how easily, in slightly different circumstances and with less personal resolution on her part, she could have become trapped in that self-condemnatory view of what she was – a carrier of bad blood, doomed. The title *Bad Blood*, then, is in some measure a labelling of the sexual censoriousness of a particular time and place from the perspective of a much more emancipated time, when many of those boundaries are gone. It draws attention to the transitory and relative nature of all constructed views of the world, although at the time of experiencing them, they are entertained as absolutes.

The title of her autobiography could be said to epitomize Sage's anguished sense of self at a particular time. The essential route to self-acceptance, some psychoanalysts are convinced, comes from the mirroring that mothers give their infants. Adam Phillips, in his lucid book, *Winnicott*, encapsulates that psychoanalyst's understanding of the process of mirroring:

> Being seen by the mother is being recognised for who one is, and what the infant is, is what he feels. The infant cannot risk looking, if looking draws a blank; he must get something of himself back from what he looks at. This makes the mother of infancy the arbiter of the infant's truth. Her responsive recognition . . . makes up his sense of himself.[4]

When a mother identifies with what her baby is feeling, the baby, looking into the mother's face, sees himself or herself in the deepest sense. In this way, babies come to identify, own and understand their feelings. Sage sees her mother as having been deeply damaged by her nurture, her own mother, Lorna's grandmother, being locked within her own narcissistic needs and her father having betrayed her at a crucial stage in adolescence when the support of a father can be of key importance. In infancy, Lorna seems to have perceived her mother, who should have been the crucial figure in her life, as a 'wraith' (8) and even by the council-house stage Sage is still commenting on 'the absent and amorphous aspect of her daily self' (126). Sage herself owns to having found eye contact with anyone difficult and, most discerningly, relates her inability to tell the time until her mid-teens to the discomfort she felt at looking people in the eye: 'The involuntary sulk that I lived in included clocks: just as I couldn't meet people's eyes, I couldn't look a clock in the face. I squinted at them so hastily and at such a weird angle that they made no sense' (130). It is hard to avoid the conclusion that these difficulties developed as a result of Sage's infant distress at having a mother characterized by 'absence and brooding' (156), continually refusing the loving eye-contact so necessary for a baby's developing sense of who s/he is. Whatever infant nurture Sage recalls seems to have come from her grandfather. From what we learn of Sage from her self-depiction in *Bad Blood*, mirroring by significant adults seems to have been singularly lacking.

Indeed, the recognition that Sage depicts as being given by other consciousnesses is in the main censorious, or casts her in the role of reprobate. She seems to be given a profoundly negative sense of what she is from her mother, who identifies in her daughter her grandfather's bad blood, which has skipped a generation. An intensely painful 'naming' by her mother takes place at the climactic chapter-ending where it has just been disclosed that Sage, at sixteen, is pregnant. Her mother rants to the effect that 'I've spoiled everything now, this house will be a shameful place like the vicarage. I've soiled and insulted her with my promiscuity, my sly, grubby lusts' (236). Lorna's headmistress, too, is intensely disapproving of Lorna's perceived lapse, which seems to eclipse, in her eyes, all Lorna's academic promise. In her early years in Whitchurch High, the only teacherly reaction to her that is described in detail is that of the gym mistress 'who came to regard [her] with real distaste' (150) and finds lice in Lorna's long hair. Unsurprisingly, then, her description of herself in adolescence seems to suggest a classic Winnicotian hunger for mirroring:

> I was in deadly earnest without [her friend Gail]. There was only the search for recognition, being reflected back (every eye was a crystal ball) so you could imagine who you were. But people frosted over the more anxiously I peered. (210)

When her interest in the opposite sex becomes urgent, it is 'the mesmerising compulsion to get boys, almost any boys, to acknowledge my existence *to make me exist*' that she records (217).

Autobiographical theorists are agreed that the memories which are retained and recorded are those which fit in with the pattern the autobiographer has discerned in her life: an author who can entitle her memoir *Bad Blood* is drawing attention to her low self-esteem in the period of life she explores. Sage just about survives. In her generally bleak landscape of punitive authority figures there is, however, one life-saving exception – Miss Roberts, her Latin teacher, who gives Sage hope and encouragement at a very difficult time.

Certainly, Sage's growing awareness of her own particular identity emerges from her relationship to a series of significant others on whom she models or against whom she defines herself. She strenuously resists the negative female scripts offered by her mother and grandmother of being a perpetual daughter. In some of the means she chooses to explore what she is, we see the truth of Susanna Egan's argument in *Patterns of Experience in Autobiography* that 'everyone . . . takes his own habits of thought for granted and perceives his bias only by contrast'.[5] She recognizes that the Rhondda would have valued her intellectual aptitudes, whereas in Whitchurch, 'clever was always too clever by half' (256). Her own solitary habits at the age of nine, straying, disappearing for hours, getting lost, and her own disorganized home are all measured against the sense of safety she absorbed from the orderly day and ways of the Edge household. However, Gail, her bosom friend throughout adolescence – 'I could never have thrown myself into the part [of being a teenager] with such conviction without her' (188) – proves to be the most useful yardstick for measuring her own idiosyncracies. As a small child: '[Gail] was simply better at inhabiting her own body than I was . . . She made me feel like an unstrung puppet' (23). Where Sage hungered for recognition by boys to feel that she existed, when Gail and she sat together in a first-floor café on a Saturday morning, Gail 'was only really interested in looking, not being looked at' (217). Gail was much more her own person who 'went her own way' and 'never even played at team games, let alone played them' (209–10). Sage herself 'couldn't resist the longing to be liked and accepted, even though it was so transparent its very intensity undermined my efforts' (209), and, to this end, even played in a hockey team. Sage's wants were global: 'I wanted to be wanted' (210), Gail's were specific and only just out of reach: 'to win her service with four impeccable aces . . . or to meet Paul Anka in person' (210). Her close friendship with Gail, then, provides a striking route to self-knowledge for someone of Sage's analytic temperament.

Compellingly, too, another figure – Grandpa – casts his long shadow over this autobiographical search for self. Implicitly, Sage explores the teasing conundrum, as she sees it, and disparagement, as her mother delivers it: 'You're just like your grandfather.' He was bookish, literary, with a desire to prove himself as a journalist. His sexual incontinence brought disrepute and distress to his family. All this could equally be said of Sage. Genetic endowment there certainly was from her grandfather: what did it then make her? *Bad Blood* as a text is an attempted answer.

Grandpa was something of an orator and people flocked to hear his sermons. As an adult, Sage seems to have been fully in the line as a charismatic lecturer, yet saw herself as being alarmingly dumb as a child. She regularly castigates herself for her perceived failure of facility and poise in speech, seeing herself handicapped to the point of being crippled by it. She has a great fellow feeling for Tarzan, one of her early literary heroes, who taught himself to read and write in the jungle, but 'he can't speak at all' (90).

Disablingly shy, Sage reckoned that she 'got more and more clumsy in speech as I grew' (90). From the time Grandpa taught her to read at the age of four, Sage retreated into obsessive reading: 'More and more I lived in books, they were my comfort, refuge, addiction, compensation for the humiliation that attended contact with the world outside' (29). She gives a sense of the inner space created by reading being a sanctuary: 'I knew how to hide in books. If need be, I could build a kind of nest out of any old scraps of print I found around' (90). Her parents looked askance at this activity; although proud of her getting into grammar school a year early, 'they were . . . convinced that my addiction to print was part of my general delinquency' (130). Indubitably, in Jungian terms, Sage is an introvert, revealed, as we have seen, in her urgent need for defended space of her own, her sense of being energized by inward reflection and her considerable preference for writing, which allows deep reflection before committing oneself, over speech.[6] Here, reading allowed a very nurturing inner withdrawal.

From the age of ten, Lorna Sage increasingly became aware of a sense of self to do with intellectual mastery: books, from being a refuge, further became a tool. She felt great pleasure – and triumph, for her father had warned her they would not find her clever at the high school – when she comes top in nearly everything at the end of the first term, 'for surely it meant that my private currency had value in the world outside' (149). The nature of her intellectual aptitude and mastery is exemplified by Latin, which she uses as shorthand for her preferred intellectual process:

> Latin, the great dead language that only existed in writing would compensate for my speechlessness, vindicate my sleepless nights and in general redeem my utter lack of social graces. Latin stood for higher education, still, in the early 1950s, a kind of litmus test for academic aptitude. (143)

Sage recounts how she became blissfully aware of the symbolic nature of all languages, and here one must feel the end-of-the-century university lecturer animating the remembered mental process of the child:

> The words, maps, lists and diagrams in my textbooks were to me classic ciphers, empty and 0 shaped – obedient, open, waiting to be filled with meaning. I'd get light-headed over the simple, blissful fact of alphabetical abstraction; the thought that the smudgy marks I made shared the same powers as the ones printed in books was a continuous miracle. (148)

The huge pleasure she is recalling is to do in part with this all being inward process, all within her control; her interpreting mind is needed to animate 'the mimic empire of signs' and 'ciphers'. Surely, too, in her reconstruction of her remembered anguish over speech, retreat into reading and pleasure in control of a fixed-because-dead language is a sense of her profound alienation from the real world at that time. When she could have been basking in the self-esteem of being top of the class, this is how she recalls feeling about herself:

> In my first high school year, I had no friends, I was mostly invisible as well as inaudible: small, grubby, uncouth, a swot and no good at sports. Then there were the bugs. We finally bought the lethal shampoo from Boots and applied it . . . And worse, much worse – during that first winter I had braces fitted to my teeth, top and bottom . . . Most people tried not to look at me nearly as hard as I tried not to look at them. (154)

In the last decade of the twentieth century, with the skills of a critic, journalist and literary academic, Lorna Sage engages in tracing the remembered nature of her interior experience in the 1940s, 1950s and early 1960s, at the same time exposing and analysing models of identity, particularly for women, which belonged to that period. In writing in general terms of perceived 'separate spheres' for males and females in the late 1950s, she describes with incredulity how 'our heroes, the Beats' (233) reinvented the same old world of male dominance, female biological destiny. Retrospectively angry, Sage comments:

> It's galling to realise that you were a creature of mythology: girls were the en-
> emies of promise, a trap for boys, although with the wisdom of hindsight you
> can see that the opposite was the case. In those seductive yarns about freedom,
> girls' wants are foreknown. Like Lucy, you are meant to stay put in one spot of
> time. (234)

Those readers who lived through the period she depicts may feel a sense of shock, then one of recognition, as Sage shapes our awareness in a way that makes us take in the constructed nature of the norms of that (as any) time. She writes, too, in an engagingly frank way of the experience of being female and how it affects what one feels about oneself. Sage, in common with others in the enlightenment of the late twentieth-century feminist revolution, demon-strates what the hormonal contribution of adolescence, pregnancy and the menstrual cycle do to her sense of identity.

In some respects, the onset of the menarche improved life for Sage: start-ing menstruating at eleven was a real status-enhancer and her father stopped beating her, retrospective interpretation suggesting that 'my adolescent breasts and curves were beginning to give the whole performance a comprom-ising sexual savour' (172). Confirmation is seen as a rite of passage merely because her new shoes necessitated proper stockings and thus a suspender belt:

> The magic of the Church no longer impressed us. Our own bodies were more
> mysterious than the wine and the wafers . . . My period came every three weeks
> in a heavy iron-smelling flood, along with backaches, headaches and cramps . . .
> Bad blood, excited blood. My nose bled too. (197–8)

She is shocked to read the confession, thirty years after the event, of Joyce Johnson, lover of Jack Kerouac, revolutionary bard of the Beat generation, which was such a feature of Sage's growing-up:

> Could he ever include a woman in his journeys . . .? Whenever I tried to raise
> the question, he'd stop me by saying that what I really wanted were babies.

That was what all women wanted and what I wanted too, even though I said I didn't. (234)

Describing this as 'claptrap', Sage records in anguished detail how far short she falls of any such longing when she becomes pregnant: 'I'd been caught out, I would have to pay. I was in trouble, I'd have no secrets any longer, I'd be exposed as a fraud, my fate wasn't my own' (236). She feels terror, believing that she is about to be found out, when, at school, a girl playfully puts her arm around her waist and observes she has put on weight: 'I was an outsider, harbouring an alien, an alien myself. Having such a secret was like having cancer – a disease which couldn't be mentioned except in shamed whispers' (246). Certainly, there is not the remotest sense of her accepting a longed-for natural state. She does not become reconciled to her situation nor ever even pay lip-service to, let alone give real assent to the patriarchal thesis that 'Biology is destiny'. She does her A levels leaking breast milk. Refused contraceptive advice by her doctor, in spite of the certainty of total abstinence she becomes obsessively terrified of a further pregnancy: 'Behind it all was a visceral dread that easily defeated common sense. Every month I was convinced, despite our abstinence, that I was, by some bad miracle, pregnant, and I raged and despaired' (271). Lorna Sage communicates vividly the struggle she had to realize what she perceives to be her deepest, intellectual identity – an identity in which she subsequently distinguished herself – against sabotage by her own female metabolism and the construction of female role and identity at that time.

In this most intelligently interpretative autobiography, I would quarrel with only one major conclusion she drew. Her reading of her mother's story was that a confident, outgoing girl was transformed into a timorous, inept and neurotic wraith by her father's betrayal of her, at the age of sixteen, when he had a relationship with her friend, Marj. Certainly the diaries of 1933 and 1934 suggest that Sage's mother, Vanna, had been close to her father at that period, although Lorna had only ever known her expressing alienation and resistance to anything to do with him. However, Sage's own childhood and what we can conclude from it of her earliest nurture, would seem to give the lie to any interpretation of a pre-existing psychological security in Vanna before the rupture caused by the Marj affair. Here is a mother whose preferred mode of being seems to be a 'miles away' abstraction which would certainly have boded ill for the comforting eye-contact of 'mirroring' for her own babies (see pp. 162–3). Analytical literature explains that in the mother–baby dyad, the nursing couple, the mother tunes in to recollections of her own experience for a sense of an appropriate way of how to be. Interestingly, Sage herself does not seem to notice that her own predilection revealed a marked similarity to her mother's habitual state: in her early unhappy years in the council house she attempted to blur the boundaries of self through plodding through the countryside:

> Try as I might to lose myself in the landscape, however, I was still only an apprentice misfit . . . And the truth was that often no amount of trudging would get me to the state of dreamy abstraction I craved. Then I was simply lonely. (105)

Sage communicates a continual sense in her narrative of being an outsider, both in her family and her social group. Her insecurity over boundaries and general unhappiness, particularly after the move to be in her mother's care at the council house, suggest a very insecure attachment to her, as Sage felt safer wandering the countryside than being at home under Vanna's abstracted and chaotic rule. In early adolescence, Sage seems happiest in the complete withdrawal of losing herself in reading.

Sage's mother is the only figure in her life continuously present throughout her growing up, yet in Sage's recollections of her early years, Grandpa stands out far more vividly. Bowlby's fascinating late collection of essays, *A Secure Base* (1988), contains a considerable body of research evidence on family circumstances which promote both secure and insecure attachment to a mother figure.[7] Although Sage describes herself as Grandpa's 'hobble' (3) during her very early years, it seems highly improbable, given the sexist ethics of the times on childcare, that he was actually involved in her management as a nappy-wearing infant; it is hard to see how Vanna could have avoided playing the central role in her early infancy.

Bowlby quotes at length Main's longitudinal study over many years which identified the sort of infant/mother relationship which produces secure attachment. Of the three categories she describes – secure attachment, anxious attachment and avoidant attachment – Sage would seem to fall firmly into the third category. Main makes clear that models of parent/child interaction are established in infancy and

> tend to persist and are so taken for granted that they come to operate at an unconscious level . . . For a relationship between any two individuals to proceed harmoniously, each must be aware of the other's point of view, his goals, feelings and intentions and each must so adjust his own behaviour that some alignment of goals is negotiated. This requires that each should have reasonably accurate models of self and other which are regularly up-dated by free communication between them. (*A Secure Base*, 130–1)

We have already seen to what a degree the 'couple myth' of her parents is divorced from any reality that Sage perceives in the material world. Further, one of the most distressing aspects of her autobiography is that, from her perception, virtually the only time she wins approval from her parents is in some public situation. Main's research makes clear that, for the most part, parents with happy early childhoods themselves have a securely attached infant 'and those who had an unhappy childhood, more or less cloaked by an inability to recall' (*A Secure Base*, 134), have children who are insecurely attached. Inability to ponder on, make sense of and thus integrate past unhappiness by bringing it firmly into consciousness, tended to produce the poor outcome of insecurely attached children. Main concludes that 'free access to, and the coherent organisation of information relevant [to their own childhood attachment] play a determining role in the development of a secure personality in adult life' (*A Secure Base*, 135).

It seems probable that Grandpa was the primary attachment figure in infancy and childhood for Vanna, Sage's mother, as well, (though, again, it would be implausible for even such a wife as his not to be driven into playing an active role in small baby management). It is highly unlikely, however, that this was a secure attachment. Sage herself recalls being left, as a three-year-old, to play with some frightening urchins in the street outside a distant pub when Grandpa was 'minding' her (15). It seems more than probable that vicious and violent quarrels were a feature of life before Grandpa and family moved to Hanmer in 1933 as, Sage later learns from her father, there was talk of another woman, and possibly an illegitimate child, while Grandpa and his family lived in the Rhondda. Had Sage's mother been securely attached to her father, it seems improbable that she would have become permanently alienated from him through the affair with Marj when she was sixteen, in spite of its new element of personal betrayal of her.

In a very interpretative autobiography, Sage's judgement of the root cause of her mother's insecurity is the only major area where she has failed to convince me, which says a great deal for the analytic self Sage has enacted. In conclusion, then, it may well be salutary to ponder on the human need which has seemed to impel the writing of this very revealing text. It is probable that Sage was aware that the confronting of ghosts was a means to laying them. Further, her 'spell-binding, jaw-dropping frankness'[8] in the telling of her story is a rejection of particular sorts of fantastical, crippling and defensive female scripts: that of her grandmother, which cushioned her from the real world at a high cost to all those around her; and that of her mother, which allowed her to be a daughter in perpetuity, 'a child dreaming of pretty things' (186).

If she guarded her threshold it was against prying eyes. Women neighbours were never allowed in, nor were their daughters, who were suspected of being fifth columnists, housework spies who'd run home and tell their mothers we didn't clean behind the sofa. (119–20)

In her forthright account, which lets the world in, Sage is daring to repudiate a matriarchal prohibition and is bringing a brutal clarity to the realm of her mother's evasions and fantasies. The start of Lorna's intimacy with Victor Sage comes when, watching a tennis game, they 'confide recklessly' in each other: 'We boasted to each other about the awfulness of life in our respective council houses and stripped off the appearances with which our parents covered their privacy' (228).

In seeking out and publishing her harsher truth, Sage demonstrated an important facet of her self at the time of writing – her analytical, authorial power. She dared to expose what she believed herself to be and how she reckoned she came to be that way. From a family that she saw as bedevilled by impotent dreaming and a strong drive towards damage limitation through pretending nothing bad had happened, Lorna Sage chose to confront publicly a painful past, to achieve her own naming of self – a naming which belied the book's title. Mortally ill for much of the period of writing this book, she chose to use much of her final life-energy to ponder on her growing-up and to try to make sense of it. Indeed, *Bad Blood* came out to widespread critical acclaim and was shortlisted for the Whitbread Book of the Year Award in the final weeks of Sage's life. Ironically, a work in which she confronted unconventional, even scandalous, elements in her own and her family's past and sought to shine light into the darkest recesses of self became the means whereby a deep and enduring need was answered: through *Bad Blood*, Lorna Sage finally achieved affirmative mirroring in the world.

8

Conclusion

In conclusion, it seems important to return to a valuable precept for any literary study – that texts are written in circumstances for purposes. A reflection on the contexts and driving impulses from which the autobiographical acts I have considered seem to have been created brings this study to a close, in the full recognition that the past is recalled from the lived reality of the present, which both shapes and colours what is written. None of the authors considered here would have declared with the Olympian certitude of Horace: 'Exegi monumentum aere perennium', 'I have created a memorial more lasting than brass', yet a need to memorialize has been at least part of the impetus that made several of my subjects autobiographers.

For R. S. Thomas, writing *The Echoes Return Slow* in the mid-1980s, important elements in his personal life and in the wider world coalesced. As he ministered to the needs of his dying wife he was forced to confront his own mortality, to reflect on the meaning of his life and on the relationships which had formed him. In the wider world, the Chernobyl disaster brought radioactive pollution to his very door. Prophet-like, he sees that the perversion of human intelligence that the nuclear bomb on Hiroshima represented might yet unleash Armageddon. Knowing that it is the human lot to die, this most introspective of men has a need to explore and understand himself and his world and to record what he finds. As he interprets his own life, he is both his unique self and Everyman.

Berry's drive in memorializing was to create a frail bulwark against the encroaching tide of annihilation, to celebrate the human qualities he had cherished in his life, and to commemorate the passing of an entire purposeful way of life and relating that had been obliterated in his lifetime with the near-extinction of the coal industry in Wales. What he creates is both time-capsule and memorial urn. He also seeks meaning in the pattern he has discerned in his life. An element in Coombes's complex drive, and his professed motivation, was to reveal to an ignorant and indifferent world the human cost of coal and, in so doing, commemorate those whose lives had been blighted or lost in the struggle to wrest it from the earth.

Part of the pain of Margiad Evans in facing an early death will have been the thought of leaving a small child motherless. In the final year of her life, she composes 'The Immortal Hospital', where she relives a blissfully happy year of childhood, during which the substitute mothering she received from Aunt Fran was the most powerful element in her sense of well-being. As she reawakens the memory of that love, as succour and consolation in a time of grief, there may indeed be the hope that the world will provide the sort of nurture for her child that had proved such a source of strength for herself. She writes *A Ray of Darkness* and 'The Nightingale Silenced' in an attempt not only to master the distress of epilepsy but also to be of use to others, while *The Wooden Doctor* is a means of trying to understand a particular life experience, a necessary catharsis, written in the hope of passing through and, perhaps, beyond it.

Probably suffering from emphysema for the seven years she took to write *Bad Blood*, Lorna Sage may well have deduced that she was unlikely to live into old age: certainly in the final years of its writing she knew herself to be dying. She seems to have been responding to a not uncommon need to make sense of one's life as one reaches the end of it. Ultimately, the literary critic and intellectual uses her formidable analytical skills to work out what she reckoned her early life had meant. In leaving so clear-sighted an analysis from her vantage point as a successful academic, someone who has won through, she offers, beyond her own death, the hope of a rich survival to others.

Gwyn Thomas seems to have written *A Few Selected Exits* because others wanted him to. At that time in the mid-1960s, *Punch* was a popular periodical and his regular stories and articles there were valued. In those stories he was often able to distance himself from the blacker thoughts his early upbringing engendered in him. Indeed, the retelling allowed him to handle the material in a cathartic way, as my analysis of 'Arrayed Like One of These' has attempted to show. Further, he had become something of a household name through such programmes as the *Brains Trust* on television and *Any Questions* on radio. When both American and British publishers simultaneously showed an interest in an autobiography, it was hard to resist. As we have seen, the introspection involved proved to be deeply painful for Thomas and the result, at times, less than satisfying.

Rhys Davies published his autobiography in 1969, the year after he had been awarded an OBE, something of an Establishment accolade. *Print of a Hare's Foot* positions him within the literary world of London and highlights his friendship with D. H. Lawrence. He presents himself as a debonair figure, a sophisticated littérateur, who has moved thoroughly beyond the crudities of Welsh flannel. In keeping with this image, he intends that the reader shall get from his work only what he has deliberately put into it. As an autobiographer he can be experienced as both controlling and manipulative. Yet he writes, as I have shown, from the vulnerability of a narcissist, in the clinical sense: for him, costly self-disclosure would have meant being perilously exposed.

Working on autobiography can give one the sense of moving deeply into other people's lives. All the subjects of this work are now dead. It has felt a privilege to come to know, to understand and even, in some cases, to love these writers who, through leaving a record of how they perceived their lives, have sent their stories forward into the future. To write searching autobiography, seeking to sound the depths of one's own complexities and re-enacting the joy, pain, wonder and struggle of one's human journey, is to bequeath a rich gift to posterity. Through tracing the meaning that others have discerned in their lives, readers of autobiography are offered the hope of ultimately making sense of their own.

Notes

1. INTRODUCTION

1 Diane Bjorklund, *Interpreting the Self: Two Hundred Years of American Autobiography* (Chicago and London: University of Chicago Press, 1998), p. 119. References are given in the introduction only when the matter considered is not alluded to again later in the work.

2 Jerome Hamilton Buckley, *The Turning Key: Autobiography and the Subjective Impulse since 1800* (Cambridge, MA, and London: Harvard University Press, 1984), p. 42.

3 For a comprehensive introduction to the extravert/introvert distinction, see Myers and Myers, *Gifts*.

4 Quoted by Buckley, *Turning Key*, p. 4.

5 Lorna Sage, *Bad Blood* (London: Fourth Estate, 2000), p. 275.

6 Quoted by Eakin, *Touching*, p. 184.

7 Roy Pascal, *Design and Truth in Autobiography* (Cambridge, MA: Harvard University Press, 1960), p. 92.

2. HARE OR HOUDINI?: RHYS DAVIES (1901–1978)

1 Rhys Davies, *Print of a Hare's Foot* (Bridgend: Seren, 1997).

2 M. Wynn Thomas, ' "Never Seek to Tell thy Love": Rhys Davies's Fiction', *Welsh Writing in English*, 4 (1998), 17.

3 D. A. Callard, 'Rhys Davies and the Welsh Expatriate Novel', *Planet*, 89, 1991, 84.

4 Sigmund Freud, *Art and Literature*, Penguin Freud Library 14 (London: Penguin, 1990), p. 214.

5 The drawings were originally commissioned for Oscar Wilde, *Salome* (Paris and London: John Lane, 1893).

6 'D1 frag.' is to be found amongst uncatalogued papers in the Rhys Davies archive in the National Library of Wales, 1–51.

'D2' is to be found in NLW MS 21532B 1, 1–174, and MS 21532B II, 175–359 (labelled Draft One on the spine).

'D3frag.' is to be found at the end of NLW MS 21532B II, 1–27.

'D4' is to be found in NLW MS 21533C, 2–292 (labelled Draft Two on the spine).

'D5' is to be found in NLW MS 21534C, 1–321 (labelled Draft Three on the spine).

7   Lejeune, 'Pact', p. 29.

8   Elizabeth W. Bruss, *Autobiographical Acts: The Changing Situation of a Literary Genre* (Baltimore and London: Johns Hopkins University Press, 1976), p. 11.

9   Mandel, 'Full', p. 66.

10   Letter written on the paper of the *Southern Review*, Baton Rouge, Louisiana, dated 16 March 1969 and signed by Donald E. Stanford (in uncatalogued private papers in the Rhys Davies archive, NLW).

11   In early drafts, Davies frequently lists two or three possible words as he tentatively formulates an idea. He often records them, one above the other, without any prioritizing. I have indicated this practice with / in my transcription. Where an alternative word appears in parenthesis, I have transcribed the parenthesis.

12   Jonathan Ceredig Davies describes this alleged tradition in his *Folklore of West and Mid-Wales* (Aberystwyth: Welsh Gazette Office, Bridge Street, 1911), pp. 41–2.

13   Cf. 'D5', 318: 'Neurosis, often bestowing a compensatory physical toughness, can be the encroaching ivy that brings a tree down. Erasmus might succeed in demolishing Rhoda.'

14   J. R. Ackerley, *My Father and Myself* (London: Bodley Head, 1968).

15   Evidence of Davies's promiscuity is documented in an interview by David Callard with Fred Urquhart, where Urquhart speaks of being aware of Davies 'having a number of "one-night stands", almost invariably with Guardsmen'; D. A. Callard, 'Rhys Davies (1901–1978)', in Dean Baldwin (ed.), *British Short Fiction Writers 1945–1980* (Detroit: Gale Research, 1994), p. 68.

16   I am deeply grateful to Jonathan Pope, a psychoanalytical psychotherapist, for indicating, in response to my analysis of the draft material, that Rhys Davies showed many of the signs of narcissism in the psychoanalytical sense. Jonathan Pope's humane and knowledgeable exposition of narcissism in a personal interview has very much extended my understanding of the state and has encouraged a rounded rather than a reductive view of Davies.

17   See Neville Symington, *Narcissism: A New Theory* (London: Karnac Books, 1993), pp. 51–9, 73–5; Otto F. Kernberg, *Borderline Conditions and Pathological Narcissism* (New York: Jason Aronson, 1975), p. 234.

18   Kernberg, *Borderline Conditions*, pp. 234–6.

19   C. Lasch, *The Culture of Narcissism* (New York: Norton, 1991), pp. 37–41.

20   Rhys Davies, *Collected Stories II*, ed. Meic Stephens (Llandysul: Gomer, 1996), p. 122, hereafter *CSII* in the text; similarly *CSI* for Rhys Davies, *Collected Stories I*, ed. Meic Stephens (Llandysul: Gomer, 1996).

21   D. A. Callard, 'Rhys Davies', p. 71.

22   See, particularly, 'The Trip to London' in *CSII*, pp. 46–53, and 'The Chosen One' *CSII*, p. 271.

23 'Resurrection', *CSI*, p. 166; 'A Man up a Tree', *CSII*, pp. 219–32; 'Mourning for Ianto', *CSI*, pp. 218–23; 'Tomorrow', *CSII*, pp. 146–54; 'Pleasures of the Table', *CSI*, pp. 277–86; 'The Last Struggle', *CSII*, pp. 32–41.

24 Heinz Kohut, *The Analysis of the Self: A Systematic Approach to the Psychoanalytic Treatment of Narcissistic Personality Disorders* (New York: International University Press, 1971), p. 117.

25 Ibid., p. 15.

3.   WRITING IT OUT: MARGIAD EVANS (1909–58)

1   Margiad Evans, *The Wooden Doctor* (Boston and New York: Houghton Mifflin Company, 1933), hereafter referenced in the text.

2   Margiad Evans, *A Ray of Darkness* (London: John Calder, 1978), hereafter referenced in the text.

3   Margiad Evans, 'The Nightingale Silenced', manuscript drafts of an unpublished autobiographical work, NLW MSS 23367B 1954, hereafter referenced in the text.

4   Margiad Evans, 'The Immortal Hospital or Recollections of our Childhood', unpublished autobiographical essay, NLW MSS 23369C 1957 referenced in the text.

5   I have been indebted to two literary biographies: Moira Dearnley, *Margiad Evans*, Writers of Wales, eds Meic Stephens and R. Brinley Jones (Cardiff: University of Wales Press, 1982), and Ceridwen Lloyd-Morgan, *Margiad Evans*, Border Lines, ed. John Powell Ward (Bridgend: Poetry Wales Press, 1998), for careful tracking of Margiad Evans's life and for some inspired interpretations of her work.

6   Margiad Evans, 'Journal 1', NLW MS 23366D, Feb. 1933–July 1934, Margiad Evans, 'Journal 2', NLW MS 23577C, Sept. 1935–Oct. 1939, hereafter referenced in the text as 'Journal 1' and 'Journal 2' respectively. The journals in the archive are not numbered.

7   Clare Morgan, 'Exile and the Kingdom: Margiad Evans and the Mythic Landscape of Wales', *Welsh Writing in English*, 6 (2000), 89–118.

8   For example, 'Journal 1', 56, 'Journal 2', 50v.

9   Margiad Evans, *Turf or Stone* (Oxford: Blackwell, 1934).

10 A. Calder Marshall, letter to W. A. Thorpe, 28 July 1963, NLW, Margiad Evans Papers 22, hereafter referenced in the text.

11 'Journal 1', 16v, 'Journal 1', 83, 'Journal 2', 52.

12 Margiad Evans, 'The Wooden Doctor, here entitled *The Divine Image*', manuscript draft, NLW MSS 23357B 1932 (?), pp. 81, 101, hereafter referenced in the text as '*The Wooden Doctor*, draft'.

13 Evans, 'Journal 1', 18.

14 'Journal 1', 5, 'Journal 1', 15, 'Journal 1', 42v.

15 'Journal 1', 1v, 2, 4, 82v.

16 Cassie Cooper, 'Psychodynamic Therapy: The Kleinian Approach', in Windy

Dryden (ed.), *Individual Therapy: A Handbook*, Open University Press Psychotherapy Handbook Series (Milton Keynes and Philadelphia: Open University Press, 1990), pp. 48–9.

[17] Bowlby, *Attach2*, pp. 278–83.

[18] Ibid., pp. 279–80.

[19] Margiad Evans, *The Old and the Young* (Bridgend: Seren, 1998), pp. 136–7.

[20] Margiad Evans, *Autobiography* (Oxford: Blackwell, 1943), p. 92, hereafter referenced in the text.

[21] Margiad Evans, 'Journal 4', NLW: Margiad Evans MS 34, 24 September 1942–14 July 1943, hereafter referenced in the text.

[22] See Myers and Myers, *Gifts*, pp. 53–6, for an exploration of introversion.

[23] Robert F. Murphy, *The Body Silent*, Phoenix House edn (London: J. M. Dent, 1987).

[24] Oliver Sacks, *The Man Who Mistook His Wife for a Hat* (London: Picador, 1986).

[25] Idris Parry, 'Margiad Evans and Tendencies in European Literature', *Transactions of the Honourable Society of Cymmrodorion* (1971), 224–36.

4. MINERS INTO WRITERS: B. L. COOMBES (1893–1974) AND RON BERRY (1920–1997)

[1] B. L. Coombes, *These Poor Hands*, Left Book Club edn (London: Victor Gollancz, 1939) hereafter referenced in the text.

[2] Ron Berry, *History is What You Live* (Llandysul: Gomer, 1998).

[3] Wolfgang Iser, *The Act of Reading: A Theory of Aesthetic Response* (London and Henley: Routledge and Kegan Paul, 1978), p. 107.

[4] The Rt. Hon. Lord Meston and B. L. Coombes, *The Life We Want*, The Life We Want 1 (London: Lund Humphries for the Liberal Party Organization, 1944).

[5] Barbara Nield, 'Bert Lewis Coombes', in Joyce M. Bellamy and John Saville (eds), *Dictionary of Labour Biography*, vol. 4 (London and Basingstoke: Macmillan, 1977).

[6] B. Jones and Chris Williams (eds), *With Dust Still in his Throat: A B. L. Coombes Anthology* (Cardiff: University of Wales Press, 1999), is an anthology of Coombes's unpublished work which has made sections of 'Home on the Hill' conveniently available. My references, for completeness, are from the typescript in the archive: B. L. Coombes, 'Home on the Hill', unpublished autobiography, South Wales Coalfield Collection, B. L. Coombes archive 1959, hereafter referenced in the text. A further work, B. Jones and Chris Williams, *B. L. Coombes*, Writers of Wales, eds Meic Stephens and R. Brinley Jones (Cardiff: University of Wales Press, 1999), a critical biography, appears to have been written with an eye firmly on the public persona of Coombes as the 'voice of the miner' and has relied, at times, on Coombes's own autobiographical writing as a source of biographical fact. My reservations about the latter aspect of the work have been explored in a review article, Barbara Prys-Williams, 'A Miner "On Message" ', *New Welsh Review*, 48, Spring 2000. For their new edition, B. L. Coombes, *These Poor*

Hands, eds Bill Jones and Chris Williams (Cardiff: University of Wales Press, 2002), Jones and Williams have now consulted the Gollancz archive.

7 B. L. Coombes, 'Then Come the Golden Moments', *Neath Guardian*, 11 October 1963.

8 A more extended account of the evolution of *These Poor Hands* is contained in Barbara Prys-Williams, 'A Difficult Man, your Coombes', *New Welsh Review*, 49, Summer 2000. This article was written within weeks of my reading the Gollancz letters, before my discovery of the Lehmann papers in Texas. I have subsequently modified my views on the nature and extent of Lehmann's influence.

9 In every case, letters between Coombes and Gollancz (sometimes Victor Gollancz in person, sometimes his firm) are to be found in the Gollancz archive, hereafter G, and those between Lehmann and Coombes in the Lehmann papers at the Harry Ransom Humanities Centre, hereafter L. The locations of the holding libraries are listed at the front of this book.

10 Coombes to Gollancz, 18 October 1937, G.

11 Coombes to Glyn Jones, 14 November 1939, NLW.

12 B. L. Coombes, 'These Poor Hands 1st draft', typescript, B. L. Coombes Archive, South Wales Coalfield Collection, 1937, hereafter referenced in the text, and B. L. Coombes, 'These Poor Hands 2nd draft', typescript, B. L. Coombes Archive, South Wales Coalfield Collection, 1937, hereafter referenced in the text.

13 Ruth Dudley Edwards, *Victor Gollancz: A Biography* (London: Victor Gollancz, 1987), pp. 245–6.

14 Coombes to Gollancz, 14 March 1938, G.

15 Space constraints prevent a detailed account of my findings. See Barbara Prys-Williams, 'Variations in the Nature of the Perceived Self in some Twentieth Century Welsh Autobiographical Writing in English' (unpublished Ph.D. thesis, University of Wales, Swansea, 2002), 105–8.

16 Adrian Wright, *John Lehmann: A Pagan Adventure* (London: Duckworth, 1998).

17 Coombes to Gollancz, 18 February 1937, G.

18 Gollancz to Coombes, 24 February 1937, G.

19 Lehmann had suggested dropping real names.

20 Coombes to Gollancz, 14 March 1938, G.

21 Coombes to Lehmann, 7 June 1939, L.

22 Coombes to Gollancz, 17 April 1938, G.

23 He refers to his 'autobiography' in letters to Gollancz of 18 October 1937, 27 October 1937, 23 January 1938 and in a letter to Lehmann of 18 April 1937.

24 Currently available in B. L. Coombes, 'Twenty Tons of Coal', in Alun Richards (ed.), *The Penguin Book of Welsh Short Stories* (Harmondsworth: Penguin, 1976). The near-verbatim transposition from 'These Poor Hands 2nd draft' forms pp. 175–83 of this publication.

25 Gollancz to Coombes, 10 March 1938, G.

26 Coombes to Gollancz, 7 April 1938, G.

27 Coombes to Gollancz, 18 February 1937, G.

28 Coombes to Lehmann, 22 December 1940, L.

29 John Lehmann, *The Whispering Gallery: Autobiography 1* (London: Longmans, Green, 1955), pp. 231–2.

30 Ibid., p. 309.

[31] Coombes, 'Then Come the Golden Moments', *Neath Guardian*, 11 October 1963.

[32] Clive John, 'He Sent the Message of the Miner around the World', *Neath Guardian*, 27 September 1963.

[33] B. L. Coombes. 'I Stayed a Miner', Radio, 11 October 1957, script in NLW: BBC Archives, Features 57.

[34] Coombes to Gollancz, 22 November 1938, G.

[35] Between 25 January 1941 and 22 April 1945 he mentions this second autobiography and the work he had been doing on it eight times. He confusingly entitles this work 'The Singing Sycamore', the title that he had also given to an earlier unpublished novel.

[36] It is indeed possible that Lehmann authorized the writing of an autobiographical novel. Coombes's letter of 12 June 1937 reads: 'I would like [you] to know about the autobiographical novel you suggested some months ago. I have gone along steadily and have about 50,000 words done now.' Unfortunately, the commissioning letter from Lehmann to Coombes does not appear to have survived.

5.   YOU'VE GOT TO LAUGH: GWYN THOMAS (1913–81)

[1] Joseph Boskin, 'The Complicity of Humor: The Life and Death of Sambo', in John Morreal (ed.), *The Philosophy of Laughter and Humor*, SUNY Series in Philosophy (Albany: State University of New York Press, 1987), p. 255.

[2] Gwyn Thomas, 'Arrayed Like One of These', *Selected Short Stories* (Bridgend: Seren, 1988), pp. 27–35, hereafter referenced in the text.

[3] Gwyn Thomas, *A Few Selected Exits* (Bridgend: Seren, 1985), hereafter referenced in the text.

[4] There are loose-leaf fragments of early drafts of *A Few Selected Exits*: NLW, Gwyn Thomas MSS and Papers, B16, *c.*1966, hereafter referenced in the text as 'Drafts'.

[5] Gwyn Thomas, 'Gwyn Thomas', in Meic Stephens (ed.), *Artists in Wales* (Llandysul: Gomer, 1971), p. 72, hereafter referenced in the text as 'Gwyn Thomas'.

[6] Bowlby, *Attach1*, Bowlby, *Attach2*, Bowlby, *Attach3*.

[7] Michael Parnell, *Laughter from the Dark: A Life of Gwyn Thomas* (Bridgend: Seren, 1997), p. 5, hereafter referenced in the text.

[8] Dilwyn Thomas, letter to Nana Thomas (transcribed by M. Parnell), undated – late 1985, NLW, Gwyn Thomas Manuscripts and Papers, J16.

[9] Michael Parnell's interview notebook from 1985 to the late 1980s has proved an invaluable resource; NLW, Gwyn Thomas MSS and Papers, M32, hereafter referenced in the text as 'NB'.

[10] Gwyn Thomas, interview by Gerry Monte, 'Wales '76', 1976, NLW, Gwyn Thomas MSS, G167.

[11] Gwyn Thomas, 'My View of Wales', talk, NLW, Gwyn Thomas MSS and Papers, G218 1966.

[12] Michael Parnell, 'Some Notes on Gwyn Thomas's Personality', NLW, Gwyn Thomas MSS and Papers, M39.

13 Gwyn Thomas, interview by Denis Mitchell, *Private Lives*, 1975, NLW, Gwyn Thomas MSS and Papers, G166, hereafter referenced in the text.

14 Dai Smith (ed.), *Gwyn Thomas (1913–1981)* (Welsh Arts Council, 1986), p. 5.

15 Gwyn Thomas, 'Not Even Then', *Gazooka and Other Stories* (London: Victor Gollancz, 1957), p. 58.

16 Gwyn Thomas, 'The Keep', in Michael Parnell (ed.), *Three Plays* (Bridgend: Seren, 1990), pp. 90–1.

17 He was later entirely dependent on his wife to provide a total life-support system, including secretarial services, every aspect of household management, complete financial oversight and to chauffeur him wherever he needed to go (*Laughter from the Dark*, 131, and 'NB', *passim*). However, the dependence seems to have been as much emotional as practical: Reg George, a teaching colleague and former pupil, found him a 'very vulnerable person . . . helpless and hopeless without [Lyn]', during a brief period she spent in hospital ('NB', 89–96).

18 Gwyn Thomas, interview by Michael Parkinson, *The Parkinson Show*, BBC Television, 28 November 1971, video.

19 'Gwyn Thomas: A Critical Reputation', BBC Wales Television, 11 May 1986. Transcript in NLW, Gwyn Thomas MSS and Papers, G 173, hereafter referenced as 'A Critical Reputation'.

20 'Any Questions', BBC radio, 5 June 1964. Transcript in NLW, Gwyn Thomas MSS and Papers, G83 13/30.

21 Wynn Thomas in 'A Critical Reputation', Alun John, 'NB', 82, Glyn Jones, 'NB', 97.

22 Gwyn Thomas, 'Change Here for Strangeness', *Punch*, 19 April 1961.

23 Lyn Thomas, interview by Michael Parnell, 3 October 1985, Gwyn Thomas MSS and Papers, M30.

24 Gwyn Thomas, interview by Frank Delaney, *Bookshelf*, BBC Radio, 1979, NLW, Gwyn Thomas MSS and Papers, G168/1.

25 Michael Parnell's widow, Mary, writes a preamble to this effect to her late husband's transcription of the notebooks: NLW, Gwyn Thomas MSS and Papers, N2.

26 These are to be found in NLW, Gwyn Thomas MSS and Papers N2; hereafter referenced in the text: *MP* for transcriptions by Michael Parnell, and *LT* for those by Lyn Thomas.

27 Further jottings: 'Sober, I am entombed. With a little alcohol laid along my veins, I float for a while in the wandering wake of Lazarus' (initialled GT, *MP*, Notebook 22, 13 June 1970, 92); in the same notebook, 'The mind is a burning house. Jump clear if you can' (initialled GT, *MP*, 95); 'Freud: "I have found little that is 'good' about human beings on the whole. In my experience, most of them are trash." Yes, yes. Rain is wet. How do you make a mac?' (*MP*, Notebook 21, 31 March 1970, 67); 'Look at the sad little fragments of experience that enter officially into the category of happiness and take sadly to drink' (*LT*, 41).

28 See, for example, 'Pathophysiology of Erectile Dysfunction', *Campbell's Urology*, 7th edn, eds P. C. Walsh et al. (Philadelphia: W. B. Saunders, 1998), p. 1169. I am grateful to Michael Rose, a former consultant urologist, for this reference.

29 The randomly assembled pile of loose-leaf typescript has some long runs of several consecutive pages, some shorter sequences and some individual sheets: the overlapping pagination suggests that there had been several drafts.

[30] Harold Harris, letter to Gwyn Thomas, 28 June 1967, NLW, Gwyn Thomas MSS and Papers, J57/19.

[31] Ibid.

[32] See, for example, a run, 143–61, of 'Drafts', almost all carrying the instruction 'stet'.

[33] Harold Sions, letter to Gwyn Thomas, 21 August 1967, NLW, Gwyn Thomas MSS and Papers, J66/7.

[34] Gwyn Thomas, letter to Harold Harris, undated (draft), in response to letter of 28 June 1967, NLW, Gwyn Thomas MSS and Papers, J57/19.

[35] Gwyn Thomas, 'A Few Selected Exits', redrafted first chapter, NLW, Gwyn Thomas MSS and Papers, B3.

[36] The redrafted chapter opens with 'Brotherly Love' (*Punch*, 12 April 1961) and concludes with 'Explosion Point' (*Punch*, 3 May 1961).

[37] Harold Sions, letter to Gwyn Thomas, 29 March 1968, NLW, Gwyn Thomas MSS and Papers, J66/11.

[38] The typescript has a holograph addition indicating the newspaper name and date of publication.

[39] Gwyn Thomas, interview by Glyn Jones, 'How I Write', *Arts Magazine*, 16 March 1950, NLW, Gwyn Thomas MSS and Papers, G161.

[40] Gwyn Thomas, 'Foreword' to *Old Barry in Photographs* (Barry: Stewart Williams, 1977).

[41] See 'NB', 24, 107.

[42] See 'NB', 7, 87.

[43] Gwyn Thomas and Keith Baxter, interview by Beata Lipman, 'Sap', 1974, NLW, Gwyn Thomas MSS and Papers, G165.

[44] Victor Golightly, '"We, Who Speak for the Workers": The Correspondence of Gwyn Thomas and Howard Fast', *Welsh Writing in English*, 6 (2000), 67–88, 76–80.

[45] Thomas taught at Cardigan County School from 1940–2.

[46] Undated draft in response to a letter from Harold Harris dated 28 June 1967, NLW, Gwyn Thomas MSS and Papers, J57/19.

[47] See Gwyn Thomas, *A Welsh Eye* (London: Hutchinson, 1964), p. 91.

6.   BURIED TO BE DUG UP: R. S. THOMAS (1913–2000)

[1] R. S. Thomas, *The Echoes Return Slow* (London: Macmillan, 1988).

[2] For example, the significance of the Troy and the Robert Graves allusion (*Echoes*, 56) became clear only after extensive reading, which included Chaucer's *Troilus and Criseyde*, Shakespeare's *Troilus and Cressida*, several biographies of Graves, one of Laura Riding and, finally, Riding's turgid novel, *A Trojan Ending*. In working through the considerable ramifications, I am grateful to Allan Prys-Williams for some assiduous preliminary excavation.

[3] R. S. Thomas, *Neb* (Caernarfon: Gwasg Gwynedd, 1985).

[4] R. S. Thomas, *Blwyddyn yn Llŷn* (Caernarfon: Gwasg Gwynedd, 1990).

[5] Translations of these texts are now available in R. S. Thomas, *Autobiographies*, trans. Jason Walford Davies (London: Dent, 1997).

6   Further exploration of Thomas's use of emblems and epitomes and of techniques that he used for creating ambiguity and indeterminacy are to be found in Barbara Prys Williams ' "Entered for Life": Some Aspects of R. S. Thomas's *The Echoes Return Slow* as Autobiography', (unpublished MA dissertation, University of Wales, Swansea, 1995), 16–22, 26–7. (NB Some of my early publications were as 'Prys Williams' (which is good Welsh but confuses indexing devices) and thus are often listed under 'Williams'. I now employ a hyphen.)

7   Translations are by me unless otherwise noted.

8   Sartre, for example, in his autobiography, *The Words*, recalls how his fatherless boy-self at last found identity through the act of writing: 'I was beginning to find myself . . . I was born of writing. Before that, there was only a play of mirrors. With my first novel, I knew that a child had got into the hall of mirrors. By writing I was existing . . . I existed only in order to write and if I said "I", that meant "I who write" '; Quoted in Eakin, *Fictions*, p. 142.

9   Olney, *Metaphors*, p. 30.

10 Ibid., p. 106.

11 R. S. Thomas, *Experimenting with an Amen* (London: Macmillan, 1988), p. 52.

12 Tony Brown, 'Eve's Ruse: Identity and Gender in the Poetry of R. S. Thomas', *English*, 49, Autumn (2000), 229–50.

13 M. Wynn Thomas, 'Keeping his Pen Clean: R. S. Thomas and Wales', in William V. Davis (ed.), *Miraculous Simplicity: Essays on R. S. Thomas* (Fayetteville: University of Arkansas Press, 1993), p. 74.

14 Bowlby, *Attach2*, pp. 297–333.

15 R. S. Thomas, 'Autobiographical Essay', in Davis (ed.), *Miraculous Simplicity*, p. 2.

16 In R. S. Thomas, 'Probings: An Interview with R. S. Thomas', *Planet*, 80, 1990, 42, Thomas again mentions this: 'I seem not to have attended school for a year or two.'

17 Bowlby, *Attach2*, pp. 304–6.

18 Alice Miller, *For Your Own Good: The Roots of Violence in Child-Rearing* (London: Virago, 1980), p. 88.

19 Cf. Tony Brown, 'Eve's Ruse', and M. Wynn Thomas, 'Keeping his Pen Clean'.

20 'Autobiographical Essay', 1.

21 'Ap Huw's Testament', R. S. Thomas, *Poetry for Supper* (London: Hart-Davis, 1958), p. 29.

22 'Autobiographical Essay', 3.

23 I am grateful to Diane Green and Allan Prys-Williams for illuminating discussion of this stanza.

24 Thomas, *Amen*, p. 52.

25 R. S. Thomas, *Mass for Hard Times* (Newcastle-upon-Tyne: Bloodaxe, 1992), p. 29.

26 Richard Perceval Graves, *The Years with Laura 1926–40* (London: Weidenfield and Nicolson, 1990), pp. 84–6; Martin Seymour-Smith, *Robert Graves: His Life and Work* (London: Hutchinson, 1982), pp. 166–7.

27 Graves, *Years with Laura*, pp. 141–2, Seymour-Smith, *Robert Graves*, pp. 233–4.

28 Graves, *Years with Laura*, p. 224.

29 Laura Riding, *A Trojan Ending* (Manchester: Carcanet, 1984), p. 239.

[30] Riding, *A Trojan Ending*, p. 323.

[31] It may be recalled that Isabel Archer's thoughts on her marriage are that 'They were strangely married at all events, and it was a horrible life': Henry James, *The Portrait of a Lady* (Harmondsworth: Penguin, 1984), p. 482.

[32] Personal recollection, *Blwyddyn yn Llŷn*, p. 28, and checked with the *South Wales Evening Post*, 29 March 1986, for the exact date.

[33] Genesis 3: 5.

[34] Erik H. Erikson, *Young Man Luther* (London: Faber, 1958), p. 108.

[35] R. S. Thomas, 'Y Llwybrau Gynt 2 [The Paths Gone By]', in Sandra Anstey (ed.), *Selected Prose* (Bridgend: Poetry Wales Press, 1986), p. 134.

[36] J. Huizinga, *The Waning of the Middle Ages* (Harmondsworth: Penguin, 1972), pp. 134–46. A personal communication from R. S. Thomas, dated 1 February 1995, confirmed that he had read the book.

[37] Personal communication to M. Wynn Thomas.

[38] See Myers and Myers, *Gifts*, pp. 53–6, for a fuller exposition of extraversion and introversion.

[39] J. Leasor, *The Sea Wolves* (London: Corgi, 1978); *The Sea Wolves*, directed by Andrew McLaglen, 1980.

[40] Olney, *Metaphors*, p. 263.

[41] 'The Word', R. S. Thomas, *Laboratories of the Spirit* (London: Macmillan, 1975), p. 3.

[42] 'A Life', *Experimenting with an Amen*, p. 52.

7.   HACKING HER WAY OUT: LORNA SAGE (1943–2001)

[1] Lorna Sage, *Bad Blood* (London: Fourth Estate, 2000).

[2] Eakin, *Touching*, p. 94.

[3] Quoted by Susan Stanford Friedman, 'Women's Autobiographical Selves: Theory and Practice', in Shari Benstock (ed.), *The Private Self: Theory and Practice of Women's Autobiographical Writings* (Chapel Hill: University of North Carolina Press, 1988), p. 38.

[4] Adam Phillips, *Winnicott*, Fontana Modern Masters, ed. Frank Kermode (London: Fontana, 1988), p. 130.

[5] Susanna Egan, *Patterns of Experience in Autobiography* (Chapel Hill and London: University of North Carolina Press, 1984), p. 22.

[6] A helpful analysis of the introvert/extravert distinction is contained in Myers and Myers, *Gifts*, pp. 53–6.

[7] John Bowlby, *A Secure Base: Clinical Applications of Attachment Theory* (London: Routledge, 1988), hereafter referenced in the text.

[8] Iain Finlayson, 'Roughing it', *The Times*, 27 September 2000.

Index